Rome's Sicilian Slave Wars

Rome's Sicilian Slave Wars

The Revolts of Eunus & Salvius 136–132 & 105–100 BC

Natale Barca

Pen & Sword
MILITARY

First published in Great Britain in 2020 by
Pen & Sword Military
An imprint of
Pen & Sword Books Ltd
Yorkshire – Philadelphia

Copyright © Natale Barca 2020

ISBN 978 1 52676 746 2

Printed and bound in the UK by TJ International Ltd, Padstow, Cornwall.

Pen & Sword Books Limited incorporates the imprints of Atlas, Archaeology,
Aviation, Discovery, Family History, Fiction, History, Maritime, Military, Military
Classics, Politics, Select, Transport, True Crime, Air World, Frontline Publishing,
Leo Cooper, Remember When, Seaforth Publishing, The Praetorian Press,
Wharncliffe Local History, Wharncliffe Transport, Wharncliffe True Crime and
White Owl.

For a complete list of Pen & Sword titles please contact

PEN & SWORD BOOKS LIMITED
47 Church Street, Barnsley, South Yorkshire, S70 2AS, England
E-mail: enquiries@pen-and-sword.co.uk
Website: www.pen-and-sword.co.uk

Or

PEN AND SWORD BOOKS
1950 Lawrence Rd, Havertown, PA 19083, USA
E-mail: Uspen-and-sword@casematepublishers.com
Website: www.penandswordbooks.com

Contents

Preface

In 136 BC the slaves at work in the Sicilian countryside revolted against their owners, quickly taking control of large parts of the island and keeping them until the intervention of the Roman legions in 131 BC. A second movement followed the first in 105 BC, with similar results. The ancient sources agree in identifying the causes of these uprisings, both in the mistreatment suffered by slaves from their masters, especially those who were required to work the land, and in the tendency of the Roman authorities to tolerate the behaviour of certain wealthy owners of estates, often senators, who armed their slave-shepherds and pushed them to commit criminal acts. The most important of such sources is Diodorus of Sicily, a Greek-speaking Sicilian aristocrat who lived in 1st century BC at Adrano, near Catania. This historian, in his main work, called the two movements of slaves cited above the Revolt of Eunus and the Revolt of Salvius, and this definition survives to this day.

While the revolts ended in 102, they left their mark on the history of Sicily as well as on that of the Roman Republic. They introduced a crisis that was both social and civil. The crisis lasted for decades, and led to the Social War (91–88 BC)[1] and the rebellion of Spartacus.

The latter broke out in 73 BC in Capua (now Santa Maria Capua Vetere), a large city located near Naples, in Campania, and raged for three years in various parts of central and southern Italy. It developed to such a large scale, and became so famous, as to obscure the memory of all other similar events.

Rome's Sicilian Slave Wars are often linked to the rebellion of Spartacus. Today they are little known by the general public, while the revolt of Spartacus is far better known. It is likely that the former did not have the same echo of the latter because Spartacus and his companions were gladiators and Spartacus himself was a charismatic leader, more so than Eunus, Salvius or Athenion.

In this book I tell the story of Rome's Sicilian Slave Wars.

I provide a detailed reconstruction of the facts – as far as it is possible to deduce from the ancient sources – framing them in the broader context of Hellenistic Sicily and the history of Rome.

I include evidence that the insurgents founded a kingdom and fought for freedom and political self-determination, and explain why this aspect – little emphasized by the ancient sources, and only to ridicule the 'king of the slaves' – is central to understand what really happened.

I also explain why the Rebellion of Spartacus was something quite different, and thus why it is inappropriate to link it to the revolts of Eunus and Salvius.

A monument to Eunus exists in Enna, Sicily, outside the ancient citadel. It is a bronze statue, about three metres high, depicting a man who screams while breaking his chains. It was erected by the local municipality in 1960 to celebrate the triumph of freedom against slavery. This initiative took a cue from the revolt of Eunus, which started in Enna and from there spread to large parts of Sicily. After being the cradle of the revolt (in spite of itself), Enna also became the theatre of its tragic epilogue.

Some final notes. The language used in this book has been made as simple as possible to make it accessible even to a non-specialized public. All dates shown are BC unless otherwise specified. So, from here on, BC will no longer be indicated for the sake of brevity, while AD will be always indicated unless it is clearly unnecessary. As for place names, the name indicated first is the original. The names in brackets are those attributed subsequently to the place considered, and the last is the modern equivalent.

Natale Barca
Trieste, Italy, March 2020

Acknowledgments

*R*ome's Sicilian Slave Wars is the result of a research project carried on by the author at the Hellenic and Roman Library (HARL) at Senate House, in London's Bloomsbury. HARL is one of the world's great libraries for the study of Greco-Roman Antiquity, a resource without parallel for international researchers. I must warmly thank Professor Greg Woolf, Director of the Institute of Classical Studies, School of Advanced Studies (ICS), University of London, for having let me frequent such a library as an academic visitor of the ICS. I am also grateful to Carlos F. Noreña, Professor of Ancient History at the University of California, Berkeley, CA, USA, and to Dr Marco Perale, University Teacher in Greek and Latin at the University of Liverpool, for having made this possible. A grateful thought also to Paul Richgruber, Professor of History at Lake Superior College, Duluth, MN, USA, for his encouragement. Many thanks also to Pen & Sword Books Ltd – particularly to Philip Sidnell, Commissioning Editor, Matthew Jones, Production Manager, and Tony Walton, who did the copy edit – for having published this book.

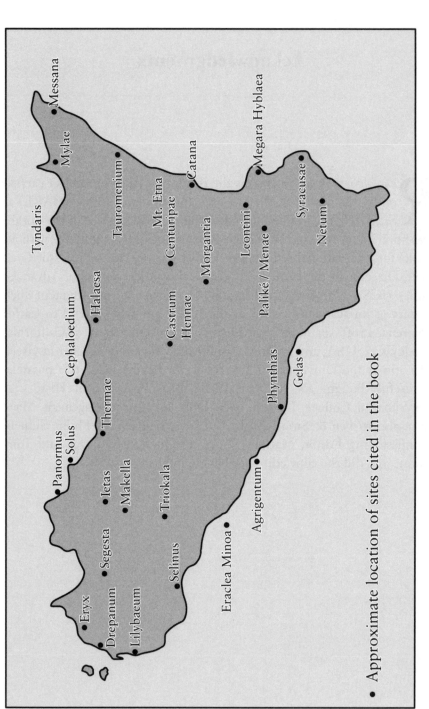

Map 1: Sicily at the time of the First and the Second Slave War.

- Approximate location of sites cited in the book

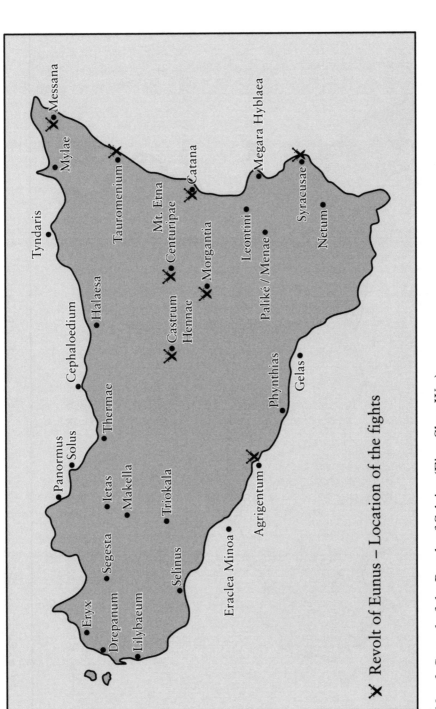

Map 2: Spread of the Revolt of Salvius (First Slave War)

✗ Revolt of Eunus – Location of the fights

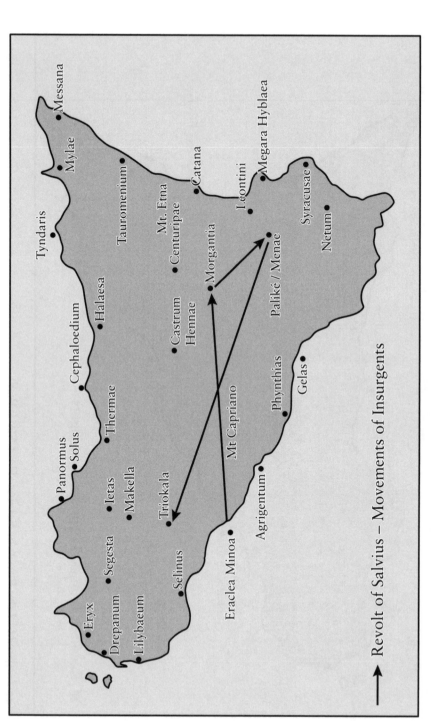

Map 3: Rebel movements in the Revolt of Salvius (Second Slave War)

→ Revolt of Salvius – Movements of Insurgents

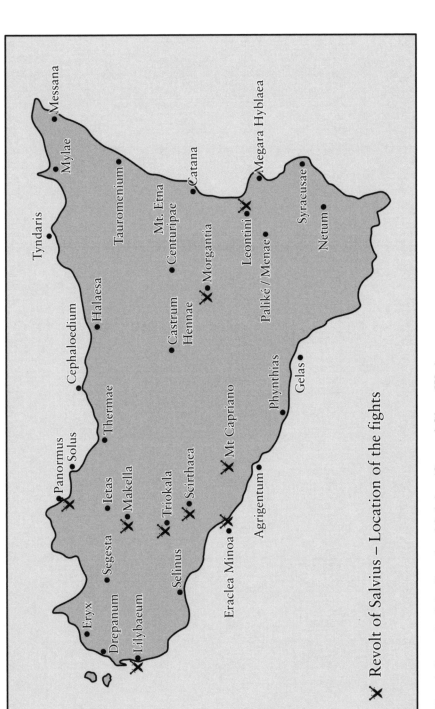

Map 4: Spread of the Revolt of Salvius (Second Slave War)

Messana

Mylae

Tyndaris

Tauromenium

Mt. Etna

Catana

Megara Hyblaea

Centuripae

Syracusae

Castrum
Hennae

Morgantia

Leontini

Netum

Halaesa

Paliké / Menae

Cephaloedium

Thermae

Phynthias

Panormus

Solus

Gelas

Ietas

Segesta

Makella

Mt Capriano

Triokala

Scirthaea

Agrigentum

Eryx

Selinus

Eraclea Minoa

Drepanum

Lilybaeum

✖ Revolt of Salvius – Location of the fights

✖ Revolt of Salvius – Location of the fights

INTRODUCTION

SLAVERY AND SLAVE REBELLIONS

Chapter 1

The Slave Trade

The infamous deals with slaves

The slaves are those unfortunates whom the worst of human conditions have touched, marked by loss of freedom and reduction to a thing that is bought and sold, and which you get rid of after having used it by reselling it or throwing it away. Enslavement degrades the human beings who suffer it. They become a valuable good that contributes to forming the patrimony of their owner. But who are the slaves? In the second half of the second century BC, in the Mediterranean world, they are those who were born as such, because procreated by slave parents, and also those who were born free and then have become slaves due to certain conditions or circumstances. Unfortunately, the risk of becoming a slave often turns into reality for children who have been abandoned by their parents, those not recognized by their father as legitimate, raised by strangers, sold by the father or even kidnapped. The same fate can await anyone who has been seized by pirates for the purpose of extortion but has been unable to pay the ransom price. He who has been condemned to a punishment that implied the permanent loss of personal liberty also becomes a slave, in appliance of the law that protects the creditors. The same can happen to he who has been kidnapped because little known and unable to prove his identity; or has been taken prisoner in war, either because a soldier or a civilian of a conquered city; or who is taken prisoner by an army marching through their homeland. These victims become slaves when they are sold to slave merchants. After that, they are sold again, privately or publicly, often time and again. The public sale takes place in specialized markets, where the human commodity is exposed to the people on a stage, with a sign hanging on their neck, indicating their origin, working capacity, merits and defects. This happened for instance at Delos.

Slave markets

Delos is an islet of the Cyclades archipelago (in the southern Aegean Sea, between mainland Greece and Crete). It is little more than a rock, mostly flat, arid and barren, but in ancient times had two great advantages. First, it was located in a favourable position with respect to the mercantile routes that intersected in the Aegean Sea. In Ancient times, there were the routes from the ports of the Black Sea, western and southern Anatolia, Cyprus and the southern Levant, and directed to Greece and the Western Mediterranean; and those from south-eastern Europe and headed to Libya and Egypt via Crete. Second, from 166 BC, it was a place which enjoyed free port status, thanks to which all commercial transactions were tax exempt. Delos was home to a populous and prosperous city of the same name. The city of Delos was a large market specialized in the slave trade, oil and wine, a first-class financial centre, and the centre of the cult of Apollo, which made it a destination for pilgrimages from all over the Hellenistic world. The slave market of Delos was a focal point of the slave trade in the Mediterranean. While perhaps exaggerated, it was said that 10,000 slaves changed hands there every day, whence arose the proverb, 'Merchant, sail in, unload your ship, everything has been sold.'[1] (This suggests a system in which the burden was acquired in advance and where slaves could not leave the ship, waiting for another merchant to take the load on it to Rome.)[2] Another large slave market was that of the port town of Side, in Pamphylia. Side (Eski Adalia) was a Hellenistic city located on the shores of the Gulf of Antalya. Its population probably descended from the Hittites and the Luwians of the region. The escaping refugees who founded Side in the seventh century after the collapse of the Neo-Hittite Empire were Sidetics, and their descendants spoke Sidetic, a variety of the Anatolian branch of Indo-European languages, which is closely related to Lycian and Piside, but had undergone a strong Hellenistic influence.[3] There were also slave markets elsewhere in the Eastern Mediterranean: at Mylasa (Milas) and Theangela, both in Caria; at Ephesos (Ephesus, Efes) and Chios, both in Ionia; at Aigina (Aegina), in the Saronic Gulf; at Athènai (Athens, Attica); at Byzantion (Byzanthium, Costantinopolis, Istanbul),[4] in Thracia; and at Anactorium, or Anaktorion, on the promontory on the Ambracian Gulf, in Acarnania.[5]

In the Western Mediterranean, there was a slave market in Rome and at Aquileia, a city in north-eastern Italy, close to the shore of Caput Adriae (the very northern end of the Adriatic Sea). Aquileia rises on the banks of the River Natisone, which can be navigated by transport ships from its mouth for more than 60 stades.[6] The city was founded in 181 by the will of the Senate of Rome as a Latin colony for trading with the Istrians, and the Illyrians who dwelled round the Danube. Local merchants dealt in marine merchandise, and used wagons to carry wine in wooden casks and oil, while others exchanged slaves, cattle, and hides.[7] But Aquileia had mainly been founded for keeping in check the barbarians dwelling higher up, that is the Celts of Noricum (a part of Bayern, southern Austria, western Slovenia, and, in Italy, a part of Friuli, and the Karst). It was a city-fortress, the focal point of the defence of Northern Italy against a possible invasion from Eastern Europe through the Carnic Alps, the Valcanale or the narrow valley of the Vipava River. It was also a launching platform for Roman military expeditions in the Western Balkans and Pannonia, which increasingly spread the dominance of Rome in central-eastern and south-eastern Europe. Such enterprises bore important war booty, including many prisoners, who were sold as slaves.

Rome was founded in Lazio in Central Italy, on the Tyrrhenian coast, near the mouth of the Tiber, one of the most important rivers in Italy. In the second half of the second century, it was entirely enclosed within a ring of fortifications, 11km long, known as the Servian Walls, after Servius Tullius (578–539), the fifth king of Rome, second of the Tarquiny dynasty, of Etruscan origin. While enclosed in these walls, Rome had a suburb, called Trans Tiberim (Trastevere) from the fact that it was located beyond the Tiber, that is on the bank of the river opposite to where the city stood, at the foot of the Gianicolo hill. The city then had more than 200,000 inhabitants. The community of Roman citizens was inhomogeneous, formed by different ethnic groups (Latins, Sabines, Etruscans). Politically, Rome was the capital of a city-state which was struggling to evolve into a territorial state. Despite its territory being extensive, it was distributed in widely spaced areas. Rome was initially governed by kings: in a span of about 250 years there had been seven kings of Rome, starting from the legendary Romulus, founder of the city. In 509, the last of them, Tarquinius the Superb, the third ruler of an Etruscan dynasty, had been driven from the city by a popular uprising. Since then Rome had been governed by a couple of consuls, by a Senate of a maximum of 300 members and by four assemblies, whose powers were balanced. Besides the consuls, there were also other magistrates, some elected by the Roman people gathered in assembly, others appointed by the Senate. The consuls and other elected magistrates changed every year. The other magistrates remained in office for a variable time, according to each case. The form of government of the Roman state established after the fall of the monarchy is called *res publica*, 'public affair'. This was not a democratic regime, but a mixture of monarchy, oligarchy and democracy, where the monarchy was represented by the consuls, the oligarchy by the Senate and the democracy by the popular assemblies.

Under the *res publica*, Rome had seen its population grow enormously. Nobody knows exactly how many inhabitants there were in Rome in the second half of the second century. The demographic censuses carried out periodically by the censors did not concern the entire population, but only the holders of Roman citizenship; the numerous foreigners and slaves remained outside the survey. On the eve of the First Punic War (265–241), 180,000 holders of Roman citizenship were living in the urban area.

Under the *res publica*, the Roman state had continued to expand in Lazio and beyond its physical borders, as it had done under the monarchy. In the second half of the second century, Rome controlled all of Italy and the surrounding islands, of which the largest were Sicily, Sardinia and Corsica, which belongs to the Roman state as *provinciae*; it also had other provinces outside Italy (two in the Iberian Peninsula, one in North Africa, one in southern France and one in the Balkan Peninsula). It also had friends and allies, including city-states, kingdoms, peoples and tribes, among which were the republic of Rhodes, the Greek cities of Anatolia and the kings of Pergamon, Bithynia, Paphlagonia, Pontus and Cappadocia. At this time the *res publica* was the most powerful state in Western Europe and the Eastern Mediterranean, where no rivals could compete with it in the economic field or military field. Those that tried were overwhelmed by the Roman army, one after the other: primarily Carthage, but also the city-state of Corinth, the kingdom of Macedonia and the Seleucid Empire.

One of the main suppliers of the slave markets was piracy. By piracy, we mean the Seven Seas pirates. According to Herodotus of Halicarnassus (484–434), a historian and Greek traveller, the Seven Seas were the Aegean Sea, Black Sea, Sea of Marmara, Red Sea, Ionian Sea, Tyrrhenian Sea and Adriatic Sea. Most of these seas are in the Mediterranean basin, and Mediterranean piracy had an important nucleus: Cilician piracy.

Suppliers. In particular, the pirates.

The name says it all: The Mediterranean is the sea 'in the middle of the lands'. It separates and at the same time unites them. Far from being an obstacle to communication between the riparian lands, it is a bridge that allows contacts and exchanges, and in a certain sense favours them. Although the Mediterranean world was crossed by a network of roads, including the consular roads, transport – commercial or not – took place mostly by sea. Therefore, vessels, people and goods of all kinds travelled along the routes of the Mediterranean. On the islands and on the coast of the mainland, the ports were equipped, or were being equipped, with mooring docks and masonry depots to cope with the development of traffic. The circulation by sea of so many riches not only attracted the interest of the public and private entrepreneurs, but also the greed of the professional predators: the pirates. The marauders of the sea made navigation a more dangerous adventure than it was in itself. They intercepted the ships, pursued them, boarded them, captured them, stripped the goods carried and kidnapped the crew and passengers for the purpose of extortion. In addition to boarding vessels at sea to rob the cargo and capture crewmen and passengers, the pirates also landed on populated coasts and went inland, seizing people of all ages, sex and social status, free or slaves, especially young children, adolescents and girls, for ransom. They also plundered towns, villages and isolated houses; even places of asylum and the inviolate shrines. There are reports of an episode of this kind that occurred on the Cycladic island of Amorgos, but also of similar misdeeds perpetrated on the mainland shores of the Aegean region of Anatolia, for example in Caria.[8] Not content with this, the pirates of the Mediterranean also performed raids for the purpose of robbery against coastal towns and villages, and, after having raided them, they disappeared into the vast sea, the immensity of which allows them to raid with impunity with their 'hit and run' tactics.

Who were the pirates of the Mediterranean? They were former fishermen, ex-labourers, deserters of any army, exiles, escaped criminals and evildoers of every realm, origin and provenance. They were the scum of society. There were many thousands of them, all thirsty for gold and blood. Their dens were located on an island or mainland coasts. They were based quite far from the most frequented routes, so they could not be seen by passing sailors, but close enough to easily intercept them. Their nests were defended so well that it was extremely difficult for anyone to storm them or even get close to them. When their ships were at sea, they raised their banners and sailed far and wide, looking for prey. To resupply they dropped anchor in small hidden coves, edged by a sandy beach and surrounded by wooded hills. The crews went ashore to stock up on water and food, then reboarded and set off to continue their raiding across the immense sea, which was treacherous and dangerous even without them. When they came across a valuable prey, they pounced on it with ferocity. Their ships could be propelled by sail or by rowing, were rather small and were able to keep at sea even in winter. They could be *hemiolae* (with a row and a half of oars), *liburnae* (with a low and stringy line, very fast), *triremes* or *quadriremes* (solid and fast). They carried out their depredations using small, fast ships, built by themselves and called *limbus*, aboard which they quickly emerged from or retreated into hidden inlets to attack heavier vessels. To camouflage themselves, these ships had the hull, mast and sail painted in black or a blue-greenish colour, with the exception of the eyes painted on the sides of the bow, just above the waterline. The single eye was coloured black, with the outer corner pointing upwards. This superstitious motif served to counteract evil influences. The major vessels were adorned with statues and relief sculptures, and with friezes of gold, silver or purple.

Piracy was a constant threat to the commercial navigation and security of the Mediterranean populations, and an industry of which the coastal populations were often, if not victims, then the protagonists. The phenomenon had ancient origins. It is probably correct that 'there was never a time when these practices were unknown, nor will they ever cease probably so long as human nature remains the same.'[9]

In the late Bronze Age, piracy was practised by individuals and entire peoples. Around 1177, the so-called Sea Peoples ravished the Hittite Empire, the kingdom of Cyprus and the small states of the southern Levant before being defeated by Pharaoh Ramesses III on the eastern threshold of Egypt. The Phoenicians were merchants or pirates according to the occasion and convenience of the moment; hence their fame for unreliability and the distrust that surrounded them abroad. At the time of the Trojan War (twelfth century), going to sea with predatory intent was no shame for the Greeks, indeed it brought a certain glory. They boasted of doing it, at least those who lived on the coasts of the continent and in the islands of the Aegean and Ionian seas. They attacked non-fortified coastal cities and villages, and began to pillage and kidnap, from which they derived their means of subsistence. Achilles was a pirate and Ulysses was honoured to have made raids for the purpose of robbery against coastal villages of Crete, with looting and massacres. A servant of Ulysses, Eumaeus, was the first to recognize the hero coming back from the Trojan War to Ithaca.[10] He was himself a victim of piracy. He had been kidnapped as a child by Phoenician pirates and enslaved, and brought back to his native country by a Phoenician woman, daughter of a wealthy man of Sidon. In turn that woman had been kidnapped and sold as a slave to Syros (Cyclades islands) by pirates who, later, had entrusted her with the child and cared for him. After several misadventures, Eumaeus had been bought by the father of Ulysses and had become his swineherd.

The fame of the pirates' boldness and brutality was so deeply rooted in the Greek world that it was even imagined that they had unsuccessfully tried to capture Dionysus, the Greek god of vegetation, linked to the lifeblood that flows in plants, but also the god of ecstasy, wine, intoxication and the liberation of the senses. The god defended himself, making use of his supernatural powers, and his terrified attackers threw themselves into the sea and were turned into dolphins.

Greek mythology is full of stories about piracy and its victims. Issipile, daughter of the king of Lemnos – a Greek island in the northern part of the Aegean Sea – and nephew of Dionysus, was captured by pirates and sold as a slave. To the god Imene, who presided at marriages, is attributed the liberation of some girls kidnapped by pirates. Bellerophon, son of Glaucus, had routed the pirates who infested the waters of Caria (a region in south western Anatolia, between Ionia in the north, Lycia in the south and Phrygia in the west). The nymph Pimplea was kidnapped by pirates and held prisoner in Phrygia, where she went to free the Sicilian shepherd Dafni, son of Mercury. Hercules made the last of his labours in the Garden of the Hesperides, a legendary place; seven nymphs had been kidnapped by pirates, whom he killed and returned the girls to their father Atlas.

Since the Bronze Age, piracy had manifested itself everywhere in the Mediterranean as an endemic plague. It had been such a widespread pheno-menon as to appear normal, and had even carved out a space in mythology: the Athenians dedicated a temple to the gods Castor and Pollux, who had freed their city from pirates. The Dioscuri, after having cleaned up the Aegean pirates, took part in the Argonauts' expedition in search of the Golden Fleece. The Argonauts were taken for pirates by the inhabitants of Kýzikos, a city in the Gallipoli peninsula (on the European shore of the Dardanelles strait, the waterway that separates Europe from Asia, connect-ing the Aegean to the Black Sea).[11]

In the Archaic Age, the inhabitants of the northern Aegean islands were pirates. The Aegean Sea, with its thousands of islands, islets and rocks, was an ideal place to practise piracy. The pirates could easily find suitable hiding places in the small islands, in Crete and in south-western Anatolia, and launch surprise attacks to loot passing merchants. Piracy was facilitated by the fact that navigation did not take place in the open sea, but under the coast. As the city-states of Greece grew in wealth and power, they adopted measures to combat piracy and, in turn, began to act as pirates, mainly to the detriment of Phoenician ships which transported amber, silver and copper. Polycrates, tyrant of Samos, an island of the Dodecanese, was the head of a pirate state (523). In the Western Mediterranean of the Archaic Age, piracy was practiced by the Etruscans and the Greeks. The Etruscans were fierce marauders of the sea: they raided throughout the Tyrrhenian Sea and went beyond the Strait of Messina, striking the Greek colonies of eastern Sicily. They continued to do so until a group of Chalcidian pirates settled in Capo Peloro, on the Sicilian shore of the Strait of Messina, taking control of local navigation. The inhabitants of Alalia (Aleria), a city in Corsica, were pirates, originally from Phokaia, a Greek city on the Aegean coast of Anatolia. To put an end to their raids, which had lasted for five years, the Etruscans and the Carthaginians allied together and faced them in a great naval battle, which took place in the Sea of Sardinia, in the 40s or 30s of the sixth century. The Phocaeans were disastrously defeated, evacuated Alalia, and headed for the Tyrrhenian coasts of southern Italy, where they founded the colony of Hyele (Elea, Velia) in Campania, south of Posidonia (Paestum).

In the Classical Age, piracy was a way of being at war without having declared it. The reaction of the Persians to a plundering raid carried out by Aristogenes, tyrant of Miletus, against the city of Sardis, after an attempt to raid the island of Naxos had failed, was one of the main causes of the Persian War, destined to end in 490 with the victory of the Greeks at the Battle of Marathon. The phenomenon of piracy experienced a pause in the period of the Athenian thalassocracy, but it resumed after the Peloponnesian War (431–404). At that time, the island of Scyros,[12] on the direct route to the Hellespont, had a bad reputation. The same could be said for the Sporades islands, notably Skyatos. According to tradition, the 'Pelasgian' natives of Lemnos carried out their pirate raids as far as the coast of Attica.[13]

So, since ancient times, all seafaring populations had fringes dedicated to piracy: the Phoenicians, Etruscans, Greeks, Illyrians, Balearics, etc. There were also pirates on the African coast, notably in Libya, Egypt. These pirates attacked ships in transit from the mainland, or moored in a harbour, or stranded at sea. The Egyptian pirates lurked on the heights that dominated the mouth of the Nile and scanned the sea waiting for their prey to appear. The great Mediterranean powers had tried to oppose pirates in certain areas, such as for example the second naval treaty between Carthage and Rome in the fourth century. But the boardings continued elsewhere. The governments of Athens, Rhodes and Alexandria launched offensives against pirates, but always in restricted areas with limited results. First Alexander the Great, then the Ptolemies and the Republic of Rhodes fought successfully against the pirates of the Aegean and Eastern Mediterranean. Piracy had grown in the Western Mediterranean because of lack of such vigilance as already exercised by Rhodes along the Eastern Mediterranean routes. At that time the largest slave market of the Mediterranean was the city of Rhodes, on the namesake island of the Dodecanese archipelago in the south-eastern Aegean. In 304, it attracted many slave traders, and more than a thousand boats would have docked there.[14]

The Romans had to use maritime trade for vital food supplies of the city. They had to adopt measures to resist boardings by pirates, initially using the penteconter galley, which was replaced with the trireme. The pirates first appeared in the history of the Romans in the fourth century. Moving from the Aeolian islands, they intercepted a trireme en route to Delphi; when they realised it was Roman, they let it free. Some decades later pirates appeared on the coast of Lazio, but they were ejected. A much more serious threat to Roman interests was represented in the third century by Teuta, queen of the Illyrians. The Illyrian coast (Dalmatia and Albania), a tangle of islands and deep bays, flanked by menacing mountains, was a land infested with pirates. The Illyrians had been practising piracy since the dawn of recorded time, so much so that their name was commonly a synonym for piracy.[15] Around 230, Teuta allowed her subjects to practise piracy in the Adriatic against Roman and Italian merchant traffic, granting 'letters of marque' to privateers, authorising them to plunder all whom they fell in with.[16] The capital of the Illyrian kingdom became one of the most famous pirates' dens in the Mediterranean. After diplomatic negotiation had failed, Rome went to war against the Illyrians (First Illyrian War, 229–228). Rome used 200 warships and 400 cargo ships, carrying troops, and forced Teuta to accept drastic limitations to the movement of Illyrian ships.

The pirates later began to support, in an indirect, para-terroristic way, the aggressive and expansionist aims of other sovereigns: Philip V of Macedonia; Nabis, tyrant of Sparta; and Antiochus III the Great, king of Syria and emperor of Thrace, Anatolia, Mesopotamia, Persia and other Asian territories. Philip V assigned ships to Dicaearchus of Aetolia to conduct war in the Aegean, while Nabis made use of Cretan pirates in the waters south of the Peloponnese. Antiochus III benefited from the contest of the pirate leader Nikandros in the Aegean and the Spartan Ibrist with the pirates of Kefalonia in the Ionian.

The Romans acted to remove those threats, winning the Second Macedonian War (200–197), the Spartan War (195) and the Syriac War (191–190). In 189, when Roman citizens were kidnapped by pirates from Crete, Rome intervened militarily against the island. Admiral Lucius Fabius Labeo rescued the kidnapped citizens, after which the Romans defeated the piracy of the Ligurians in the Western Mediterranean (182–181), that of the Illyrians in the Adriatic and the upper Ionian (178 and 168), and that of the Balearics along the Mediterranean routes to the Iberian peninsula (123–122).

The Cilician piracy

The wealth and power of Rhodes had declined after 167, due to the creation of the free port of Delos. The Senate of Rome had established this port for the specific purpose of punishing Rhodes for its ambiguous attitude in the Third Macedonian War (171–168). Rhodes could not compete with Delos commercially and its economy fell into ruin. One of the consequences of the decline in Rhodes' maritime trade was that it failed to control piracy along the maritime routes as it had previously done. After the downsizing of Rhodes, piracy resumed in force, developing in particular in the Mediterranean region of Anatolia east of Lycia (Pamphylia, Cilicia), facing Cyprus, and ended up also infesting the Western Mediterranean. The economies of Pamphylia and Cilicia were now based mainly on the proceeds of piracy and on the slave trade.

Pamphylia was part of the Mediterranean region of Anatolia. It bordered to the west with Lycia, to the north with Pisidia, to the north-west with Lycaonia and to the east with Cilicia. To the south, it was bathed by the Eastern Mediterranean.

Cilicia wedged between Pamphylia to the west, Licaonia to the north and Syria to the east, its coast stretching from Korakesion (Alanya) to the Syrian border, a little further east of Alexandria of Issus (Iskenderun). One of the ranges of the Taurus, known as Amanus, was a natural frontier between Cilicia and the northern limit of the Syrian plain. Cilicia was divided into two parts, separated by a river: Cilicia Trachaea to the west and Cilicia Pedias to the east. Cilicia Trachaea was a rugged, mountainous district formed by the Taurus spurs, often ending in rocky headlands, with small protected harbours and cities. Located just above Cyprus, this region was wild, poor and abandoned, where communications were very difficult, except for those along the Calycadnus valley (Göksu valley). Usually, the settlements were small villages inhabited by hard and brutal men. On the other hand, communication for the maritime ports was quite easy when sea conditions permitted. Here were the cities of Elaiussa/Sebaste, Antioch ad Calycadnum and Iotape. Cilicia Pedias, by contrast, was flat, a crucial location in communications between Anatolia and Syria or Mesopotamia. This territory had experienced early urbanisation and was home to cities, generally quite large, remodelled in the Hellenistic era, with a fertile countryside, well cultivated and peaceful. Among other centres, there was Olbia, Seleucia and Tarsus, but the main city was Tarsus, in the western part of the plain, on the banks of the River Cydnus (Tarsus Chai), which descends from the Taurus mountains and unloads into the sea at Cape Zepyirius, after having formed impressive waterfalls north of the city. Traditionally, the inhabitants of Tarsus were interested in all branches of science and literature, as well as philosophy, in imitation of the Athenians and Alexandrians. The city was home to a 'university' and a philosophical school, open to contributions from members of all the currents of thought: Stoics, Epicureans, Platonics, Cynics. When, in 333, Alexander the Great attacked the Persians, crossing the Taurus range from the central Anatolian plateau through the Cilician Gates, without resistance, the city was already large and rich. The Cilician Gates crossed the Taurus north of Tarsus; Alexander had found them open through the betrayal of a local lord, a Persian vassal. The river at Tarsus was the Cydnus. Its waters are very cold, and to get across it, Alexander risked death.

Another pass of strategic importance crosses the Amanus at the Amanian Gate (Bahçe Pass). In 333, in the foothills along the coast between the Cilician Gates and the Amanian Gate, Alexander the Great defeated Darius III Codomannus, emperor of the Persians. The Battle of Issus – the second great battle of Alexander's conquest of Asia, subsequent to the Granicus – was fought near the mouth of the Pinarus River and south of the ancient town of Issus. To celebrate victory, Alexander founded the city of Alexandria of Issus (Iskenderun). After Alexander's death in 323, Cilicia was long disputed between sovereigns and rival military commanders; it fell into the hands of the Ptolemies and then passed to the Seleucids, who, however, had never been able to fully control the region's western parts. The Seleucids rebuilt Tarsus. They decorated it with prestigious monuments and great roads, allowed the arts and culture to flourish, and kept it autonomous, letting it coin its own money. Cilicia remained under the dominion of the Seleucids until Antiochus III, in execution of the Treaty of Apamea (188), abandoned all his possessions north of the Taurus and withdrew to Syria. Rome had distributed these territories among its client-states. It was then that Cilicia Trachea saw the pirates settling on its shores. The criminal story of the Mediterranean region of Anatolia flourished after the Peace of Apamea, which, in putting an end to the Syrian War (192–188), forced Antiochus III, emperor of Anatolia, Syria, Mesopotamia and Persia, to yield to the victors (Rome, Pergamon and Rhodes) Anatolia west of the Taurus. Around 140, the pretender to the Seleucid throne, Diodotus Tryphon, occupied the abandoned fortresses of Cilicia Trachea and that of Korakesion, making them the base of his pirate raids.

Korakesion (Alanya) is a fortified port town located on a jagged coastline, closed behind by rough mountains. At that point of the coast, a promontory stretches out into the sea, beginning with a low and narrow isthmus and ending with rocky cliffs. On the most advanced part of the cape was a fortress, which overlooked the sea. The fortress had been built on top of a peak, on precipitous rocks, in the Hellenistic period following the area's conquest by Alexander the Great.[17] While the fortress of Korakesion is located on the promontory, the port town of Korakesion is at the root, on the slope that leads to the fortress.

With the passing of time that first nucleus of pirates grew through the aggregation of local populations and of men who came from many parts – Syrians, Cypriots, Cretans, Pontics, Pamphylians, Lycians – so much so that Cilician piracy had risen to significantly affect the management of crises and conflicts throughout the Mediterranean. Korakesion became the largest Cilician port and the main haunt of piracy in the Eastern Mediterranean. At that time, Pamphylia – which had been included among the provinces annexed by the Romans to the dominions of Eumenes II Soter (197–159), king of Pergamon – also became a centre for criminal activity. The port town of Side, about 50 nautical miles from the dens of the Cilician pirates, became the chief centre of the Pamphylian pirates and the most important slave market of the Eastern Mediterranean, in competition with Delos.

The fundamental impulse to the extraordinary development of that piracy came from the immense amount of resources devolved to this end by Mithridates VI (134–63), king of Pontus. Cilician piracy played a role of considerable importance in the Mithridatic Wars (fought between 88 and 63), when the pirate chiefs Isidorus and Seleucus distinguished themselves for daring and ferocity.[18] After 146, since the control of the sea that was previously operated by Carthage had failed, the pirates also reappeared in the Western Mediterranean. The pirates were a sword of Damocles for ships that crossed the Strait of Sicily to bring African grain to Rome. The danger from the pirates was so great that the sea transporters and their passengers were terrified of encountering them. Shipowners would not venture to finance transport by sea, which had a huge effect on maritime trade.

In the second half of the second century, the activity of the Mediterranean pirates was no longer aimed at obtaining the means of subsistence, as in the past, but was a real industry, in the hands of criminal organizations based at strategic points. This industry, providing unransomed prisoners to slave traders, was practised in order to make money on the cruel fate of many unfortunates, but originated mainly from the craving of the ruling elites to own slaves, for various reasons: whether economic or psychological (one of the reasons that pushed the buying of slaves was the drive to dominate other men).

The participation of the Roman army in the slave trade

Rome was strongly interested in the slave trade because its economy required the employment of large numbers of slaves, to be used for work in the fields and for farming. One of the reasons why its politics was based on territorial expansion was to get the slave labour it needed. From this we can see that the Roman Army was one of the main protagonists of the slave trade, along with Mediterranean pirates. After each victory, the Army sold prisoners of war to merchants who followed the legions during their campaigns, who staying outside the entrenched camps, together with other civilians, for example prostitutes. Those who had been taken prisoner in war, either as soldiers or as defenders or members of the civilian population of a conquered city, as well as those who lived in regions traversed by a marching army, were considered a constituent element of the spoils of war, in the same way as treasures in gold, silver and coinage, artistic masterpieces, lands, livestock and moveable goods accumulated through the looting of an enemy country. Like other spoils of war, they were the property of the victorious commander, who could share them with his officers and soldiers, who would keep their share of loot for themselves or sell some or all of it to merchants. Traders bought to resell and earn the difference between the price spent and that received. Therefore, all the goods purchased by merchants from the military were resold: the human ones, mainly in the slave markets. The size of the trade in the sale of prisoners of war was huge, and the sums of money obtained were immense. We can get an idea of the magnitude of the profits of the traffic in slaves if we consider that, between 200 and 150, Rome captured about 250,000 prisoners of war, including Celts, Macedonians, Greeks, Epirotes, Anatolians and Syrians.[19] Just to give an example, after the Battle of Pydna in 168, Lucius Aemilius Paullus Macedonicus captured 150,000 Epirotes, for the most part Molossians.[20]

Chapter 2

First Uprisings

The slaves of the Romans

The Romans, like other people in the world, used slaves as labour in various activities, depending on their abilities, physical strength and education. Slaves that were worth less were used as labour in farms, industries, shipyards and weapons factories. Those with a high level of education were bought for a higher price – sometimes an exorbitant price – and employed in homes and public offices as servants, doctors, tutors, secretaries or scribes. The destiny of individual slaves depended on imponderable factors, including chance or fortune. Everything depended on the owner, whether or not he was animated by good feelings and was without prejudice. Many Romans despised slaves, considering them mere 'animals with words'; in their eyes, slaves were not noble men, generous of spirit, but cruel, greedy, violent and fanatical individuals.

However, among the Romans, slavery was a condition from which one could be redeemed. Roman law allowed a slave to be freed, that is released from his master. The freedman (as was called the freed slave) remained linked to his former master – who become his patron – by mutual obligations. The liberation took place through the application of a special juridical institution called *manumissio*. The single freedman, upon release, could acquire Roman citizenship, or be a *latinus junianus* or a *dediticius*. He became a Roman citizen if his master requested his enrolment in a territorial tribe. The *Latini juniani* were holders of the citizenship of Latin law; they could operate freely in the business world (trade, crafts, industry, currency exchange, management of contracts, etc.), but could not make a will, nor receive a legacy, let alone be appointed guardians in a will. They were also excluded from a career as a magistrate and from voting for the renewal of magistrates (the right to elect could be purchased by their grandchildren). The *dediticii* were all the ex-slaves who regained their liberty without becoming either Roman citizens with full rights or Latins. Some freedmen received loans from their patrons to buy, educate, train and then resell other slaves, or to act in a deal on behalf and in the interest of another person, who preferred not to appear, as 'straw men'. If they were particularly skilled, they could become rich without limit.

Bad masters

Some masters treated their slaves with humanity, fed them sufficiently and dressed them, leaving them free to profess the cult they preferred. They even allowed them to be part of colleges and associations formed by people having the same work, to defend their common interests, under the protection of a tutelary deity. The most numerous of these colleges and associations were the guilds of arts and crafts, which included actors, boatmen, carpenters, tanners, leather-goods makers, flautists, bakers, writers, school teachers, doctors, merchants, muleteers, jewellers, painters, sculptors, weavers, dyers, potters, etc. Usually, the deities venerated by slaves were the chthonic ones (generally female, linked to the cults of the divinities of the subsoil that triggered earthquakes and volcanic eruptions), the Lares and the god Silvanus, as well as those called by the Romans Diana, Iupiter, Dionysus and Helius. The latter was the god and personification of the sun in Greek mythology, called Helios by Greeks and revered in many parts of the Hellenistic world as a symbol of justice and equality, albeit with different names: Apollon in Rhodes, Shamash in Syria, Baal in the southern Levant. Generally, Helius is depicted driving the sun chariot, in the act of leading it from east to west. Dionysus was the Greek god of wine, of ecstasy and of the liberation of the senses. He represented the state of natural man, his primordial, animal, savage, instinctive part, which remains present even in the most civilized man, as an insuppressible original part. He was the god of the excluded, of the humble and the oppressed, for whom he represented a hope of redemption from poverty and liberation from chains. Some masters even agreed to pass over the differences between the free and the enslaved, when, during the *Saturnalia*, the roles were reversed and the slaves were served at the table by their masters. The *Saturnalia* was a festive cycle of traditional Roman religion dedicated to the god Saturn and the mythical Golden Age. It took place every year, in December, with the preparation of large banquets and exchanges of greetings and gifts.

Other masters, however, were arrogant, proud and treated their slaves with harshness and cruelty. At the time of purchase they marked them with fire as they did their cattle and then chained them, a cruel fate for all, but especially for those born free. Such owners made them work like animals, giving them little to eat and nothing to wear. They held their fate in their hands, punishing them for the slightest infraction, whipping or torturing them and throwing them into prison. If the slaves rebelled, they killed them. When the slaves became old or sick, they simply got rid of them, as they would useless goods.

The inhuman treatment of slaves in the countryside

Slaves serving households in towns were usually not treated too badly, at least not in a manner that made them want to escape or revolt. The fate of slaves employed in the countryside, and in the quarries and mines, was far different. These unfortunate people hoed the land, tended animals, broke stones, toiled all day long, and were treated without a shred of humanity by their masters, who sometimes even had fun in mistreating them. In moments of rest, however unhappy, they let off steam. They blasphemed against their common fate, plotted and dreamed of revenge. Sometimes, driven by despair, they revolted, especially if they had been born free. Slave revolts were usually acts of rebellion by individuals, who were immediately opposed and severely punished (according to Roman law, if a slave killed his master, he would be put to death along with all the other slaves owned by the victim; if he fled and was captured, he would be tortured and crucified or thrown from a cliff). Occasionally there were collective upheavals against order and established power: however, they were spontaneous actions, only small or not very extensive and disorganized.

The involvement of slaves in political conspiracies

The first revolts of slaves in Rome had taken place in 501 and 500. They must be placed in the broader context of the attempt of Tarquinius Superbus, seventh and last king of Rome and third of the Etruscan dynasty of the Tarquins, to resume power. Tarquinius was overthrown by an uprising of the Roman people, who did not forgive the many acts of arrogance by himself and his parents and relatives. The last straw had been the rape of the wife of a cousin of Tarquinius, by the son of Tarquinius himself. Behind the popular revolt, however, it seems that there was a political design: Lars Porsenna, king of Clevsi (Chiusi), an Etruscan city in the Tiber Valley, wanted to usurp the throne of Rome. After the expulsion of Tarquinius, Porsenna besieged Rome, but failed to take it. He retired immediately after Mucius Scaevola had given him a demonstration of the moral temperament of the Romans, which had deeply impressed him. Meanwhile, Tarquinius had asked for and obtained the help of his father-in-law, Octavius Mamilius, lord of Tusculum (Tuscolo), to recover the throne. The Latins were intolerant of the hegemony of Rome. However, to hope to defeat the Romans was beyond Tarquinius, even with the exiles from Fidenae and Cameria, who were also putting pressure on Mamilius.

In 501 and 500, Mamilius and Tarquinius hatched two successive conspiracies against Rome, both of which failed. These involved the most disadvantaged and influential parts of the population – free citizens in misery and slaves – who were understandably willing to do anything to gain freedom, prosperity and money; but also some Latins, as well as the followers of the Tarquins, belonging to the Etruscan component of the Roman people. In the first case the slaves were in the minority. The 501 plot was unveiled by some informers; the consuls Postumius Cominius and Titus Lartius ordered the gates to be closed and the knights occupied Rome's fortifications. The slaves who had been conspirators were rounded up and then tortured and crucified.

In 500, Mamilius and Tarquinius instigated the poor of the city to rise up against the rich because of the infamous activity of the moneylenders, and they again involved, first and foremost, several slaves. The conspiracy was discovered through the betrayal of two conspirators, two Tarquinii, Publius and Marcus, both of Laurentum (Castelporziano), who as their reward received citizenship, money and land. It seems that Tarquinius later attempted to regain power again, with the help of Aristodemus, tyrant of Cumae (Cuma), a city in Campania, and with the connivance of the Roman plebs of the lower class and the slaves of Rome. The hypothesis is corroborated by the fact that Tarquinius finished his days in Cumae, a guest of Aristodemus.

The slaves of Rome also appear as accomplices in an attempt to overthrow the *res publica* in the uprising of Appius Erdonius Sabinus in 460. Erdonius placed himself at the head of citizens of Sabina, Roman plebeians overburdened by debts, the Roman people (the *capite censes*, the lowest social stratum of Roman society) and Roman slaves – 4,000 men in all – and took both the Capitolium and the Arx by surprise. The enterprise failed because of the reaction of the consul Valerius, who fell bravely while leading an assault on one of Rome's hills, and that of the citizens of Tusculum, who came to Rome's aid. Erdonius, after having done slaughter around him, died struck by countless arrows, while few of his allies were taken alive, most killing themselves. In 419 another revolt happened in Greece. Some slaves slaughtered their masters, together with their wives, looting and starting fires. It was a serious but episodic event. Nothing like that had happened before, and it would be 300 years before it was repeated.

A long interval separated the conspiracy of the servants of 419 from similar events which occurred in 259 in Rome, and one wonders if it was not due to a lack of news, but rather to a newfound social peace, given that there were four such conspiracies from 501–419. A third possibility is that historians may have overlooked slave revolts and the plots in which slaves were involved because more important events took place contemporaneously, and they concentrated on the latter. Among these events were the Sack of Rome of 390 or 386, which suspended the territorial expansion of Rome in the region of Lazio; the Samnite Wars and the Latin War, which expanded Rome's influence in Campania and subdued the Samnites; the Pyrrhic War, by which Rome expanded to the Ionian coast, submitting the cities founded in Italy as Greek colonies in the sixth century, collectively known as *Magna Graecia*;[1] the struggles between patricians and plebeians, which lasted until 287; the advance of the Roman legions to Rhegion (Rhegium, Reggio Calabria) at the southern tip of Italy, on the shore of the Strait of Messina that separates the continent from Sicily; and finally, in 265, the outbreak of the First Punic War.

In 259, Rome was in very serious danger, which could have sent it to ruin, at a time when the war with Carthage in Sicily was going badly. Three thousand slaves and 4,000 *socii navales* (naval allies) wanted to take advantage of Rome's weakness to massacre Roman citizens.[2] The slaves involved were prisoners of war sold to Roman citizens living in Rome, Carthaginian for the most part. The remainder included prisoners of war captured and sold to slave traders after the conquest of Akragas (Agrigentum, Agrigento) in 261, and the Samnite, Lucanian and Bruttian prisoners of war captured over previous decades. The *socii navales* were workers who came to Rome from the territories of its allies to help build a large fleet, including quinqueremes, and form the crews of the ships, perhaps even the troops embarked on them. They were probably for the most part Samnites from Neapolis (Napoli), Pompeii and Pithekoussai (Pithecusae, Ischia). It seems they conspired to escape from the harsh conditions of life in navy service. while others (mainly Carthaginians and Samnites) were driven by hostile feelings towards Rome. Their plan failed due to the commander of the allies, Erius Potilius, who had pretended to be an accomplice to investigate and foil the plot. Summoned by the Senate, he unveiled the plot. The Roman authorities intervened in silence, at night, without bloodshed, dismissing the allies and having the slaves taken from their masters[3] (one can well imagine what could have happened in the Italian territories if news had spread that a revolt had broken out in Rome).

Another attempt at revolt in which slaves were involved took place during the Second Punic War. In 217, a spy of Carthaginian nationality was captured and twenty-five slaves were crucified for their part in the conspiracy.[4] It is uncertain whether the two facts were connected. The slaves could have been agents or collaborators of the spy, to whom they provided information of military interest, or by whom they were instigated to revolt against their masters, possibly against the state, and create riots. It is likely that they were living in Rome, but they could have been foreigners, even Carthaginian. It seems that the spy was at work for two years. The plot was discovered thanks to an informer, another slave, who was rewarded by being freed and the payment of a sum of money. It is unknown whether he was a slave who was spying for the Carthaginians, along with the other twenty-five, who betrayed his companions. It is likely that the Campo Marzio – understood as the slopes of the Pincio, Quirinale and Campidoglio, as far as *amnis Petronia*, the Via Flaminia and the Tiber, including the Flaminia meadow – was where the slaves gathered to conspire. Their councils could have gone unnoticed in such a busy and confusing place, where there were continuous assembly meetings, military exercises and troops reviewed by their commanders, military recruitment, census operations, naval shipments and foreign legations. The place itself may be indicative of the quality of the conspirators and of the information provided. It cannot be ruled out that they were public slaves, shipyard or temple workers. In that case they could provide information concerning troops, naval expeditions and the tenor of topics dealt with, and the agreements concluded, between the Roman state and the foreign legations.[5]

Another conspiracy in which slaves were enlisted took place in 198 in Lower Lazio. A group of hostages of the Romans were held in Setia (Sezze Romano), with stringent limitations of personal freedom. Setia was a small town on a high hill commanding the Pontine plain, about 65km (40 miles) south of Rome and 10km (6 miles) from the coast.[6] The hostages belonged to noble families of Carthage. The servants were personal servants of the hostages and slaves of local inhabitants; former prisoners of war, they were all North African – Carthaginians, Libyans, Numidians and maybe others, belonging to tribes that had fought against Rome during the Second Punic War as allies of Carthage. They conspired to foment a slave revolt in Setia itself and the nearby cities of Norba (Norma) and Circeii (San Felice al Circeo).[7] Judging by what happened, they were all people of high rank with political-organizational skills. The conspirators aimed to take control of a stretch of the Appian Way, a base on the coast (Circeii) and a stronghold in the mountains dominating the Pontine Marshes (Norba). However, their plans were foiled. Two slaves and one free man revealed the plot, receiving a cash prize and the slaves their freedom.[8] The praetor Lucius Cornelius Lentulus received the information in Rome and quickly reached Setia, enlisting a militia along the way. He captured the leaders of the conspiracy and later the other conspirators and slaves involved, who had fled.[9]

Soon after, a new revolt threatened to break out in Praeneste (Palestrina),[10] a fortified city in the same region, that had always been a refuge for exiles and political fugitives. Praeneste, with its celebrated temple and oracle of Fortune, is about 23 miles from Rome. It was said to be founded by Greeks, being formerly named Polystephanus. A fortified citadel was located on a lofty mountain, which overhangs the town. In addition to its natural defences, the city was served by subterranean passages, linking it to the plains. Some such tunnels served to convey water, while others formed secret ways.[11] Five hundred slaves were executed at Praeneste. In order to avoid the risk of contagion, the Latin cities were exhorted to keep the hostages locked up and to guard the chained prisoners.

Only two years after the plot of Setia, in 197, a slave movement took place in Etruria (Tuscany). This was bloodily put down by the Roman army, led by the praetor Marcus Acilius Glabrio. Many rebels were killed, the leaders of the revolt were scourged and then crucified, the others being given back to their masters.[12] It is worthy to note that the military intervention of Glabrio took place in the territory of the Etruscan allies, under the guise of protecting the local communities. The main aim was actually to prevent the rebels from interfering with communities between Rome and the Po Valley, where Rome was at war against the Celtic Boii tribe.

In 185–184, a revolt of slave-shepherds occurred in Apulia (Puglia),[13] in connection with a scandal of the religious rites in honour of Dionysus (Bacchanalia), which plunged many Romans into panic.[14] The cult of Dionysus, mysterious and orgiastic, was born in Crete, from where it had spread to Attica and then to *Magna Graecia*. Later it had reached Rome, where it had been first assimilated to the god Bacchus and then to the god Liber.[15] In the beginning the Roman authorities had restricted the practice of such a cult to women, foreigners and slaves. Then they had been disinterested for a long time, until, in 186, they did not forbid it, but only allowed it in exceptional cases and placed controls on it. They also set up a commission of inquiry with judicial powers, that sentenced to death many people convicted of plotting to commit acts of immorality and other crimes, and incarcerated others convicted of similar offences.[16]

It is important to stress that the slave risings mentioned above were exceptional. They took place in the second century, in Southern Italy, and in areas where there was a high concentration of slaves and weak surveillance.[17] They showed the ability of slaves to rebel not only against their masters, but also against the Roman state, at the risk of their lives. Some define them as revolts, while others incline to think that groups of slaves rose up at the instigation of free men, for whom they served as a tactical mass.[18]

Certainly such movements were not comparable to the slave uprisings that took place later in Sicily and in Italy, that were large enough to be able to be called wars. These started in Sicily in the second half of the second century, when the island was a Roman *provincia*, the foreign policy of Rome was marked by the Spanish War and its interior policy was about to be occupied by Tiberius Sempronius Gracchus, whose tribunate of the plebeians would be a turning point in the history of the Late Republic.

PART I

HELLENISTIC SICILY

Chapter 3

A Large Triangle-Shaped Island

Physical geography

Sicily is a large, populous and prosperous island, with many cities and good ports. It is close to Italy, from which it is separated by the Strait of Messina; and it is only 145km (90 miles) from North Africa, from which it is separated by the Channel or Strait of Sicily. The Strait of Messina, at its narrowest point, is 3.1km (1.9 miles) wide and is at most 250 metres (820ft) deep. Looking at it from the slopes of the mountains facing each other from Sicily and Calabria (the southernmost region of the Italian peninsula), it seems to be a very large river that flows between the shores. From the western end of the island, the nearest coast of Africa was a day's trip away. Some say that, on days when the sky is blue and clear, from Mount Erice, looking towards the sea, it is possible to glimpse the coast of North Africa in the distance. When travelling from Palermo if you turn to the west, along the northern coast of Sicily, you come in sight of Monte Erice, after having rounded the promontory of Monte Cofano. It stands alone on a vast flat terrace, facing west to the Sicilian Channel and the town of Trapani. Sicily is in the centre of the Mediterranean. In fact, conventionally, the Strait of Messina separates the Eastern Mediterranean from the Western Mediterranean. Sicily is thus at the centre between Europe and Africa, and between the East and West. Its geographical position is extremely privileged. It has made Sicily the point of intersection of all traffic currents, from north to south, and east to west, of the immense Mediterranean basin. The island has always been a major target for trade or for conquering armies. Dominating Sicily was a primary strategic requirement.

Mount Etna

The island has a roughly triangular shape, and for this reason the Greeks called it *Trinacria*, '(the land of the) three capes'.[2] The landscape is dominated by Mount Etna (3,326 metres high, or 10,912ft), the highest mountain in Italy south of the Alps, rising in the middle of the eastern part of the island. The immense size of the mountain looms over a great plain (Plain of Catania), of which it occupies the edge, lapped by the Ionian Sea. It stands out against the backdrop of an almost always blue sky and offers a magnificent spectacle. It can be seen from the Tyrrhenian coast of Calabria and dominates the entire coastal arch of Sicily from Syracuse to Messina, as well as central Sicily up to at least Enna. Mount Etna is covered up to midway by woods of chestnut, oak and fir, and at higher altitudes by meadows and rocks, covered by snow in winter. In its various environments many animals find suitable conditions for living, mainly rabbits, foxes, birds, hares and partridges. The mountain is a place of mythological and poetic suggestion, like many other places in Sicily. The smithy of Hephaestus is believed to be situated beneath it. Hephaestus was the Greek god of fire and smithery, the son of Zeus and Hera (the Roman Iupiter and Iuno), and the husband both of Maia and Aphrodite (Venus for the Romans). His Roman counterpart was Vulcan, god of fire, including the fire of volcanoes, metalworking and the forge. The Etruscan name is Sethlans.

Mount Etna is also the home of the legendary Cyclopes, members of a race of giants, sons of Poseidon (Neptune for the Romans), the Greek god of the sea and earthquakes, to whom horses were sacred. The Cyclopes lived in a wooded and unexplored environment, and were herdsmen or shepherds. Odysseus, king of Itaca, a hero of the Trojan War, and his companions were said to have met one of them, Polyphemus, after landing in Sicily during their journey back home from Troy. The Greek poet Homer (who possibly lived in the eighth century BC), in his epic poem *Odyssey*, tells that they met Polyphemus in his cave on the slopes of Mount Etna. To defend themselves from him, after he had killed some of them, they made him drunk, and stuck a pointed pine trunk in his one eye before escaping. Odysseus had previously told Polyphemus that his name was 'Nobody'. Crazed with pain, Polyphemus summoned the other Cyclopes, his brothers, shouting that he had been blinded by Nobody and urging them to hunt him down; they were perplexed, for how could Polyphemus be blinded by nobody? In the meantime, Polyphemus blindly hurled large boulders, trying to hit the fugitives. According to another tradition, some of those boulders, falling into the sea, formed the islets which can still be seen in the sea off Aci Trezza, north of Catania.

The Greek lyric poet Pindar (517–438) – who lived around 470 in Sicily in Syrakousai (Syracusae, Siracusa) and Akragas (Agrigentum,

Agrigento), both in Sicily, among the tyrants Hiero and Theron – describes Mount Etna in his *Pythian* as follows:

> And the pillar of the sky holds him down, snow-covered Aetna, year-round nurse of bitter frost, from whose inmost caves belch forth the purest streams of unapproachable fire. In the daytime her rivers roll out a fiery flood of smoke, while in the darkness of night the crimson flame hurls rocks down to the deep plain of the sea with a crashing roar. That monster shoots up the most terrible jets of fire; it is a marvellous wonder to see, and a marvel even to hear about when men are present. Such a creature is bound beneath the dark and leafy heights of Aetna and beneath the plain, and his bed scratches and goads the whole length of his back stretched out against it.[3]

These words clarify the nature of Mount Etna from a geological point of view. It is the largest volcano in Europe and one of the most active volcanoes in the world. Its many craters scattered on its top and slopes indicate eruptions of basaltic lava alternated with periods of calm of differing duration. Usually, a white column of gas rises from the main crater: this is the 'breath' of the volcano, indicating that the mountain is active, alive, but 'sleeps'. The 'awakening' is signalled by ground tremors. The white cloud grows in size and becomes dark grey in colour. It is fed by terrifying explosions, which project into the sky fumes, vapours, lava, boulders, ash and lapilli. The erupted solid materials rise up to great height, then rain back down around the top of the mountain, while a veil of ash covers the slopes, along with the plain, coast and sea below. The sky darkens, an acrid smell of sulphur spreads in the air, and lava overflows from the craters. The lava, creating long trails of fire and vapours, first descends from the mountain in liquid form, sometimes running along a tunnel; then, cooling, it congeals and gradually reduces speed, but still advances unstoppably. At night, the tongues of fire that descend from the mountain can be seen from afar, creating a real spectacle.

Rarely, the lava descends to lower altitudes and the Plain of Catania, covering the cultivated fields. Everything depends on the strength of the eruption, which is variable and sometimes very powerful. Occasionally the lava flows even advance to the Ionian coast and into the sea. When it enters the properties, the locals philosophically comment that 'He' – as they call the volcano – has regained possession of what is his own, and welcome lava as a special guest. In this way, with a mixture of faith and superstition, evil is exorcised. But not all evil creates harm. The passage of lava fertilizes the land, feeding new crops, especially the vines. No other area of Sicily produces a wine of the same quality, and Sicilian wines are famed far and wide outside Sicily.[4] Once the volcano has calmed down, there sprouts from the mantle of lava tufts of red, yellow and blue flowers, showing nature's great perseverance. Man and nature are said to resume their dialogue, like the rhythm of the seasons. This has happened periodically on Mount Etna since time immemorial, by law of nature. Nature is said to be the volcano, and nature's law is its law, to which all things living on its slopes and around it are subjected.

The surrounding islands and submarine volcanoes

Mount Etna is the southern end of a line of volcanoes (a part of which is submarine) extending from Campania (the region of Southern Italy, with Naples its main centre) to Sicily, passing through the Lower Tyrrhenian Sea. This is dramatically evident in the Aeolians, a small archipelago in the Lower Thyrrenian Sea, north of Messina.[5] In those islands there are two active volcanoes, Stromboli and Vulcano, of which the first erupts continuously, with lava fountains, while the other alternates long periods of apparent calm with terrifying, explosive eruptions. The Aeolians are known as islands of wind and fire, wild lands, made of lavic rock, black with a reddish, rusty patina, that the sun's warmth turns brown; but they are also known as a land of myths, because Homer, in his *Iliad*, locates there the realm of Aeolus, king of the winds and friend of Odysseus. According to Homer, Aeolus hosted Odysseus during his long and tormented journey home, and on his departure from the island of Lipari, the largest of the Aeolian islands, gave him a vase in which he had enclosed all the winds, to facilitate his navigation, with the recommendation not to open it. But the vase was opened and immediately the winds rose furiously in a terrible storm, which slammed the ship of Odysseus against the island of the sorceress Circe … but this is another story.

Further volcanoes rise from the depths of the Tyrrhenian Sea north of the Aeolians. Apparently they are extinct for the most part. One of them, almost as big as Mount Etna, is called Marsili and it is said could erupt at any time.

But it is not only the Lower Tyrrhenian that has volcanoes above and below the water's surface. A group of submarine volcanoes is spread in the middle of the Strait of Sicily, lying under the water, south of Agrigento. One of those volcanoes is also comparable in size to Etna. It has derived its name, Empedocles, from the Greek pre-Socratic philosopher (*c.* 490–430), a scientist and citizen of Akragas (Agrigentum, Agrigento). It is an active volcano: one of its cones erupts occasionally, with a dark, steaming lava that emerges on the surface in a pit of fire, smoke, ashes and gas. It creates short-lived islets that cannot resist the force of the waves. It could thus be said that, in the middle of the Strait of Sicily, there is a land which appears and disappears, a ghost island.

The landscape of the interior of Sicily varies according to the region: there is the northern mountain range, Etna, the undulations of the central area, the Iblei mountains in the south-east, the flat western part and the staggered plateaus in the south. The northern mountain range – the Peloritani and the Nebrodi, partly covered with woods, and in winter with snow – is a continuation of the long chain of the Apennines, which is the back bone of the Italian peninsula. There are many springs and torrents, but only a few rivers. The most important river is the Simeto, which crosses the Plain of Catania and flows into the Ionian Sea.

Population, economy and cultural framework

In the second half of the second century, the Sicilian population ranged from 600,000 to one million.[6] The greatest population density was found in the interior of the island and in the south-east, and a tendency towards population growth occurred in the north-west. Approximately half a million people derived their livelihoods from cereal agriculture and breeding livestock. Agriculture was the main economic activity. Of the main cities, those located on the coast developed maritime trade, whether by inshore navigation, from one port to another, with small cargo boats and small businesses, or across the open sea and over long distances. Its ports were characterized by a continuous coming and going of ships from nearby or distant ports, scattered among the islands and mainland shores of the Mediterranean. Ships had a rounded stern and bow, a sailing propulsion system, side rudders rotating on an axle, a large hold, possibly one or more covered intermediate bridges, and a stern cabin. They loaded mainly wine and oil, but also shingles, tiles, sulphur loaves, lead ingots, pottery, etc. In some cases they also embarked passengers and armed men.

The Sicilians were a mosaic of five different ethnic groups, which in the past had strong divergences marked by wars, but in the historical period considered coexisted without major problems. There were the descendants of the Phoenician/Punic and Greek settlers, and also the indigenous Sicels, Sicani (or Sicanians) and Elymians, who had been living on the island since the Iron Age.[7] To these groups were added Romans and Italics, in service or permanently resident. The Sicans had inhabited Sicily for a long time when the Phoenicians arrived.[8] They were spread in the western part of the island, except the north-western corner. The Sicels came to Sicily from central Italy and lived in the eastern part of the island.[9] The origin of the Elymians is uncertain. According to a Greek tradition, adopted by the Greek historian Thucydides, who lived in the fifth century, the founders were a band of Trojan fugitives from the destruction of their home city, Troy. Trojans fleeing from their burning city were said to have landed on Sicily after a long sea journey. They built four cities in the north-western corner of the island: Eryx (Erice), Egesta (Segesta), Entella and Iaitias (Ietas, Monte Iato). Their physical and cultural mixing with the Sicans gave life to the ethnos of the Elymians. Another tradition, however, says the Elymians came from mainland Italy.[10] Others say that the Elymians were a distinct people, already existing in north-estern Sicily when the Trojans arrived. There is, however, another story, according to which Segesta was founded by a band of Phocaeans (migrants from Phocaea, a Greek city in the Aegean region of Anatolia).

The cultural framework of Sicily was, therefore, composite and in some ways unclear. It remained such despite the processes of Romanization – acculturation, integration, assimilation – having begun immediately after the Roman conquest, with the administrative reorganization of the territory and the increasing insertion in local communities of Latin and Italic elements. The culture of the Greek-speaking populations continued to be that of the Greek Sicily of the past. Not only the ruling class, but the entire community was attached to the Greek-Hellenistic matrix culture and tried to maintain a living relationship with Greece, and in general with the Hellenistic world.[11] In those communities the language of use was Greek, or rather the dialect of the metropolis that founded the particular city. For example, at *Syracusae* (the Latin name of the Greek city of *Syrakousai*), the language of use was the Doric dialect, because the first settlers came from Corinth. Latin, the language of the Romans, was spoken only on official occasions. The Roman magistrates spoke normally in Latin, but they often used Greek. The sentences issued by the courts were in Latin, but Greek was used in the trial phase of the judicial proceedings. A Phoenician-Punic tradition – Elymian, Sicel or Sican, according to the particular case, persisted in the panhellenic populations. The Greek-Hellenistic culture, however, tended to also spread in the territories that did not have a Greek tradition and to acquire prevalence there. We can conclude that the second-century island now belonged to the Romans, but maintained a prevalent Greek cultural imprint; thus it would be more appropriate to talk about a Hellenistic Sicily than a Roman Sicily.

Chapter 4

From the Phoenicians to the Romans

Sicily before the Romans

Phoenician merchants and navigators 'discovered' Sicily during the height of their culture and marine power, *c.* 1200–800. They were supplied with precious metals in Sardinia and Spain, and Sicily was on their maritime routes. Sicily supplied them with minerals – namely sulphur – and was a market for their goods, so the Phoenicians established along the Sicilian coasts many places of commerce, factories and markets to trade with the natives.[1] The Phoenicians had also founded maritime colonies in North Africa, Sardinia and the Iberian peninsula. The most important of those settlements was *Qart-ḥadašt* (Karchēdōn, Carthago, now commonly Carthage). Carthage was located in North Africa, on the shores of Lake Tunis, and, with the passing of time, became a major centre of a republican-oligarchic regime city-state, inhabited by hundreds of thousands of people.

Carthage was the hub of a maritime empire and was able to compete with the Etruscans, Romans and Greeks for supremacy in mercantile trade across the Western Mediterranean. All the Phoenician urban communities of Sicily had links with Carthage, as well as with the Greek cities of the Eastern Mediterranean and southern Italy.

Many Greeks arrived in Sicily in the eighth century from continental Greece, the islands of the Aegean and the shores of the Anatolian mainland. First they were sailor-traders and beat the trade routes. Then masses of settlers arrived in Sicily, driven by the need to colonize new territories essential to their survival and that of their community of origin. Mainly they came from city-states like Chalcis, Athens, Corinth and Megara. This phenomenon did not only concern Sicily, but also the Aeolian islands, southern Italy (from the Ionian to the Tyrrhenian Sea, passing through the Strait of Messina) and even Sardinia, Corsica, southern France, southern Spain and Cyrenaica. Settlers built numerous cities, mainly beside the sea, and took possession of territories of increasing size, starting by the coast. This was coherent with the Greek idea of a city, intended as a city-state, which implied the appropriation usually of a large area necessary for the needs of the community and its prosperity, and presupposed the sovereignty of the city and the overwhelming of the previous occupants. This does not necessarily mean that the natives were physically removed; if they submitted to the newcomers, they could survive within the city-state and even integrate themselves into the new socio-political structure, while remaining in a subordinate position.

In Sicily, the Phoenicians did not oppose Greek colonization, since their main economic interests were related to maritime trade and this activity needed peace, not to mention that the Greeks were now customers of the Phoenicians and partners in commercial enterprises. They had abandoned all their positions in Sicily and moved to the north-west, where – with the consent of the Elymians – they built three walled cities: Mtw (Motye, Mozia), Zyz (Panormos, Panormus, Palermo) and Kfr (Solus, Soluntum, Solunto).[2]

Mtw stood on a flat islet in a coastal lagoon, now known as Stagnone di Marsala. It was connected to the promontory of Birgi by a road that crossed the lagoon, and enclosed within a 2.5 metre (8.2ft) wall, reinforced by square-based towers. The inhabitants were a thriving community devoted mainly to maritime trade, but also to the production of ceramics and textiles. Many of them lived in beautiful houses and the city was richly ornamented. Zyz had the most beautiful port of Sicily, so much so that the Greeks took inspiration from this to call the city Panormos, 'all port'.[3] Kfr was about 16km (10 miles) east of Zyz, on the south-east side of Monte Catalfano, commanding a fine view from a high, naturally strong situation.

Another story is that of the impact of the Dorian settlers with the Sicels, of which an emblematic episode was the violent end of the kingdom of Hybla (Pantalica?), caused by the territorial expansion of the Syracusans along the coast towards Eloros (Elorum, Eloro) and inland towards Akrai (Palazzolo Acreide) in the last quarter of the eighth century.

In the second half of the seventh century, the Greek city of Megara Hyblaia, in south-east Sicily, north of Syracuse, had established the coastal colony of Selinus (Selinunte) along the southern coast of Sicily, west of the River Platani. It seems likely that the name of the colony was derived from the wild celery (in Greek: σέλινον, selinon) which grew there in abundance. This was why coins minted in Selinus bore a celery leaf. Selinus was the most western of the Greek city-states in Sicily. It was located between two rivers, on two lofty areas connected by a saddle. The southern area, nearest to the sea, was occupied by the acropolis, based around two intersecting streets and containing many temples. The northern area, further inland, was the urban area, containing housing on the Hippodamian plan. There were also two necropoleis. The rivers that bordered the city each housed a port at their mouth. The course of the Platani marked the political border between the territory of Selinus and that of another Greek city-state, Akragas.

In the marly landscape of the southern coast at the mouth of the Platani, 25km west of Akragas, Selinus later established the sub-colony of Heraklea (Eraclea Minoa, Cattolica Eraclea). The city was placed at the mouth of the river, on a terrace that ends at the sea with a white rock wall, high and steep. It was a walled city and had a magnificent theatre, though smaller than that of Segesta. The name of this city was connected with the legends of its origin. Eraclea calls Heracles, son of Zeus and Alcmena, the mythical owner of the whole of western Sicily (having vanquished the local hero Eryx in a wrestling match). According to Greek mythology, Eryx was the son of Bute – one of the Argonauts – and Aphrodite, the goddess of love, beauty, conception and fertility. He would have reigned on Mount Erice.

Legend has it that Eryx had extraordinary physical strength and used it to challenge anyone to a wrestling match, often killing his opponent. One day he challenged the hero and demigod Heracles, also endowed with a superhuman strength, who was passing through Sicily. The stakes were the kingdom of Eryx if Heracles had won; while if Eryx had won he would take the herd of Gerion, which Heracles had brought with him. The contest ended with the death of Eryx, who was buried in the temple that he himself had dedicated to his mother on Mount Erice (Temple of Venus Ericina). Heracles did not want to kill Eryx, nor did he want his kingdom, which he left to the locals, telling them to keep it until a descendant came to take possession of it. Passing from mythology to history, we can perhaps say that Eryx was a king of the Sicani, who practised the cult of the goddess of love on Mount Erice. As we have said, the Sicani would have welcomed a group of Trojan refugees on Mount Erice, and the immigrants would have children with local women and exchanged their ideas and experiences with those of the natives. From this process of physical mixing and cultural exchange, the Elymian people would be born.

Selinus aimed to expand northwards, along the Platani valley, in order to obtain an outlet on the Tyrrhenian Sea, at Castellammare del Golfo. Segesta, a city located in that valley, barred the passage to Selinus. Relations between Selinus and Segesta deteriorated due to border disputes. In 580, a contingent of Greek settlers, coming from Rhodes and led by Pentathlus of Cnidus, landed at Selinus and, together with the inhabitants of the city, attempted to found a city on Mount Erice. The Elymians opposed them and a battle took place, in which Péntathlos and many Rhodians were killed.[4]

In 415, Selinus, supported by Syracuse, decided again to expand northwards, along the Platani Valley. Segesta asked for help from Athens, which sent a great army to Sicily and attacked Syracuse, but after two years of bloody clashes lost the war ruinously. The Syracusans imprisoned the Athenian survivors in quarries, known as Latomie; and left them to die of hunger and thirst.[5]

The last episode of the lengthy confrontation between Segesta and Selinus, and their respective allies, had taken place in 409. Segesta asked for help from Carthage, which sent an army to Sicily. Carthage had been expanding territorially in Sardinia and Corsica, as well as in the south-west of the Iberian peninsula, where it had founded colonies. The Carthaginian army of 100,000 men, led by Hannibal Mago, landed at Capo Lilibeo on the western coast and marched to Selinus. The city was unprepared to face so powerful an army. Its walls were, in many places, in disrepair, and the armed forces promised by Syracuse, Akragas and Gelas did not arrive in time. The desperate resistance of the Selinuntines was broken after a ten-day siege. Some 16,000 of the citizens of Selinus were killed, 5,000 were taken prisoner, and only 2,600 were able to escape to Akragas. The proud city was sacked and its walls destroyed. Subsequently, Hannibal allowed the survivors and fugitives to return and occupy the city, paying tribute to Carthage.

At that time the Carthaginians occupied a large part of western Sicily. Later, unavoidably, they clashed with the Syracusans, who had risen in defence of the Siceliotes (the Greeks of Sicily) and headed a coalition. Carthage and Syracuse had contended each other for supremacy in Sicily for 250 years, constantly waging war and involving their allies in confrontations. In 265, Rome became one of the parties involved.

At that time, the Romans hegemonized a number of peoples, city-states and tribes, linked to these allies by contracts of association, called in Latin *foedus* (pl. *foedera*). What kept together Rome and its *socii* was the binding effectiveness of the *foedera*, based on the good faith of the contractors, but above all by the strength of the Roman legions.

The Roman Conquest

Rome, in the first half of the third century, had already expanded in southern Italy up to Rhegion (Rhegium, Reggio Calabria) and the shores of the Strait of Messina. But never satisfied by their territorial conquests, the

Romans as always wanted more[6] and looked with greed to Sicily. They were attracted by the Sicilian cities – ancient in tradition, rich and flourishing – and their harbours, fertile land and abundant agricultural production. The excuse to set foot on the island was offered by the 'Mamertine Crisis'. The Mamertines were Campanian mercenaries of Oscan language. After being in the service of Agathocles of Syracuse until his death, they had been fired by his successor, and had taken possession of Messene (Messana, Messina), where they ruled.

In 265, 20,000 men, led by Hiero II (308–215, king of Syracuse from 270–215), tried to expel the Mamertines from Messene, but were defeated in battle at Mylae (Milazzo) and went south of Messene, where they encamped waiting to assault the city. The Mamertines were allied with the Carthaginians, who had arrived with a fleet and landed north of Messene; they held off the Syracusans, but when the Carthaginians left, the Mamertines appealed to Rome in 264. Some Roman senators were opposed to helping the Mamertines, but one of them, Appius Claudius Caudex, persuaded the others to support him, and he led an armed force to Messene, where he met only symbolic resistance, as the Mamertines had convinced the Carthaginians to withdraw. The Mamertines delivered the city to the Romans, but the Carthaginians – mostly Celtic, Greek and Libyan mercenaries – returned and laid siege to Messina. Claudius tried to negotiate with both the Carthaginians and the Syracusans, but was ignored. He then led his troop outside the city, while Hiero retreated back to Syracuse, where he later signed a treaty of friendship and alliance with the Romans. The next day Claudius' two legions faced the Carthaginians at Kurkourakis (Curcuraci), near Messene, a small centre of agricultural and pastoral activities on the heights of Capo Peloro. From that position the Romans could dominate the surrounding area and the low peninsula which leads toward the opposite bank of the Strait and constitutes the north-eastern corner of the Sicilian triangle. The Carthaginians were more numerous, but disorganized and poorly motivated. Initially they resisted the Romans, which deluded their commander, Hanno, that he could defeat their opponents, and he ordered his men to fight in the open field. When the Carthaginians jumped out of their trenches, the Romans decimated them and won the battle.[7] Claudius Caudex later unsuccessfully laid siege to Echetla – a town located between the Carthaginian and Syracusan territories[8] – but was forced to withdraw to Messene in 263 after suffering heavy losses.[9]

Meanwhile, the armed intervention of the Romans alongside the Mamertines had caused the outbreak of the First Punic War (264–241). Syracuse did not participate in that conflict, although giving support to the Romans in terms of the supply of war machines and money, under the terms of the treaty signed with them. The fighting ceased in 241 with the final victory of the Romans. Under the Peace of Catulus (so called after the name of the victorious Roman commander), the Carthaginian army had evacuated Sicily. The Phoenician-Punic cities of Sicily were handed over to the Romans, as well as the Greek cities, except Syracuse. Thus a new Roman territory was formed, comprising most of Sicily and the surrounding Aeolian and Aegadian islands. It was first organized by the praetor Valerius and the former consul Quintus Lutatius Catulus Cerco, and became the first Roman *provincia* (province), called Sicilia. At that time the Romans intended that a *provincia* as a territory should be under the jurisdiction of an annual magistrate. In the case of Sicily, the magistrate was a quaestor based in Lylibaeum (formerly Lilýbaion, modern-day Marsala).

Shaping the Sicilian *provincia*

Rome had no experience of provincial government, nor the necessary personnel, desire or other valid reasons for changing the general situation of its newly acquired territories. It did not consider itself to 'own' its *provinciae* and their officials, but sought to control from a distance the political and economical policies of the defeated enemies. In regards to Sicily, the governor had a territorial militia, assigned to him from Rome, or from its federates, to patrol the island, which did not necessarily constitute military control, nor close control of Sicilian administration. This explains why, after the Roman conquest of Sicily, the economic and social structure, cultural framework, legislation and civil law of the Sicilians remained much as they were before. This is proved, for example, by the keeping of the law in force in the Greek cities that excluded from ownership of land anyone who was not a citizen of these cities, including the other Greeks of Sicily (the exclusion applied only to private land ownership, so did not work with respect to the *ager publicus populi romanorum*, 'soil owned by the Roman people', i.e. state property). The only changes concerned the local administration system: not the autonomy of the cities – which was confirmed, with some exceptions – but the political institutions and tax system. Political institutions were modified in the area of diffusion of Greek culture, since they had often triggered the degeneration of power. All the cities were endowed with a *senatus*, or *curia*, composed of aristocrats, which were holders of consultative functions, active administration and possibly of control. The supreme magistrate, who retained his Greek name, was placed in charge of a commission, which was composed of between two and ten people, according to the importance of the city. He was competent to deal with business and the management of public affairs, and represented the local community in the Senate of Rome. This institutional and administrative structure was extended to Syracuse after 212.

Tax system

The tax system remained that which had evolved over the centuries, in different ways, according to the Phoenician-Punic, Sicel or Elymian cities. Those Sicilians who had been dominated by the Carthaginians had paid taxes to Carthage, which imposed a fixed tribute in money; moreover, every Sicilian city-state imposed its own taxes on residents.

In Syracuse, the principal tax was the tithe, which was equal to one tenth of the agricultural crops (wheat, barley, wine, olives, fruit, vegetables). It was collected on the farms after harvest, so it was paid in kind. The tax collectors were the local agents of the contractors of the tax service. The selection procedure of the contractors was governed by sectoral regulations, with improvements made by Hiero II.

The Romans, before 212, subjected the Sicilian cities to the tax levy according to a complex mechanism of rewards and penalties, applying conditions more favourable to those with which they had entered into a treaty of friendship and alliance (*foedus*). The cities were classified in three categories: *liberae et foederatae* (this status was attributed to Messana, Tauromenium and Netum), *liberae et immunae* (Centurĭpae, Halaesa, Segesta, Halyciae and Panormus) and *decumanae* (all others). Each city's attitude either for or against Rome at the time of the conquest was taken into consideration. In the case of Segesta, its classification had been dictated by a sentimental reason, which nevertheless had a solid political justification. Segesta was an Elymian city, and the Elymians – like the Romans – boasted a Trojan descent. Rome exempted the Sicilian *civitates liberae et foederatae* and *liberae et immunae* from tax payment. In addition, it imposed on all Sicilian cities the obligation to contribute to the costs for the defence of the island, through the payment of the *tributum*. The *tributum* was a tax burden that weighed on all cities in the *provinciae*, as well as the colonies and the friendly and allied cities. It was originally weighed on Roman citizens, but was revoked for them in 167 due to the enrichment of the Roman state from the conquest of Macedonia. It was used to cover expenses for the construction and maintenance of ships, and for the maintenance, equipment and armament of soldiers. It could be paid either in cash or by providing support troops, ships and crews to Rome. This system was extended to Syracuse after the taking of this city and suppression of the Syracusan state, both of which occurred in 212.

In 218 the Carthaginian general Hannibal Barca conquered Arse (Saguntum, Sagunto), a Hispanic city located in the Spanish Levant that was allied with Rome, setting in motion the Second Punic War. This conflict was a great military enterprise on a scale never seen before. Hannibal crossed the Alps with a large army reinforced by dozens of war elephants in order to invade Italy. Two years later the Maltese archipelago was added to the Roman *provincia* of Sicily. Meanwhile, Hiero II of Syracuse had died and his successor, Hieroymous, deserted from the alliance with Rome and formed a connection with Carthage. In 215 the Romans besieged Syracuse. The city was powerfully fortified, defended by numerous troops and equipped with a large number of war machines (ballistas and catapults – the former throwing heavy iron bolts, the latter large boulders). Collaborating with the defence was the famous scientist and inventor Archimedes, who derived his love of sciences from his father, a Syracusan astronomer called Pheidías. During his long life, Archimedes had been linked to Hiero II and in touch with the scholars and scientists of Alexandria in Egypt, making major contributions to the progress of mathematics and physics. He had calculated the surface and volume of a sphere, perceived the laws that regulate the floating of bodies, and discovered and exploited the principles of operation of levers. He also invented numerous machines and devices, including the hydraulic screw. He took an active part in the preparations for war, inventing and constructing grandiose devices and war machines capable of nullifying the efforts of the Romans. Among other things, it was said that he invented a process whereby mirrors converged the sun's rays on the hulls and sails of enemy ships so that they caught fire.

The Syracusans resisted the Roman besiegers for three years, but in 212 it was taken through treason, with immense slaughter and plunder. Archimedes was one of the countless victims during the hours after the irruption of the Romans into the city, killed by a Roman soldier who had broken into his home while he was intensely focused on solving a problem of geometry. The legionnaire did not recognize the old man as the renowned inventor, whom the Roman commander in chief, Marcus Claudius Marcellus, had ordered spared. The soldier requested Archimedes to follow him, but the old man did not answer so the Roman, irritated, stabbed him with his spear. The survivors of the massacre were sold to slave traders in their tens of thousands. All the riches and works of art of the city were removed, with many sent to Rome to beautify the city and the houses of the rich. The Syracusan state was suppressed, with its territory incorporated into the Roman *provincia* of Sicily. The name of the city was later Latinized to *Syracusae*. Parts of the city damaged during the siege and storming were repaired, and the city became a Roman one in all respects. As it was the greatest city of Sicily, it was chosen as the seat of the island's Roman governor. As time passed, the questor of Sicily was replaced by a praetor, a magistrate of higher rank. Later, the praetor was joined by two quaestors, hierarchically subordinated to him, with one in Syracuse and the other in Lilybaeum.

In subsequent years, the Romans extended the imposition of the tithe to the whole island. Syracuse was classified as *civitas decumana* and had to change its institutions. Other taxes due to Rome were added to the *tributum* and tithe. Some *civitates decumanae* had also to pay a fixed tax, for the simple use of the lands they owned, which had been requisitioned after the surrender and then returned. Cities that had rebelled against Rome during the Second Punic War[10] were called *censoriae*, as their fixed tax was contracted in Rome by the censors. Local taxes affected only certain categories of economic operators and were paid to the cities, in compliance with the decisions of the local authorities and the declarations of the Sicilian censors, to enable them to bear the costs for the maintenance of public buildings, water supplies, worship and the execution of public utility works. In this case the tax levy took place outside Roman interference. The Sicilian censors should not be confused with the Roman ones. There were two of them, like the Roman ones; but unlike those, who were elected by the Roman people on the proposal of the Senate of Rome, and changed every eighteen months, the Sicilian censors were instead elected by the individual urban communities at regular intervals, with the primary task of verifying the patrimonial situation of their fellow citizens, through five-year censuses.

Finally, Rome imposed limits on the export of grain from Sicily, which could only take place to Rome, and reserved for itself the right to make purchases in Sicily at a price established unilaterally by the Senate, within the limit of a tenth of the harvests, for military and government needs. This right could be exercised against any city. It had been exercised in 190 in order to supply a Roman army fighting in Greece, again in 189, and then in 171 to supply the army in Macedonia. It had also been exercised for the maintenance of the Sicilian province's governmental apparatus.

Chapter 5

A Vibrant Urban Life

Dozens of cities

There were dozens of cities in the Hellenistic Sicily.[1] They were particularly numerous along the coast and, for the most part, they were originally Greek or Phoenician-Punic colonies. The settlements of the Sicels and Sicani were villages, often fortified, while the Elymians had cities worthy of the name. Of various sizes, the cities served as commercial hubs for the agricultural production of the countryside, where surplus crops, as well as small-scale manufacturing and cottage-industry handicrafts, were collected and sold. Their relatively high number was due to the fact that farmers tended not to live in the countryside, but concentrated themselves in the cities, together with the artisans and other inhabitants of the city, essentially for security reasons. Usually, in fact, the countryside was insecure, due to brigandage, while the cities were safer, because surrounded by fortification walls. Each morning, before sunrise, the land workers went out in long lines from the cities, with straw hats on their heads and work tools on their shoulders, heading for the fields, often walking long distances. They worked all day and returned home each evening.

East

The eastern Sicilian coast has narrow beaches, which often become jagged, with inlets, bays and rugged cliffs; further south, there is a wide gulf with a sandy beach, then a rocky coast, with a series of indentations, then another large bay and a gulf, and finally the coast was again sandy. In the Hellenistic age, the main cities of this part of the island, there were the coastal ones of Syrakousai/Syracusae (Siracusa)[2] and Eloros/Elorum (Eloro), while those of Akrai/Acre (Palazzolo Acreide), Leontinoi/Leontini (Lentini) and Neaiton/Neetum, or Netum (Noto Antica) were all inland. All these cities were populous and prosperous, except Leontinoi, which was going through a period of stagnation, having barely survived, because of serious material damage and loss of life suffered during the Punic Wars.

Syracusae, formerly Syrakousai

Syracusae was the most important city because of its glorious tradition, but above all because it was the seat of the governor of the Roman *provincia*. Located on the south-eastern corner of the island, facing the Ionian Sea its urban area was called Pentapolis, 'Five cities', because it was made up of five distinct areas: Ortygia, Akradina, Tycha, Neapolis and Epipolis. Except for Ortygia, which was an islet, the districts formed a triangle, having the vertex facing inward. Akradina ran along the sea. Immediately to the south of it was Ortygia, which was fortified. In the creek between Akradina and Ortygia was the smaller of the two ports of the city. The major port occupied the banks of the inlet that cut into the coast south of Syrakousai, between Ortygia and the mouth of the Anapo. Epipolis was the plateau that dominated the rest of the city. At its end (the summit of the triangle) was the powerful bulwark of the Euryalus fortress. In it branched a series of covered passages, carved into the rock, which allowed rapid movement of the defenders from one point to another. This was the point of the city most distant from the sea, dominating the road to the countryside and the interior of the island. The primitive nucleus of the city was formed on a small island emerging from crystalline waters close to the south-eastern coast, from which it was separated by a narrow channel. The name of the islet, Ortygia, is derived from the Greek *ortyx* (ὄρτυξ), 'Quail', related to a mythological episode. It is said that a quail had thrown itself into the sea. That event, quite trivial, would not have attracted the attention of the mythographers if the quail in question had not been Asteria, the sister of Leto, mother of the deities called Apollo and Artemis by the Greeks, Apollo and Diana by the Romans. These references to Greek mythology were justified by the fact that Greek settlers had founded in Ortygia the city of Συράουσαι, transliterated into Syrakousai. This had happened in 734–733, in the wider context of the early Greek colonization of islands and mainland shores of the Western Mediterranean. The site had been vacated by the Phoenician occupants. It lent itself to being inhabited because there was a source of fresh water, which flowed right to the seashore. This source was called the Arethusa, which it was said was a chaste nymph transformed into water by Artemis in order to protect her from the erotic desires of a river divinity, who pursued her. This legend came from Kòrinthos (Corinth), the city of origin of the settlers who had populated Syrakousai initially (the remaining colonists came from Tenea,[3] near Kòrinthos). Syrakousai developed as the hub of a city-state and expanded on the coast. It was destined to become one of the largest, most populous, rich, powerful and glorious cities of the Mediterranean, adorned with wonderful monuments; the capital of a maritime empire, able to compete with Carthage; a cradle of the sciences, arts and philosophy, comparable to Athens, and Alexandria in Egypt. It was well known throughout the Hellenistic world for the victories of its champions at the Olympics. Syracusan rulers were often a tyrant or a king. They exercised absolute power, acted as despotic master and founded dynasties. Gelon had been tyrant of Gelas from 491–490, then, in 485 or 484, became the first tyrant of Syrakousai (until his death in 478). His first successor was his brother Hiero, in office from 478–467. The tyranny at Syracuse continued with Trasybulus, the last tyrant of the Dinomedes dynasty, for only a year or so after Hiero's death. Then it was overthrown and substituted by a democracy, which lasted until 430, when it was in turn overthrown by Dionysius I The Great.

Meanwhile, between 465 and 430, it had developed the politics of Ducetius, or Douketios. He was a native Sicilian, likely born in the Mineo area, but his education was Greek and he was strongly influenced by Greek civilization. In 460 a war had broken out between Syracuse and its former colony, the city-state of Katane (Catania). Ducetius assisted Syrakousai because Katane had occupied the land of the Sicels, and together they defeated Katane. Ducetius went on to found the city of Menai (Mineo) and occupy Morgantia (Morgantina). By 452 he had founded a united Sicilian state, the only advanced and centralized state organization ever held by natives in Sicily, becoming the sovereign of the Sicels. Then he founded numerous other cities, among which was Paliké, the political capital of his kingdom[4], near Lake Naftia, a place near Palagonia, which took its name by the presence of two holy crater lakes located near Palagonia, where stood a sanctuary of a pair of Sicel gods, the Palici. Paliké grew quickly, becoming a place of refuge for runaway slaves, while the sanctuary became more famous and was frequented increasingly. Ducetius then conquered Aetna, south-west of Mount Etna, before moving into Akragas (Agrigento). Syrakousai, although an ally of Ducetius, became concerned by his unchecked expansion. When, in 451, Ducetius took Motyon, a small town or fortress in the territory of Akragas, Syrakousai decided to assist the latter, and in 450 Ducetius was decisively defeated at Nomai. Ducetius was taken to Syrakousai, was tried by a popular assembly and was exiled to Kòrinthos for life. He never returned in Sicily and died in 440.

Dionysius I The Great (430–367) commanded both the army and the allies in the Third and Fourth Greek-Punic Wars[5] against the Italiote League. He enclosed Syrakousai, from 402 onwards, within a grandiose system of fortifications, the Wall of Dionysius, including the castle of Euryalus. Dionysius I was a cruel man, but also a scholar and a patron. He hosted many philosophers in Syrakousai: Plato (a pupil of Socrates and teacher of Aristotle, one of the founders of Western thought), Aeschines Socraticus, Philoxenus of Cythera and Aristippus of Cyrene. He attracted many skilled artisans and esteemed scholars to the city. Subsequent Syracusan autocrats followed his example. Their court hosted the best intellects of the culture and art of Italy and Sicily. Among those who visited Syrakousai were the tragedian Aeschylus, the playwright Epicharmus of Kos, the rhetoricians Tisias and Corax, the poets Ibycus, Pindar and Theocritos, the astronomers Hicetas and Ecphantus the Pythagorean, and the historian Xenophon. When, in 409, the Greek city of Selinus, on the southern coast of Sicily, tried to expand along the Belice valley to the north coast, the Elymian city of Segesta felt threatened. The Carthaginians intervened militarily to rescue the latter, destroyed two major cities – Selinon (Selinus, Selinunte) and Himera (Imera) – and pushed their control of the southern coast up to the River Platani.[6]

From 400–397, Dionysius I assaulted the Punic cities of Western Sicily. The most illustrious victim of that offensive was Mtw (Motye, Mozia), the defensive pivot of Carthaginian possessions in Sicily. Dionysius I conquered it after a siege, with immense slaughter, then heavily plundered it and razed it to the ground. Later, the refugees from Mtw founded a new city – Lilýbaion (Lilybaeum, Marsala)– on the western coast of Sicily at Capo Lilibeo.

Mégara Hybláia

The site of Mégara Hybláia is a little north of Syracuse. The city was one of the most ancient Greek colonies in Sicily, founded in the same period as Syrakousai and Leontinoi, thanks to an agreement concluded with the Sicelian king Hyblon. It had flourished mainly in the sixth century. A hundred years after its own foundation it had founded the sub-colony of Selinon. In 438 it was destroyed by Gelon, tyrant of Syrakousai, together with Kamarina and Gelas.[7] After remaining abandoned for 150 years, the site was occupied by the Syracusans, who, in 425–414, during their war against Athens, built a fort there. It had been rebuilt and repopulated in 340 by Timoleon, as a colony of Syrakousai, and provided with solid walls. In 213, during the preliminary operations for the siege of Syrakousai, it had been destroyed again, this time by the Romans, led by the consul Marcus Claudius Marcellus. After that, it was never rebuilt,[8] with only isolated farms settled on its territory. But it was an area where the memory of Daedalus still survived.

Leontini, formerly Leontinoi

Leontinoi is north-west of Megara Hyblaia, on the border of the city-state, in a primary position for possession of the plain of Catania. It occupied two hills with steep slopes; on top of the hills were houses and temples, in the valley between the hills was the agora with the main public buildings, and at the two ends of the valley were the gates of the city, the south one leading towards Syrakousai and that in the north towards the Leontini fields. There were dwellings carved into the rock, two necropolises to the south and north of the city, and sacred areas within the city and outside of it.[9] The history of Leontinoi started in 729, when a colony was founded by the Chalcidians in an area previously occupied by a village community of Sicels (which had been expelled), in order to control the Catania plain, famous for its abundant cereal harvests. Its subsequent development was strongly influenced by the relationship with Syrakousai, a neighbour and rival. That relationship had varied widely. It also recorded episodes of depopulation, abandonment, repopulation and forced migration of the unarmed population. Walls of fortification were often made, destroyed and remade. Dionysius I, tyrant of Syrakousai from 405–367, fortified the acropolis and built granaries in it to store the harvest.[10] A radical new intervention to strengthen the defence of the city, with the use of artillery, was brought forward by King Agathocles, tyrant of Syrakousai from 317/316 and king of Sicilia from 307 (or 304) until his death. A new type of tower was added in the southern fortification, to the eastern side of the gate and on the south edge of the Colle San Mauro, while the action was more radical in the northern gate. The defence of the main gate of the city was completely reconstructed and strengthened by a new solid wall and a large tower with internal cross-walls. Only at the end of the third century, however, when Hieronymus, king of Syrakousai from 215–214, was in Leontinoi to face the Roman army, was a complete circuit-wall built. This curtain wall with square towers was probably destroyed during the siege by the consul Marcus Claudius Marcellus in 214, when the city was taken by the Romans and heavily plundered. It later became a *civitas decumana* and lost control of the *Campi Leontini*, and thus the wealth which it derived from the economic exploitation of the territory. Its land, for the most part, became *ager publicus*, 'soil of collective property of the Roman people', and was rented to farmers from the nearby city of Kentoripa (Centuripae, Centuripe).

Catana, formerly Katane

Along the Ionic coast were located, from south to north: Katane (Catana, Catania), at the foot of Mount Etna, on the edge of the homonymous plain,[11] then Naxos (Giardini Naxos), Tauromenion (Tauromenium, Taormina) and Messene (Messana, Messina).[12] The most populated was Katane, followed by Messene and then Tauromenion.[13] All these cities were initially Greek colonies.

Katane was one of the first Greek foundations in the West. It was founded by a group of Euboean settlers from Chalkís (Chalkìda) in 729, a little after that of the Sicilian Naxos and Leontinoi by other Euboeans. The settlement began on the hill of Montevergine, east of the Amenanus river. It developed through time and became a large and prosperous city. Katane had an important school of law and a lively cultural life. Personalities such as the philosopher Empledocles and the poets Stesichorus and Ibycus visited the city. The most important exponent of the school of law was the mythic Charondas, perhaps a pupil of the philosopher Pythagoras. Originally written in verses by Charondas, the laws of Katane were adopted by other Chalcidic colonies in Sicily and Italy, for example by Rhegion (Rhegium, Reggio Calabria). It was said that Charondas established in the city the celebrated first gymnasium for free men using state expenses. He killed himself because he entered the public assembly wearing a sword, which was a violation of his own law.[14] In 476, the tyrant of Syrakousai, Hiero I, former tyrant of Gelas (Gela), conquered Katane, deported its inhabitants to Leontinoi, repopulated the city with a large number of Doric people of Syracusan and Peloponnesian origin, and renamed it Aitna. After Hiero's death, the Chalcidians returned to Katane and the city regained its original name. In 413, Katane supported the Athenian expedition body against Syrakousai and paid for its ruinous defeat. Dionysius I exiled or sold as slaves many inhabitants, and mixed the rest with groups of Campanian mercenaries. In 263 Katane submitted to the Romans; it became a *civitas decumana* and retained its ancient municipal institutions. It is then that its name was changed again, becoming Catana. Afterwards it maintained friendly relations with Rome and rose to a position of great prosperity. In the Late Republic it was a wealthy and flourishing city, and one of the main ports of Sicily.

Naxos

About 40km south of Messina, close to Capo Sant'Andrea, the Ionian coast of Sicily begins to draw a succession of gulfs, bays and jagged cliffs coloured by the green of dense vegetation, while the sea is tinged with a thousand shades of blue and green. Capo Sant'Andrea and the subsequent

Capo Taormina create a series of inlets that shape the cliffs. Between the first and the second, a small island covered with dense vegetation emerges from emerald waters, like a natural monument. It is called Isola Bella, 'Beautiful Island', and is very close to the coast, to which it is connected by an isthmus. After Capo Taormina the lavas of Etna, from various eruptions and stretched to the sea, have created a low promontory called Capo Schisò. This is a large inlet, bordered by a beach of fine, golden sand, with a thick Mediterranean scrub. Between the sea shore and a large cultivable plain, on a plateau adjacent to the port, a group of Chalcidian migrants and other Cycladic migrants founded the city of Naxos in 734–733. The settlement bore the same name as the Cycladic island of Naxos, in the southern Aegean. It grew with a dense network of houses, separated by narrow alleys, and had been surrounded by walls in polygonal blocks of stone, in whose southern stretch, facing the sea, two gates opened. It was a small city, but had great symbolic importance because it was one of the first colonies of the Greeks in Sicily. Its altar at Apollon Archegetes, 'the Founder' or 'Forefather', located outside the city, in the port area, was the place where people dedicated to the gods a propitiatory sacrifice for good navigation before sailing for Greece. Among its temples, that of Aphrodite was famous. To the south-east of this were some brick kilns and, in the same area, near the northern port, the oldest houses in the city. In the port area, within the city walls, was the naval arsenal.

During the Peloponnesian War (431–404), Sicilian Naxos took the side of Athinài (Athens). The disaster of the Athenian expedition against Syrakousai exposed it to the vengeance of Dionysius I. The last hours of Naxos played out in 403, when Dionysius conquered the city after a siege and razed it to the ground, starting with the fortification walls. The inhabitants were killed, sold to slave traders or dispersed. The territory of the city was donated to the Sicels of the area. Under the reign of Hiero II of Syrakousai, Naxos was rebuilt.[15]

Tauromenium

Tauromenium, formerly Tauromenion, is charming. There is everything that seems created on earth to seduce the eyes, the mind and the imagination. It lies 200 metres above sea level, on a narrow terrace on the slopes of Monte Tauro. It faces south and overlooks the coast on one side, with Capo Schisò, and on the other a valley. From that position you can enjoy a very wide view: behind it, Mount Tauro and the peak of Mola; on the left, the Ionian Sea; in front, in the distance, the high mass of Etna, steaming and covered with snow. On the opposite side of the Taormina terrace, the view embraces Isola Bella and the thin isthmus that connects this islet to the coast; the entrance from the south of the Strait of Messina, and a dense series of parallel reliefs, sloping down towards the sea and interspersed with rivers. The ancient city was originally called Tauromenion and was founded in 359 by a group of Greek settlers led by the Greek Andromachus. It was born as the urban centre of a colony of Greek language and culture, and was destined to flourish. In 212 it was taken by the Romans and changed its name in Tauromenium.

Coming from the North, you entered the city through the urban gate, to the right of which was a Hellenistic temple, dedicated to Serapid Iupiter, constructed of large square blocks. Of the public buildings, the largest was the theatre, connected to a small sanctuary and used for the representation of tragedies, comedies and mimes. The *cavea* (seats) were dug into the rock, while the scene had the Ionian Sea and Etna as its background. Today, anyone who sits in the circle of higher seats, cannot help but think that perhaps no other spectator could ever enjoy such a show: 'Theatre offers the most pleasant expanse of sight, on which the human eye can rest and that can be imagined';[16] 'On the right, above fortresses, fortresses rise; down below, the city. … The gaze, moreover, embraces all the long mountain back of Etna, and, on the left, the beach up to Catania, even up to Syracuse.'[17]

Messana, formerly Messene, originally Zankle

Large and wealthy, Messene was strategically positioned on the Sicilian shore of the Strait of Messina, a route essential for trade. It was the most ancient Greek colony in Sicily, the second of the most ancient Greek foundations in the Western Mediterranean, preceded by Pythekoussai, in the island of Ischia, Campania, and had originated from its port. Unlike the pre-Greek settlements, located more inland, at the foot of hills, the Greek settlers of 757 instead installed themselves between the natural harbour and its non-peninsular *continuum*, between the Portalegni and Boccetta torrents. The harbour had a large inlet, protected by a slender offshoot, low and sandy, shaped like a scythe's tongue. The most ancient of the Greek names for the city, Zancle (in Greek, Ζάγκλης), recalls a Sicel term, meaning 'scythe'. The body of water inside the scythe's tongue is the widest and deepest anchorage in Sicily, and one of the largest and most important in the Mediterranean, able to offer a safe haven for ships. It was used for commercial and military purposes. There were workshops and a dry dock. Messene, in 265, became a *civitas foederata ac immunis*, called Messana. Such a status reflects the very high consideration in which it was held by the Senate of Rome. In Sicily, Rome attributed this honour to only three cities: Messana, Tauromenium and Netum. From the walls that run along the Portalegni and Boccetta begin two roads along the coast, named Pompea and Valeria by their Roman builders, the first heading south and the second heading west.

North-West

The northern coast of Sicily is often high and rocky, with frequent and wide inlets, and a couple of peninsulas, as well as long beaches. Along this shore survived several cities of ancient origin. From Messina, towards the west were, in order, Tyndaris (Tyndarium, Tindari), Halaesa (Alhaesa, Tusa), Kephaloidion (Cephaloedium, Cefalù), Thermai Himeraìai (Thermae Himerae, Termini Imerese), Solus (originally Kfr, then Soluntum, Solunto),[18] and Panormos (originally Zyz, then Panormus, Palermo).[19] In the west, the most important cities are Lilýbaion (Lylibaeum, Marsala) and Drepanon (Trapani), both on the coast, on the edge of a flat terrace which extends from the slopes of Mount Erice into the sea. A famous sanctuary of Aphrodite was located on the slopes of Mount Erice, where sacred prostitution was practised. The Romans put this in charge of a religious confederation of seventeen Sicilian cities. A fire was kept burning at night: visible from afar, it served to guide sailors. Other cities are Egesta (Segesta, near Calatafimi) and Halykiai (Alicyae, Salemi?), both located inland, in a hilly landscape. All these cities were initially Greek or Punic foundations. Other cities in northern Sicily instead developed from village communities formed by nuclei of native populations (Sicels, Sicans, Elymians). One of these was Iaitai (Ietas, Monte Iato), near Panormus. Soluntum, Ietas, Segesta, Tyndaris and Alhaesa were places that demonstrated considerable prosperity. They had important civic buildings: active theatres, *stoai* (porticoes) and most importantly *bouleuteria* (assembly houses).

Drepanum, formerly Drepanon

Over time *Drepanum* had been Sican, Elymian, Phoenician, Greek and Carthaginian. The Greeks called it Drepanon, from the word δρεπανη, 'scythe', with reference to the arched narrow tongue of land on which it was built. In the fourth century, Drepanon was disputed between Carthage and Syracuse. At that time it occupied a central position for maritime traffic. Its decline began when the Sicilian archipelago and Maltese islands passed to the Romans, after the First Punic War. Rome did not forgive it for remaining faithful to Carthage and punished it, classifying it among the cities that had resisted it most obstinately. Drepanon became Drepanum and its commercial record passed to Lilybaeum.

Lilybaeum, formerly Lilýbaion

Lilybaeum was located on the southern shore of the Stagnone di Marsala, called Capo Lilibeo. It had been founded by the Carthaginians to give a new homeland to refugees from the nearby Mtw (Motye, Mozia), a Phoenician-Punic colony, which had been destroyed in 400 by Dionysius I, tyrant of Syrakousai. Lilýbaion was to replace Mtw as a defensive pivot of the Punic province of Sicily and starting point for reaching Carthage from Sicily. The location was excellent from a defensive point of view. The presence of sandbanks and shallow waters around Capo Lilibeo, as well as along the whole coast between Drepanon and Lilýbaion, made landing difficult. Moreover, the rocky nature of the land guaranted the solidity of fortifications, while the presence of springs guaranted a water supply even in case of siege.

Lilýbaion had been built as a coastal fortress, equipped with mighty city walls. Its urban area was a large quadrilateral, crossed by five axes orthogonally cut, at regular intervals of 35 metres, by twenty-one minor axes. In 277, its fortification works were reinforced by the construction of towers and the excavation of a moat, which barred access to the city from the mainland. Pyrrhus, king of Epirus from 306 to 300 and from 298 to 272, attacked Lilýbaion at the time of his offensive against Carthage. He besieged the city for two months, after which, unable to conquer it, he withdrew, frustrated by his failure. During the Second Punic War (218–202), the Romans, advised by their ally Ieron of Syracuse, committed themselves to defending Lilýbaion from the Carthaginians, while the Carthaginians tried in vain to regain its possession.[20] The Romans carried out a naval blockade. The city was besieged again, but resisted every assault, thanks to the powerful defensive system that made it a solid bastion.

Under the Romans, the city continued to be the main centre of western Sicily, a military base and an important centre of trade. It received impetus and prosperity from being conveniently located relative to one of the main trade routes of the Mediterranean (Cyprus, Crete, Malta, Sicily, Sardinia, Hispania), and from its three ports. It was rich in public buildings and villas, and fully integrated into the cultural koiné of the Hellenistic world. Its population was ethnically heterogeneous, but the Greek component prevailed.

Segesta, formerly Egesta

Egesta is located on the slopes of Mount Bàrbaro, near Calatafimi. It was the result of the reconstruction, made after the destruction of Agathocles of Syrakousai in 307, and had a regular plan, built in part on terraces to overcome the natural sloping terrain. It was protected by steep slopes on several sides, and by walls on the more gentle slope towards a valley; and controlled several major roads between the coast to the north and the hinterland. Its Elymian inhabitants, in the late fifth century, built a magnificent Greek-style temple at the top of Mount Bàrbaro, some 300 metres above the sea, and another unfinished one on a nearby isolated hill. Both showed that the Hellenization of the city started very early and had a profound effect on its inabitants. The theatre had a *cavea* of twenty steps, subdivided in seven sectors. It was dug on the slopes of a hill and, on the western side, was supported by a stone wall. Its architecture was part Greek and part Roman. From its *cavea* you could see a wide undulating panorama, extending to the Gulf of Castellammare, on which, about 10km distant, the Segestans had a port or *emporium*. After the destruction by Agathocles of Syrakousai, Egesta remained in the Carthaginian orbit until 206, when it passed under the Romans. The Romans changed the name of the city to Segesta and claimed to be twins of the Segestans, with reference to the alleged Trojan origin common to both, although Segesta's origins are actually unclear.

South-East

The southern coast is mostly low, with generally wide and often wild beaches, and white cliffs. In the past there flourished along it a number of important Greek cities. Such cities were those that suffered the worst effects of the First and Second Punic Wars. Some of them no longer existed in the second century: from east to west, Kamarina, founded in 598/597 as a sub-colony of Syracuse, was destroyed by the Romans in 258; Gelas (formerly Lindos, Gela) – founded in 688 by settlers from Rhodes, particularly from Lindos, but also from Crete[21] – had been destroyed in 285 by Phintias, tyrant of Akragas; Akragas itself (Agrigentum, Agrigento), which began *c*. 580 as a sub-colony of Gelas, was destroyed twice, in 255 and definitively in 210, though later it had been repopulated by Roman settlers; Herakleia (Eraclea Minoa, Cattolica Eraclea), founded in 570 as an outpost of Kfr between Akragas and Selinon, was devasted and was recovering with difficulty, remaining depopulated for a long period;[22] and Selinon, begun in 650 as a sub-colony of Megara Hyblaia, and already in crisis for some time, had been abandoned in 250, its inhabitants moving to Lilýbaion. Moreover, many indigenous settlements – sicanians – disappeared during the Pyrrhic Wars (280–275).

Gelas

Gelas was founded in an area inhabited by groups of Sicels and Sicani, who occupied the hills northwards. It developed partly on a low, long and narrow coastal hill, west of the mouth of the Gela river, and partly on the surrounding flood plain. It soon expanded territorially, clashing with the indigenous people and founding the sub-colony of Akragas further west along the south-east coast. Its most flourishing period was the early fifth century, when the city was ruled by the tyrant Hippokrates. At that time it started an empire extending to Kamarina and Messene, and even dominated Syrakousai, and was a large and powerful city. In 424, Gelas played a political role on the eve of the titanic clash between Athènai and Syrakousai. In 405 it was reached by the Carthaginians, who were again on the offensive in Sicily, after having destroyed Selinon and Himera in 409; in turn, it was totally destroyed by them. In 338 it was rebuilt by the Syracusan Timoleon, but in 282 it was definitively destroyed by Phintias, tyrant of Akragas. The city was then abandoned, its refugees transferred to Phintias (Licata), a new town established by Phintias near Licata. Under the Romans, Gelas was a modest village on the road linking Syrakousai to Agrigentum, and a number of rural settlements were scattered in the Gela Plain.[23]

Agrigentum, formerly Akragas

Akragas was located 3.2km from the sea, on a series of rocky hills, 350 metres high, in the middle of a flourishing agricultural area, specializing in the cultivation of wheat and vines. Two rivers – the Akragas and the Hypsas – flanked the urban area, which was enclosed within mighty city walls, with numerous gates. The city had an extremely regular urban plan, with roads up to 4–5 metres in width, intersecting orthogonally, forming *insulae* (apartment properties) 35 metres wide and of variable length. It also had two agora (squares) and as many public areas, one of which was monumental with a Roman temple and the *bouleuterion* (assembly) in the centre. In the Hellenistic-Roman district of Agrigentum was a thermal system adjoining a house, with mosaic floors and wall decorations. Nearby was a Hellenistic theatre. The acropolis towered above the city: its outer part was bordered by an inaccessible ravine, while the inner part had a unique access from the lower city. The latter extended to the edge of a rocky ridge, along which were three temples, dedicated to Herakles, Hera Licinia/Iuno and Concordia. Another temple, that of Zeus, was majestic and colossal, the biggest in Sicily and one of the largest in the Hellenistic world.

The fifth century was the apex of the military and political glory of Akragas. At that time the city was governed by tyrants and developed its economy as well art and culture. In 490, Pyndar, in his XII *Pythian*, described Akragas as 'the most beautiful city of the world'. It did not take part in the war between Syrakousai and Athènai (415–413), but later it had been the most illustrious Sicilian victim of the Greek and Roman Punic Wars. In 409, the Carthaginians invaded Sicily, destroyed Selinon and Himera, and took Akragas by treason. The population sought refuge at Gelas and Leontinoi. In 406 the Carthaginians destroyed the city, but in 388 it was rebuilt by the Syracusan Timoleon and thrived again. In 276 the city and its territory were occupied by Pyrrhus, king of Epirus, then fell again under the domination of the Carthaginians and suffered the tragic consequences of the First and Second Roman Punic Wars. In 262 the Romans besieged Akragas for more than five months before being defeated by the Carthaginians, who had received reinforcements from their homeland. The Carthaginians then abandoned the city by night and at dawn the next day the Romans entered the city, plundered it and enslaved all the inabitants, some 25,000. In 255 the Carthaginians reconquered Akragas, burning the houses and demolishing the fortifications. In 219 the Romans again besieged Akragas, took it by treason, brutally looted it and once more sold the citizens as slaves. After that, the city's name was changed to Agrigentum, thereafter enjoying lasting peace and a remarkable economic recovery. In 214 it was occupied again by the Carthaginian army, then in 207 was repopulated by Roman settlers. By the second century, many Romans lived in Agrigentum in peace and harmony with the natives. The port of Agrigentum was located at the mouth of the San Leone river, on a large sandy beach. It was frequented mainly by ships loading grain to be transported to Rome and sulphur extracted from the mines in the central area of the island.

Eraclea Minoa, formerly Herakleia

Herakleia, further west along the coast from Akragas, was for a long time a land of clashes between Greeks and Carthaginians, falling into the hands of one and then the other. First it was overthrown by Carthage, later becoming a border town of Akragas. It passed into Carthaginian hands under a treaty of 405, was won back in 397 by Dionysius I in the first Greek–Punic War, but was recovered by Carthage in 383. It was here that Dion landed in 357 when he attacked Syrakousai. The Agrigentines won it back in 309, but it soon fell under the power of Agathocles. It was temporarily recovered for Greece by Pyrrhus in 277. Later, in the third century, it became a Roman colony, with the name Eraclea Minoa. The Roman city had kept the Greek name, but added the name Minoa, recalling Minos, king of Crete, who died in Sicily, where he had landed to pursue Daedalus and had founded a city, at the mouth of the Halycus river (according to another version of the story, the city was established by his followers, after the death of Minos himself). According to Greek mythology, Daedalus was a Greek architect and sculptor. He had worked for Minos, for whom he had planned and directed the work of construction of the Labyrinth, a complex subterranean structure. Minos had exiled both the Minotaur and Daedalus in that dark and gloomy site; the former because he was a monstrous being, a man–eating half–man and half–bull, the latter because he knew the secrets of the structure and could reveal them. After Theseus, son of Aegeus, king of Athens, had killed the Minotaur, Daedalus had fled from Crete together with his son Icarus. But Icarus had flown too high, his wax wings had melted in the heat of the sun and he crashed into the Aegean. Daedalus survived, landed in Sicily and built works there. Minos then arrived in Sicily with a war fleet, demanding that Kokalos, king of the Sicani, who housed Daedalus, give up the fugitive to him. Kokalos' daughters drew Minos into a trap and killed him, boiling him alive in a bath.

Central area

The central area of Sicily offers a rolling landscape, rich in woods and cultivated fields, irrigated by perennial watercourses. Verdant in winter, it gradually fades as summer approaches. When the ripening wheat is ready for harvest, it resembles a sea, the immense expanse of spikes, moved by the wind, moving sinuously like the waves. A mountain about 1,000 metres high emerges from this golden 'sea'. It is characterized by three rocky outcrops, which dominated the city of Castrum Hennae (formerly Henna, Enna), hence forth Henna, which was surrounded by large high plains that lent themselves to cultivation. The site was a natural fortress, but was further protected by high stone curtain walls, with towers, ditches and drains, and six arched gates. The urban area was a forest of small houses climbing the hill, leaning against each other and separated by winding lanes, or inner courtyards, cramped, interspersed with arches, bridges, stairways and narrow passages. The inhabitants kept the use of the language and traditions of their ancestors. The city was founded by Syracusan settlers, led by Ennus, seventy years after Syrakousai had been established (according to another tradition, in the fourth year of the twenty-eighth Olympiad, i.e. in 665). In the beginning it was under the dominion of Syrakousai. Gelon built a temple to Ceres there in gratitude for his military victories. After the death of Gelon, the king of the Sicels, Ducetius, seized the city. About fifty years later, Dionysius I, wanting to add Henna and other cities to his domains, seized the land around Henna. He persuaded Acimnestus, a citizen of Henna, to betray his city, promising in return that he could rule. Taking the city, Acimnestus forbade Dionysius from entering it. Furious, the latter urged the inhabitants of Henna to recover their freedom by offering them the head of the traitor. Aided by his followers, he entered Henna, captured Acimnestus and handed him over to the citizens to be executed. Dionysius left without causing any damage to the city. However, soon after, Dionysius, with an army of Carthaginian mercenaries, occupied Henna again, this time with the help of a traitor.[24]

In 212, the taking of Henna by Roman soldiers was one of the most difficult undertakings that they ever conducted in Sicily: they had to resort to the network of sewers to infiltrate to the top of the mountain and seize the stronghold. Roman Henna was the main centre of production and export of Sicilian wheat. It was also the centre of the cult of Ceres, the Latin goddess of the harvest, equivalent to Demeter of the Greeks. Ceres was the protector of crops, flowers, fruits and children. It was she who had taught agriculture to men, through Triptolemus, king of Eleusis. A sanctuary of Ceres occupied the top of one of the summits of Mount Henna.[25] The devotees worshipped there a glorious image of the goddess, in which she appeared as a severe and majestic mother, beautiful and affable, surrounded by a crown of ears of corn, with a torch in one hand and a basket full of wheat and fruit in the other. Opposite the temple was an altar and two colossal statues: one of Ceres, bearing a statue of Victory, and one of Triptolemus. The path to the temple was punctuated by minor shrines and niches with statues carved into the rock. The sanctuary was accessed by steps carved into the rock. The large sacred area embraced two spaces, connected to each other by special paths, full of votive shrines and water sources. Henna had been conquered by the Romans during the First Punic War in 258. In 212 its inhabitants tried to rebel, but the attempt was thwarted, with many citizens massacred. The commander of the local Roman garrison, Lucius Pinarius, ordered the massacre on the suspicion that the population wanted to join the Carthaginian commander Hanno, as had already happened in many other places in Sicily. The victims were taking part in an assembly in a theatre, guarded by Roman soldiers, who, on an agreed signal, threw themselves into the crowd with their drawn swords, killing many people. Livy says: 'The bodies were piled up not only for the massacre, but also for the escape of those who tried to escape from it, some fell on the others, the unharmed on the wounded, the living on the dead.' Then the Romans scattered through the streets, pursuing the fleeing people and continuing to kill them as the city was sacked.[26]

Morgantia

Morgantia (in the lands of Cittadella and Serra d'Orlando, near Adone) was about 40km from Henna, to the south-east, on an undulating, elongated plateau, steep at the sides and culminating in Mount Cittadella (578 metres above sea level). At the foot of the mountain is a lowland plain, with extensive rich pasture. The site, bordering the Simeto valley and the tributaries of this river, controlled a vast area, being an obligatory passage between the east coast and the interior. Morgantia was a Hellenistic city, rich with public and private buildings, and statues. After the Second Punic War (218–202), it had shrunk considerably, its walls having been demolished. However, the local community maintained a flourishing production of earthenware, cereals, wine and oil in the second century. The Romans built a market for the exchange of local agricultural products in the upper terrace of the agora, using many public and private buildings to carry out administrative activities that involved contact with the public and the practice of trade, mainly the provision of cooked food, wine and bread.

The site of Morgantina was occupied for the first time in the Bronze Age. In the early decades of the first millennium it became the seat of an Ausonian village, in which is recognized the foundation of the Morgetes. The Morgetes were a legendary people, descendants of the Oenotrians, who had migrated to southern Italy from Arcadia in the Greek Peloponnese. They moved to Sicily from the Ionian and Tyrrhenian coasts of Calabria, mingling with the Sicanian natives. Around 575–570, the Ausonian village community of Morgantina mingled with Greek settlers from Chalcis. At the end of the sixth century the settlement was devasted by Hippocrates, tyrant of Gelas. Rebuilt, it was destroyed again in 459 by Ducetius,[27] a Hellenized leader of the Sicels, founder of a united Sicilian state and numerous cities. The settlement was revived at Serra d'Orlando, named Morgantia and rebuilt in Hellenistic fashion, with a regular plan, in which later there was an agora and residential blocks. After the final defeat of Ducetius at Nomai by the Syracusans in 450, Morgantia entered the Syracusan area of influence, then in 424 it passed to Kamarina. In 396 it was conquered by Dionysius I, tyrant of Syrakousai, remaining for a long time in its dominion. King Hiero II of Syrakousai was particularly close to Morgantia, apparently because the city was the birthplace of his mother. Morgantia was then enriched with the construction of fine buildings in the area of the agora (which had been divided into two terraces) and became a city capable of competing with others of the same magnitude in the Hellenistic world. Among the new buildings, it is worth mentioning the *stoai* and a public fountain in the upper terrace, a granary, a *bouleterion* and a theatre. The terraces were linked by a staircase, which served as a meeting place. The surrounding territory produced wheat, grapes and wine. It provided Syrakousai with wheat and exported this cereal through its port. In 212–211, when the Romans conquered Syrakousai after a siege, Morgantia and the conquered city's other territory became part of the Roman province of Sicily. Morgantia was given to the Spanish troops who had participated in the siege of Syrakousai, becoming a military colony. The beginning of the city's decline dated back to this time.

Centuripae, formerly Kentoripa

The city of Centurĭpae was about 60km north-east of Henna and about 30km from Catana, on top of a hill (over 700 metres above sea level), from which you can see in the distance the western side of Etna, the Simeto valley and part of the Catania Plain. It was a Hellenized Sicilian centre, founded before the tenth century in a naturally defensible place. In the Greek period of the history of Sicily there was an alternation of tyrannical and democratic government in a framework of varying alliances and armed confrontations with Syracuse, which had always been resolved in favour of the latter. In 404, the tyranny of Damon allied with Dionysius I of Syracuse; in 339, the tyranny of Nicodemus was overthrown by the Syracusan Timoleon, who deported the local population to Syracuse and repopulated Centurĭpae with a colony; in 312, the Syracusan Agathocles occupied the city, establishing a Syracusan military garrison. In the second half of the fourth century the city became an important centre for the production of artistic ceramics, which continued for some time. In 263 it spontaneously submitted itself to Rome and was recognized as a *civitas immunis ac libera*, that is allied and exempt from taxation. Since then it had experienced a great development and became one of the main cities of Sicily in the Hellenistic period. The vast territory of Centurĭpae, almost entirely mountainous, extended between the valleys of Dittaino and Salso. One advantage was that it was on an important road, used to transport loads of grain destined for export to Rome through the local ports. This road started at Catana, passed through Leontini and reached Henna, from where it continued northwards, reaching the Tyrrhenian coast and stopping at Thermae (Termini Imerese).

Chapter 6

Grain, Slaves and Banditry

Latifondistic economy and monoculture

The first sixty years of the Roman domination of Sicily were relatively happy,[1] generally marked by peace and prosperity. The rural landscape included large estates, with pasturelands, orchards and small farms. Civic life was very lively, reflected by the various monuments in many cities. After the Second Punic War about 2,000 merchants and businessmen, Latin and Italic, established themselves on the island. The enriched plebeians were attracted both by the plans of reconstruction of the provincial government (the Hannibalic War had ruined cities and devastated the countryside) and the enormous availability of slave labour, at a very low price. They acquired large estates,[2] much property and large portions of *ager publicus*[3] in rent. They also developed herding – the herds and flocks were grazed in the mountains in summer and on the plains in winter – as well as agricultural activity for the cultivation of cereals, imposed by the scarcity of irrigated water. Among the cereals, the most cultivated in Sicily became spelt: this type of wheat was the basis of Roman food, mainly used to prepare bread, flat bread and polenta. The word 'flour' comes from spelt, as the Latin word *confarreatio* derives from the fact that spouses ate a muffin made from spelt wheat.[4]

Among the great landowners, many were extremely wealthy and possessed properties scattered over various parts of the Roman world. Often they were of prominent, senatorial families living in Rome, not in Sicily. It is important to note that, among the large landowners, there were many wealthy Sicilian families, who thrived in the shadow of Roman rule. The new production investments had the effect of accentuating the latifondistic (landowner) connotation of the agricultural economy, cereal and grazing, and the monoculture phenomenon. Moreover, it brought to Sicily a very large number of slaves. As time passed, the agricultural economy became an economy of large estates, based on a major use of slave labour, as this kind of economy required a large labour and the servile labour had a very low cost, because the market was swamped with slaves, so numerous were they.

This exacerbated the subjection of the Sicilian economy with respect to external needs, mainly with respect to the food supply of Rome, and ensured that slaves in the countryside grew in number from day to day. All this produced considerable change in the island's economy and society. Peasant masses were impoverished. Many small farmers failed because they could not compete with large landowners, who were able to produce more at lower prices. Many workers lost their job, or the chance of finding a job, because large landowners preferred to employ slaves in their estates to save on labour costs.

A granary of Rome

After 146 – therefore after both the Third Punic War and the Achaian War – the population of Rome had increased considerably, exceeding 200,000 and approaching 375,000. The population growth was accompanied by unbridled housing speculation, which availed itself of an abundant amount of slave labour for the construction of *insulae*, houses and entire neighbourhoods.[5] The population estimates are only approximate. What is certain is that the inhabitants of Rome cannot have been more than 400,000, the maximum capacity of the area included within the Servian Walls, which extended for 460 hectares. Any large population requires a constant supply of large quantities of foodstuffs. Rome's supply of food consisted mainly of imports of wheat and its derivatives,[6] since the feeding of the Romans was based largely on the consumption of wheat bread. The rural district of Rome does not produce wheat, so this cereal had to be imported. In part it was bought by *mercatores*, 'wholesalers', in the place of production, so it was privately owned. In part it represented the payment in kind of the tithe (the indirect tax on agricultural production, levied in the colonies under Latin law, allied cities and *provinciae*), therefore it was public grain.

Wheat importation mostly occured by sea. Loads of wheat reached their destination on board roundish, square-sailed vessels, used specifically for grain transportation and called granary ships. The largest tonnage of these vessels had a capacity of over 10,000 amphorae, equivalent to about 70,000 bushels (450/500 tons). The cereal was stowed in sacks lain loose on mezzanines and other wooden structures, mounted in such a way as to facilitate aeration.[7] The navigation of the granary ships to Italy could be direct and rapid, or slow and inshore, depending on the direction of the winds and sea conditions. Once arrived at Puteolis (Pozzuoli) – a port on the coast of Campania, the most important in Italy for imports from the West – the loads of wheat destined for Rome were transferred to ships of smaller tonnage and continued their journey. The ships went back to the Tyrrhenian coast to Ostia and then up the Tiber to Emporium, the largest and busiest port of the urban area of Rome. The fluvial ports of that area were the following: portus Tiberinus, Emporium, portus Vinarius and a fourth, located in Marmorata.[8] They were all downstream of the Tiber Island, on both banks of the Tiber, mainly on the left.

Portus Tiberinus,[9] the oldest facility, was on the left bank, in the bend that faced the Velabro and the Forum Boarium, a short distance from the Forum Olitorium and Forum Boarium. The Forum Olitorium was a fruit and vegetable market, while the Forum Boarium was a livestock market, where it was possible to buy live or already slaughtered animals.[10] Portus Vinarius was on the shore of Campo Marzio and, as the name implies, specialized in the landing and storage of wine.[11] The Marmorata area was used for the landing and storage of marble and other stone materials.[12] Emporium was the new fluvial port of Rome, where imported goods arrived via Ostia to be stored, distributed in the city or sorted to other destinations. It was on the left bank, in the area of the Forum Boarium, between the Aventine Hill and the Testaccio, in a large open, flat space.[13] It was built to receive the increasing flow of goods arriving in the city by sea, since Portus Tiberinus was no longer sufficient to support the traffic and could not be enlarged because it was wedged between areas intensely built up. The construction works were started in 193 by the *aediles* Lucius Aemilius Laepidus and Lucius Aemilius Paullus, the future *macedonicus*. They received a strong impulse from Lucius Aemilius Paullus Macedonicus, censor in 164. The port consisted of a long quay and a couple of large buildings, located near the quay and called Porticus Aemilia[14] and Horrea Sulpicia.[15] The quay was 150 metres long and paved with travertine slabs, which ran along the shore, with inclined planes, stairs and mooring rings. Porticus Aemilia was an arsenal, shipyard and naval base, about 90 metres from the river and built in *opus incertum*, made of peperino (a kind of marble, common around Rome) and tuff, with the floor of clay. It was 487 metres long and 60 metres wide, was divided into a series of areas by 294 pillars, and was equipped with steps and ramps down to the river, sloping down to the Tiber. The pillars were arranged in seven rows, which formed fifty naves, covered with barrel vaults. Each aisle was 8.30 metres wide. The total covered area was 25,000 square metres. The construction works of Porticus Aemilia were started in 193 by the builders of the port and were completed in 174 by the censors

Quintus Fulvius Flaccus and Aulus Postumius Albinus. It is called Horrea Sulpicia, a complex of buildings made up of warehouses, destined for the storage of goods, with on one side slave dwellings (in Latin, *ergastula*) and another building, in *opus reticulatum* of tuff, organized around three large rectangular courtyards, arcades, on which long rooms open.

In both Puteolis and Emporium the comings and goings of boats, sailors, slaves, goods and vehicles never stopped. During the day it happened in the light of the sun; at night, by the flare of torches and lamps. The unloaders went up and down the ships, in long lines, using rickety wooden walkways, connected to ramps and masonry staircases, which climbed up the gentle slope to the warehouses. The banks of the Tiber, from Ostia to Rome, were also intensely used, the vessels transporting grain towed by pairs of oxen, which proceeded along the shore, and which, once they reached Emporium, returned to Ostia for repeat the journey. Wheat from wholesalers was resold in Rome to retailers at the market price, with good profits. As for the public grain, a part was distributed to the army, while the remainder was set aside to prevent manipulation and price speculation. The food supply of Rome depended on the coming and going of grain ships to and from Sicily, Egypt, Thessaly (on the north-eastern Greek mainland), North Africa, Sardinia and southern Spain. Sicily was thus of great strategic importance for Rome, along with the city's other 'granaries'.

Sicilian wheat was mainly produced in the central area and the plains of Gela and Catania. The Plain of Catania is located at the foot of Mount Etna, in the eastern part of the island. It is the most extensive plain in Sicily, and one of the largest of Italy. It has been formed by the accumulation of alluvial deposits of the rivers Dittaino, Gornalunga, Simeto and their tributaries, and is surrounded by mountains and hills. Very fertile, it was cultivated with wheat, legumes and olive trees, and was surrounded by small and large settlements, of which the main one was the city of Catana, located on the eastern edge on the coast. The plain was also called the *Campi Leontini*, as it was controlled by the nearby Greek city of Leontini. Sicily's second largest plain extends along the southern coast, is surrounded by hills and derives its name from the city of Gelas. This plain was also very fertile and well irrigated, so that, like the plain of Catania, it had a strong agricultural vocation. This was the legendary country of the Laestrygonians, a tribe of man-eating giants, neighbours of the Cyclops, whom Odysseus was said to have come across before meeting Polyphemus. According to Homer, the giant ate many of Odysseus' men and destroyed eleven of his twelve ships by launching rocks from high cliffs. The plain of Gela was formed by the accumulation of alluvial deposits transported by the swirling River Gela, the Dirillo and their tributaries, which still cross it, together with the Ippari river, which runs all year round. It was covered by vast woods and was one of the most fertile areas of Sicily, particularly suitable for the cultivation of wheat, legumes, olives and vines. It was intensively cultivated, especially with grain production, making it one of the most important agricultural areas of Sicily. Such had been the case since ancient times. The tragedian Aeschylus, who lived and died in Gelas in the fifth century, mentioned the plain of Gela as 'rich in harvest'. Countless slaves were put to work in all these grain-growing regions on the large estates, or *latifundia*.

Slave labour and bad masters

It is difficult to comprehend just how many slaves were put to work in Sicily in the second half of the second century. For the most part the slaves were Syrians, but there were also many Assyrians and those from elsewhere in the Syrio-Palestine region.[16] Most were also former prisoners of war and had been bought and sold at the market of Delos.[17] They reflected the result of Roman victories against the Seleucid Empire, along with the trade of slaves by Cilician pirates and the actions of the sovereigns of Cyprus and Egypt, who were enemies of the Syrians. The Republic of Rhodes, while no friend of the kingdom of Cyprus nor Hellenistic Egypt, also contributed to the enslaving of Syrians. While it was not good practice to buy too many slaves from one area, the slave supply depended on the places where people were being enslaved in great number, and in the second century this was Syria, Thrace and Gaul.[18] Not only were there large numbers of Syrian slaves on the market, but Sicilian land-owners would favour those slaves over any other.[19]

The living conditions of slaves and their degree of exploitation were horrendous. By day they worked hard in the countryside, while at night they were locked up in establishments called *ergastula*. Not only deprived of their liberty and personal identity, they were also ill-treated: fed little and badly, they were dressed worse, punished severely for every indiscretion, no matter how small, often for no other reason than to satisfy the sadism of their masters. Many owners could be cruel and negligent in the maintenance of their slaves, even ruthless. These owners were mainly of Italic origin, but the richest of the Sicilians could compete with them in arrogance and cruelty. These guardians of the flocks – who were many, the Sicilian economy being largely pastoral – were largely uncontrolled. They were left in the open both day and night, were armed and had a most frightful and terrible appearance. They carried clubs and spears, had shepherds' sticks and packs of dogs, and dressed in the same manner, being covered with the skins of wolves and wild boars, almost like they were going to war. In any case, their condition was miserable. Some of their masters went so far as to give them neither food nor clothes, and encourage them to procure these by organizing themselves in gangs, attacking and stripping wayfarers and plundering isolated farms. Some big landowners even used their slave-shepherds to perform violence and aggression, to regulate conflicts with neighbours or to enlarge their own territory at others' expense. For example, if the neighbours were small farmers, minors or single women, with no other weapons to oppose them than to turn to state justice, many ruthless landowners took advantage of this. Given the lack of scruples of many landowners, it was not surprising that many of them behaved like bandits, or showed impunity to bandits on his lands, in a relationship of mutual convenience. Some even recruited criminals to monitor the boundaries of their property against trespassing by the flocks and herds of others, and carry out all sorts of rural theft, in return for being able to use them for oppression, abuse and revenge. There were also landowners who, not wishing to dirty their hands, used armed bands of outlaws to commit crimes and even murders, receiving in exchange protection from justice. In sum, many slaves were violent, socially dangerous individuals, were armed by their masters and, like bandits, were used for committing criminal acts.

Banditry and maladministration

Banditry has been an endemic phenomenon in Sicily for up to 3,000 years. It was linked to the importance of the pastoral economy and jeopardized the security of the countryside and mountain areas, where gangs of bandits roamed practically undisturbed. Bandits were thieves, murderers and common criminals, who had often escaped execution after a death sentence; many were youngsters attracted by the most vulgar reasons: a taste for an unbridled life, lust for booty, thirst for blood or desire for revenge against personal enemies. Banditry was nourished, before the Roman conquest of the island, by the recruitment of illegally paid mercenaries and slavery. With the arrival of the Romans, Sicily had become a place of deportation for Italics and a place of refuge for fugitive slaves, who lived by banditry. Valerius Levinus, proconsul of Sicily in 210, brought 4,000 bandits and

Popilius Laenas nine hundred and ten. Because of the presence of so many criminals, the Sicilian countryside – unlike the cities, which were largely quiet and safe – was a dangerous place. At night, the roads were dangerous for solitary or very small groups of travellers. Isolated houses and farms risked continuously being attacked and plundered, and for this reason were often fortified. Everywhere there was rapine, robberies and murders. Insecurity spread, and with it fear, without anyone being able to stop them. The state of insecurity of the countryside was fuelled by the fact that the criminal behaviour of big landowners and their slave-shepherds was often not prosecuted, or not prosecuted as it should be.[20] Magistrates and their commissioners often did not activate criminal actions, either because they were not capable, indolent or were paralyzed by fear, since the owner they were pursuing (in cases of indirect responsibility, in order to punish the crime of one of his slaves) was a Roman senator, a relative or parent of a senator, or boasted high-level friendships, and may take revenge by hindering or impeding the course of their career.[21]

PART II

THE REVOLT OF EUNUS

Chapter 7

The Slave Insurgency in Henna

Eunus, the Syrian soothsayer

The Orontes[1] river originates in the Beqā valley, just north of Baalbek, in Phoenicia (Lebanon). After having received the waters of numerous tributaries, which reached it from Mount Lebanon and the Antiliban, it crossed Antioch (Antiochia) and flowed into the Mediterranean at Samandag in Syria. Another Syrian city – Apameia (Afāmiyā) – was at the top of a hill overlooking the Orontes valley. It remained one of the most important cities of the Near East, after have been a capital of the Seleucid Empire. It had a Hellenistic urban layout as well as a strong military imprint, given by the Seleucids, who concentrated their cavalry in it. Its acropolis was a fortified citadel. Apameia was the hometown of an elderly slave called Eunus, who lived in Henna in Sicily. He had Apameia in his heart and remembered it with nostalgia, which helped him overcome his depression. Since it is the master who gave the name to any slave, it is unlikely that Eunus was his real name. Non-Greek slaves often received Greek names in order to be sold at a higher price.[2] Eunus had been a free man and a very important person, apparently a high-ranking priest.[3] He was kidnapped and sold at the slave market of Delos together with his wife or concubine. That woman, also Syrian, shared his fate (those who enslaved them did not separate them). They were both owned by Antigenes, one of the richest citizens of Henna. Antigenes possessed boundless lands and innumerable herds and slaves. He, his wife and their young daughter all resided in a country house, since many large landowners of Sicily had houses in both the countryside and the city.

Eunus was a fortune teller in the sanctuary of Demeter/Ceres in Henna. He retained for himself a share of the remuneration he received, while the remainder went to his master. Thus he was a privileged slave, perhaps even quite rich. In order to justify his ability in divination, he usually said that a world of voices was crowded around him, with rumours that resonated to him as real as if they were those of a friend or enemy; he could not reduce the volume and did not know how to shut them up. Such voices allowed him to predict the future. Eunus also claimed to be in mystical communion with the gods, in particular with Atargatis, the Syrian divinity of love, the equivalent of Aphrodite to the Greeks and Venus to the Romans. Atargatis was usually depicted as a fish-woman or mermaid. Her cult was born in the Syrian city-sanctuary of Hierapolis Bambyce, from where it had spread to Greece, conveyed by priests and navigators/merchants. The former travelled from one city to another to collect alms, while the latter passed through the large commercial ports of the Mediterranean and explained that their welfare was due to the protection of the goddess. The cult of Atargatis had been introduced to Sicily by Syrian slaves, who were devoted to Atargatis and believed that she interceded for them. There was nothing that united them more than the cult of Atargatis. Eunus said that Atargatis had appeared to him in a dream and announced to him the advent of a kingdom, of which he would be the king. He seemed an exalted mystic and many considered him a madman. But Eunus was not crazy at all. On the contrary, he was intelligent and lucid. Eunus was not the first sane man to say he hears voices. Of the precedents, the most illustrious was Publius Cornelius Scipio Africanus, victor of the Battle of Zama, the final episode of the Second Punic War. Scipio, at critical moments, used to linger in the Temple of Iupiter Optimus Maximus on the Capitolium in Rome,[4] and spread the word that he spoke with Iupiter, the god of the civilized community, tutelary deity of Rome and guarantor of its destiny. He cleverly took advantage of the naivety of his soldiers to make his commands appear to be prompted by divine warnings. The inspiration to behave in such a way came to him from having been assimilated into the political and cultural innovations of the Greek world, where politicians, since the time of Alexander the Great, had used propaganda and religion to strengthen their power. Of those who considered Eunus an imposter, the first was his owner, Antigenes. When he heard Eunus speak, he laughed out loud. Also, on festive evenings, when his guests drank heavily and gorged themselves on food, Antigenes sent for Eunus and ironically questioned him about his future reign and the treatment that, once king, he would reserve for the guests present. The guests would laugh uncontrollably, saying they feared his rule. But Eunus reassured them: he would be a good and gracious king. 'He's a nice buffoon,' they said. The 'game' continued with the roles reversed, one of the diners serving Eunus at the table and begging him to remember him when he became king, causing all to again break out in laughter.

The sedition

Eunus was a passionate man, thirsty for freedom and eager for revenge, with an infinite resentment for his servile condition and those who obliged him. He had a plan in mind: to foment a slave revolt to recover the freedom that was taken from him by force. He carried on his sedition, speaking with other slaves of nationalism, religion, revenge and race, freedom, perhaps even of the abolition of slavery. He repeats continuously the story of the voices which inspired him, of his special relation with Atargatis, of the prophecy that the goddess revealed to him of the advent of a kingdom of which Eunus himself would be the king. He often met his companions in misfortune at the sanctuary of Demeter in Henna, in particular at the asylum, a place where people facing persecution could seek refuge (in both the Greek and Roman world, some temples, altars, sacred groves and statues of the gods possessed the privilege of protecting slaves, debtors and criminals who fled to them for refuge). Eunus' goal was to change the state of mind of the other slaves, oppressed by the deprivation of every right and freedom, and appeal to their propensity to follow anyone who offered a prospect of liberation. It must be remembered that the slaves were mostly ex-prisoners of war, who in the past had lived as free men, so were particularly sensitive to such overtures. To give more strength to his words, he set up a stratagem. He hid in his mouth two half-shells of a walnut, pierced and containing embers wrapped in leaves, which when he blew emitted flames. By this he aimed to get his comrades to associate him with Dionysus, the Greek god whose tongue was considered a destructive fire in the Near East. As we noted earlier, Dionysus was the god of wine, ecstasy and liberation of the senses, but also of the excluded, of the humble and the oppressed, for whom he represented a hope of redemption from poverty and liberation from chains. In Sicily, the cult of Dionysus was often joined with that of Demeter/Ceres, so the sanctuary of Demeter in Henna was the ideal setting to evoke both gods through his stratagem. Eunus was a great speaker and had great success, inspiring his comrades to such an extent that they became fanatical and convinced that they wanted to break their chains whatever the cost.

A blast of blind violence

Damóphylos, a Sicilian man living in Henna, owned a large estate, a vast stock of cattle, much silver utensils and precious carpets and many slaves.

As well as being rich, he was known for being uncouth and uneducated, proud and arrogant beyond measure, a lover of luxury and licentiousness. He travelled through Sicily in a horse-drawn coach escorted by armed guards, in the company of beautiful boys, flatterers and parasites. He held magnificent feasts and entertainments, at great expense, acting as though he was a king. He was also severe to his slaves, cruel and ruthless. He abused them unrestrainedly, marking on the neck those that were free-born in their own country and taken captive in war. Every day he whipped someone, often without reason, or bound them in fetters. He provided neither sufficient food nor clothing to those he ordered to keep his livestock. Should any of them complain, he had them beaten cruelly.[5] His wife, Megallis, was as bad as her husband, even worse. Her face was said to be as bleak as that of a bear.[6] The slaves owned by this pair of villains were treated cruelly and inhumanely by them, like wild beasts. However, it seems that these masters were no worse than many others, so the subsequent revolt can be seen as not only a vengeance against them, but against the inhuman ferocity that animated so many of the slave masters.

The slaves owned by Damóphylos and Megallis plotted to revolt and cut their throats. One day[7] they consulted Eunus to find out if the gods would support their plan if it were put into practice. Eunus first listened to them in silence, then closed his eyes and began to speak nonsense. He behaved as if possessed by supernatural forces, those around him looking on in dismay, but also excited. After a while, Eunus opened his eyes and suddenly shouted: 'The gods agree that you rebel, they want it, the sky screams revenge!' Having said the gods approved, the slaves' long-suppressed anxiety exploded joyfully as they embraced Eunus and each other. This was the spark that ignited the fire. When evening fell, 400 slaves gathered in a field outside Henna, clutching lighted torches, sticks, axes, batons, clubs, daggers, slings, scythes, spits and anything else they could gather as weapons. Swearing to stick together in their mutiny, they headed for the city, led by Eunus. They climbed the city walls and broke in, then gave vent to their long-repressed anger in an orgy of killing. Going to where they knew that their owners lived, they broke down the front doors with their shoulders or axes, burst inside and killed anyone who opposed, raping, looting and setting fire to everything. They made such great slaughter that they did not even spare suckling children, plucking them violently from their mothers' breasts and dashing them against the ground. To satisfy their lusts, they abused the men's wives in the presence of their husbands. Having unleashed their rage on their masters, they moved on to kill others.[8]

Blood soon ran throughout the city, spreading through the streets and squares in streams and pools, while smoke and the acrid smell of fires filled the air. Some masters managed to survive, either because they found an escape route or they had not been staying in Henna, but in nearby country houses. But they were deluding themselves that they could get away scot-free. They were hunted down, caught and led into a theatre to be tried in the presence of the insurgents, assembled to enjoy the spectacle. In the meantime, the nucleus of revolutionaries had been joined by a multitude of other slaves in the city.

The punishment of the bad masters

Obviously the 'trial' of the captured slave owners was no regular judicial procedure. Yet the improvised judges distinguished among the defendants those known for the humane treatment of slaves, setting them free. Among those who were released were some friends of Antigenes. They were freed by the intercession of Eunus, who remembered an episode which stood in their favour. Eunus had once been shown to them while they were sitting at table, and they offered him food and showed interest in his prophecies.[9] However, Damóphylos, Megallis and their young daughter were caught in an orchard near Henna. They were taken to the city and into the theatre with their hands tied behind their backs, suffering many insults and much ill-treatment along the way.[10] Damóphylos begged to be spared and some were moved by his pleas. But two of his rebellious slaves, Ermeias and Zeuxis, hurled a slew of accusations at him, labelling him a liar. Without waiting for the assembly to judge him, they threw themselves at him, and while one stabbed him with a sword the other cut off his head with an axe.[11] The assembly exploded in applause. Megallis underwent a fate no less bitter. She was handed over to their servants, whom she had mistreated for so long, for them to take their revenge. She was tortured and, still alive, thrown to her death down a steep cliff.[12] The young daughter of the couple, unlike her parents, had always sympathized with the slaves and tried to help them. She was respected for this and escorted to Catana, where she was delivered unharmed to relatives.[13] Antigenes received special treatment. Eunus killed him with his own hands, then did the same with a certain Phyton.[14] As for the other prisoners, showing no subtlety in his position of strength, he proposed to select, chain and start to work those that could be used to manufacture weapons, then to kill all the others.[15] His proposal was accept with shouts of enthusiasm.

Chapter 8

The Birth of a Kingdom

The establishment of the Western Kingdom of the Syrians

The insurgents gathered in an assembly to hail Eunus as their king, 'not for his value, nor for his qualities as a leader, but, expressly, for his magical power, for having initiated the insurrection, and because his name contains a wish of benevolence towards his subjects'[1] (*eunous*, in Greek, signifies a number or assortment of good things). Moreover, they attributed to him absolute power to order and dispose of all things as he pleased. This point deserves to be stressed. The insurgents, in equipping themselves with a leader, created a head of state, legitimized by an election and provided with all powers (making laws, governing the state, commanding the army, administering justice), an absolute king to rule until death, when the next in line inherits the throne. In other words, they established a monarchy and allowed he who ruled to freely exercise sovereignty without observing any limit but that which he himself established, except being bound to respect various social and religious norms. The term 'absolute', in fact, means 'dissolved from any external constraint', and is linked to the concept that the authority of a ruler derives directly from God. The absolute monarch should not be confused with a gang leader, nor with a tyrant; the first leads an association or group of criminals, that claims an area as its territory and defends it against other gangs or unaffiliated criminals; the second is one who governs without legitimacy or limits. One could argue whether Henna's insurgents were an association of criminals, since, in seizing the city, they had committed all sorts of crimes; certainly they were such before the Roman law, perhaps even against the divine law, but in their way of viewing things they were not such at all because they believed they had fought for freedom and political self-determination, throwing themselves only against bad masters, without, that is, acting indiscriminately against the whole population. A monarchy presupposes a nation-state to be governed, an independent political organization with a centralized government that maintains a monopoly on the legitimate use of force within a certain territory, and whose people mostly share a common identity. This explains why, in his speech of thanks, Eunus proclaimed the birth of a kingdom. He also pointed out that this reflected Hellenistic realms in terms of appearance, organization and ideology. He called it the Western Kingdom of the Syrians, an ethnonym that identified Eunus and all his companions, or at least most of them, and chose for himself the royal name of Antiochus.[2] It was evident that the adjective 'Western', associated to the words 'Kingdom of the Syrians', served to differentiate the reign of Eunus/King Antiochus from the contemporary Kingdom of Syria (a part of the Seleucid Empire), ruled by Antiochus VII Evergetes Sidetes (138–129), with which it was related.[3] Specifically, there were all the conditions for founding a nation-state: a territory; a people, who mostly shared a common history and culture; and the juridical quality pertaining to any state as original power and independent of any other power (sovereignty). It is hardly necessary to note that the Western Kingdom of the Syrians, to exist, did not need to be recognized by other states, since it did not exist in international law (there was a law of nations, but it was 'a reasoned compliance with standards of international conduct',[4] so something different).

At that moment, the first condition (that any state needs a territory) was satisfied because the insurgents controlled Henna and its surroundings. The second condition (that any state needs a people who mostly share a common history and culture) was satisfied by the Syrian insurgents and by anyone who had chosen or would choose freely to become responsible for their actions. Concerning sovereignty, in the case of the Western Kingdom of the Syrians, it derived directly from Atargatis. Any state needs sovereignty primarily to enact laws and to defend its people. The Western Kingdom of the Syrians, with regard to its organization, its functioning, the rights and duties of its citizens, and its relations with other states, would be ordained according to the rules that King Antiochus and his heirs and successors brought into being in the exercise of legislative power. This power would shortly be exercised for establishing an advisory body, having the task of assisting the king in dealing with governmental affairs, and for transferring to the insurgents the rights and property of their former masters.

External signs connected to the ritual of sovereignity and court ceremonial

Being a Hellenistic king meant practising the ritual of sovereignty connected to external signs. The ritual in question was that of the Achaemenid monarchy, borrowed from Alexander the Great and 'inherited' from the Diadochi (the rival generals, family members and friends of Alexander who fought for control of his empire after his death) and their heirs and successors, with particular reference to Seleucid practices.[5] King Antiochus therefore dressed in regal purple and assumed the insignia of Hellenistic royalty. He wrapped the diadem: a broad ribbon of white cloth edged on both sides and adorned with gold, tied at the back, with the fringed ends hanging over the nape. He wore a red chiton (a tunic). He slipped on his finger a ring, which bore specific insignia and, as well as a personal ornament, also served as a seal, to authenticate both the most important acts of government and his own private acts. On official occasions, he sat on the throne beneath a golden canopy, wearing the royal headdress, or tiara. He dressed in a chlamys (a cloak) in red-purple, tightened at the waist with a belt. He held a sceptre. In his military campaigns, he would be housed in a rich red-purple field tent. The court ceremonial of Hellenistic kings was also a derivation of the Persian one. It provided for the appointment of a chamberlain (*eisangeleus*). From then on, anyone who wanted an audience with King Antiochus must address the request to the chamberlain in charge and wait to be received. Only the closest collaborators of the king had free access to his presence. The only difference between the court ceremonial adopted by King Antiochus and that of the Hellenistic sovereigns was the lack of royal worship, given the special position of Eunus as a servant of Atargatis,[6] the goddess on behalf of whom the insurgents had gone together to assault Henna.[7] Consequently, it did not provide the *proskynēsis*, nor the prostration, which symbolized the condition of the subject with respect to his lord, and was a gesture of servile devotion, by non-free people in front of their divine master, and whoever did it submitted to his law. *Proskynēsis* consisted of all those who were admitted to the presence of the king, except his closest collaborators, being obliged to put their hand to their lips and to bow lightly (among the Greeks, this was seen as a gesture of veneration in front of the gods). Prostration was different, in that the applicant begged for a grace or protection by throwing himself at the feet of the powerful.

First acts of government

A king must have a consort of equal rank at his side; therefore King Antiochus raised his partner to the dignity of queen. Then he surrounded himself with a 'Council of Sages', a court – including the inevitable fool – and a large personal guard, that would grow in time up to 1,000 men.

It seems that the bodyguard of Antiochus were Gauls, Galatians in particular. Warriors of Gallic ethnicity were usually chosen for the role of bodyguard at this time. Galatians were a people of Celtic tradition, living in central Anatolia (where the Syrian language was also spoken). Finally, Antiochus chose his service staff, including a chef, baker and barber.[8] The administration of Hellenistic sovereigns was in charge of managing the state and providing for the personal security of the king, the defence of the state against enemies and the preparation for war. His court administration, besides the chamberlain, also included a viceroy, secretary and treasurer.

At the time of Alexander the Great, both the Macedonians and the Achaemenids had a figure called in Persian *hazarapatiš*, 'chief of the thousand', and in Greek *chiliarchos*. This was the commander of the Royal Army, someone who, in case of the absence or impediment of the king, deputized for him in the exercise of his functions as head of state. After 330, Alexander incorporated the Royal Guard into the imperial army and inserted the *chiliarchia* into the imperial administration. Office and security duties were entrusted to Hephaestion, the closest friend of Alexander, who also commanded the division of cavalry. Alexander's chamberlain was Chares of Mytilene, who was mainly concerned with meeting the king's needs, with the audience in the royal tent and with the use of the pages. Later, the government of Queen Roxane's (Alexander's wife) household was added to his duties. On his return to Mesopotamia, Chares was able to extend his duties to the administration of the Palace. The secretary of Alexander was Eumenes of Cardia, who had already served his father, Philip II, as personal secretary (*grammatos*). Eumenes was assisted by archivists, who were in charge of keeping correspondence. The treasures accumulated by Alexander during his conquests were entrusted to the custody of a friend of his youth, Harpalus, who also directed the treasury and tax services, and was responsible for beating (manufacturing) money. Beating money was one of the prerogatives of kings. It served to provide the administration of the state and the army with the financial means necessary for their operation and their investments, and was a powerful stimulus to the development of trade.

King Antiochus instituted a mint in Henna.[9] This would produce many bronze coins, possibly designed to elicit a response from the people of Sicily in support of their revolt, mainly by the cities and towns in the east of the island. Antiochus also hoped that these would prove an effective communication tool. There were at least four issues of bronze coinage by this mint. Two bore on the obverse (the side unusally reserved for Zeus) a male head, bearded and diademed, without inscription; and on the reverse a winged thunderbolt or a lit torch on a pedestal, a club or a quiver. The head could be that of Eunus himself, Zeus or Heracles. It showed how King Antiochus wanted himself to be seen. The head was diademed, which was common among Hellenistic kings. Even in Sicily, it wasn't the first time that a coin portrayed a king on the obverse. The Syracusan king Hiero II placed the head of his son Gelon on the obverse of coins that had on the reverse a winged thunderbolt, and Hieroymus did the same for himself. It is interesting to note that, in Sicily, the town of Kentoripa (Centurĭpae, Centuripae) minted coins featuring Zeus on the obverse and a winged lightning bolt on the reverse from the third century until the mid-second century. The image of a club on the reverse of Eunus' issues would indicate a link to Heracles, while a quiver would be linked to Artemis. The quiver appears on coins of Demetrius I Soter and one from Halaesa dateable to after 241. Moreover, coins from Halaesa, Syracuse and Morgantia from after 210, during the period of Hispanic occupation, all feature Artemis. A third issue of coinage from the mint of Eunus had on the obverse a head, helmeted, and a club on the reverse. The helmeted head, if that of a man, could be that of Ares/Mars, while the club would invoke Heracles. If that of a woman, it could be Athena, as in a series of coins from Agyrium, minted in 339, where both the motives (Athena and a club) appear. However, another coin from Agyrium, dated to the same years, has been suggested to show the helmeted head of Ares on the obverse and a club on the reverse. We can be fairly certain that the club is a reference to Heracles from several examples of coinage from Aluntium, Cale Acte, Centurĭpae, Cephaloedium and Menaenum, all of which minted coins with Heracles on the obverse and a club on the reverse, dated from 241 to the second century. It is important to note that Athena was a deity typically associated with Hellenistic monarchies. Thus it seems more likely that the head is that of Athena rather than Heracles. The fourth issue of coinage of Eunus' mint at Henna bore the head of Demeter, veiled, on the obverse, and an ear of barley on the reverse and the inscription *basileus Antĭochos*, 'king Antiochus'.[10] It is similar to a coin type from Henna minted at some point after 340, which also had a head of Demeter on the obverse and an ear of barley on the reverse, and similar coins from Centurĭpae, Hybla Magna and Leontinoi into the second century. It is useful to remember the close association of Henna with Demeter, which emerged with the sanctuary of this goddess at Henna and the importance of the city as the main market of weath in Sicily. It assigned to Eunus a gold stater, on the obverse of which was a diademed male head and Nike, and, on the reverse side, a figure seated on the left on a pile of weapons with a stick to his left and a sword in his right hand.

Eunus said to his fellows gathered in assembly what had been prophesied by Atargatis and what started in Henna could not be considered as a protest against slavery, their mistreatment, bad food and inadequate clothing, as that would be a trade union action, culminating in a strike of disgruntled workers. Rather it was an armed insurgency carried on by fugitive slaves, with looting, violence, murder and fire. The insurgents had gone too far, and they could not back down as no one would forgive them. Any reconciliation was impossible and it was good to keep that in mind, in case anyone deluded himself about the possible attitude of the Romans. According to Roman law, he remembered, fugitive slaves captured and judged responsible for crimes were crucified or thrown off a cliff. There was thus no return from the action taken by the insurgents at Henna. They all knew what Romans were like: they hated disorder more than anything else, and could not leave fugitive slaves roaming free, particularly those guilty of blood crimes; least of all could they leave even a crumb of the provincial territory in their hands. Therefore the provincial magistrates would not remain inert: there would be a violent reaction. The restoration of public order and security rested with the local authorities, namely with the municipal authorities, who usually for this purpose used a territorial militia, a sort of police, more or less well organized, and not soldiers, let alone legionnaires (there were no legions in Sicily anymore, they having been withdrawn after the establishment of the province). However, the *duumviri* (the board of two notables who served as mayor) and the members of the municipal council no longer existed in Henna, having been swept away by the insurrection. The insurgents had cleared away the command of the city, and all power was now concentrated in the hands of King Antiochus. Therefore it was reasonable to expect the provincial government to intervene directly, using provincial troops for this purpose. It followed that the insurgents had to prepare to face such a reaction. This meant first of all replacing the improper weapons used so far – kitchen utensils and work tools – with weapons of war, but also strengthening their numbers by attracting new supporters, both in the countryside and in the cities, and accepting anyone who shared the cause of the insurgency and wanted to join them. The rebels could not assign too much importance to whether these extra supporters were victims of injustice or individuals who had committed crimes that justified their fate: thieves, rapists and other criminals. It was also necessary to organize and train for combat, with equipment appropriate for soldiers, to take care of logistics, infiltrate spies among enemies and agitators in the cities, create lines of communication and decide on their tactics and strategy.

But there was more to it than that. People go to war because they have goals and think that these can only be achieved through the use of force. Precisely because the insurgents had nothing left to lose, it was worth seeking everything possible, setting as a goal their freedom, independence, equality and justice. King Antiochus had clear ideas how to do this, and outlined a plan of action. He had an ambitious political project. Given that the insurgents had gained their freedom and political independence by the force, and were ready to fight to maintain and enforce their conquests, he proposed to lead them to extend the land they controlled, snatching it from the Romans and anybody else who opposed them, until they held the entire island. Driving the Romans from Sicily, depriving them of their own province, replacing them in the domain and the economic exploitation of such actions might all appear a crazy idea, but less so if you take into account several things: Sicily is a large island; it was inhabited by various peoples, all different from each other and from the Latins, all conquered and subjugated by the Romans, and certainly not happy to have them as rulers, barring exceptions; and things you could achieve in Sicily would be impossible in Italy, nearer Rome. The primitive social movement became something new, leading to the establishment of a nation–state inside Roman Sicily which had unleashed a war against the Romans. The people of the new state were mainly born and raised in Syria, or were not Syrians but spoke Syrian. They did not seek to return to Syria. Instead, they planned to take root in Sicily and live as free citizens in their new homeland, one conquered with arms. They could not cross the sea to return to Syria: they had neither the ships nor the crews, nor were they able to create crews – you do not become a sailor overnight – or have control of the ports. Moreover, they could not wait for help from the inhabitants of coastal cities, because these detested them as fugitive slaves usually, and the punishment for those who helped such insurgents was very harsh.

Achaios' suggestions

One of the insurgents was named Achaios, an Achaean by birth, and thus a Greek. Achaios was a prisoner of war when he was sold to slave traders at the time of the destruction of Corinth after Rome's victory in the Achaean War in 146. Like his fellow adventurers, he was a rancorous and desperate man, thinking of nothing but revenge. But his mind was clear: he was an educated person, who thought with his head rather than his heart. Achaios was part of the *consilium* of King Antiochus, since he was a man known for his wisdom and foresight. He gave Antiochus useful suggestions. First of all, that of hitting the big landowners, wherever they were, and, in order to enlarge the territory they controlled, alternating guerrilla tactics and clashes in the open field, according to the convenience of the moment, widening gradually the field of action.

Guerrilla warfare involves ambushes, nocturnal attacks, rapid lunges and tactical retreats, carried out by small groups of fighters, scattered and very mobile, in a rugged terrain of forests, gorges and mountains. Practising such tactics requires dividing one's own forces into small bands, some well organized and others less so, operating in many areas. The units must be equipped and armed lightly, and be very mobile and autonomous, but able to act in concert with the framework of a pre-established strategy. It also involves not striking the population in the countryside, because they represent 'the water that allows the fish to swim' (in the sense that the guerrillas will tend to find support and connivance among them). Combat units are ordered to avoid clashes in the open field, between armies; rather they must practise guerrilla fighting. The guerrillas keep at a distance from large enemy forces, except to attack them with continuous minor actions on limited and always changing fronts. They set goals when conditions are favourable, preferring those that are secondary and less protected. To hinder the enemy's movement, they pollute pastures and water sources, causing shortages. They attack isolated contingents and supply convoys. They strike at night and in difficult terrain – forests, swamps, mountains – preferably where the climate, semi-desert landscape or rough ground hinder the enemy's movements, exploiting their knowledge of the ground. As soon as the enemy stiffens its defence and prepares to counterattack, or before it receives reinforcements, they disengage from combat and disappear into the dark. Then they hide, mix with the population, blend into the woods and swamps, hide in caves and ravines, and remain there, immobile, ready to strike again at the first opportunity. To demoralize the enemy and undermine his fighting spirit, they blind their prisoners before abandoning them to die under the sun, or threaten to attack him, but never engage in decisive combat. The most effective countermeasure to guerrilla warfare is to quickly pacify the territory. As guerrillas are small fish, to overcome them you need to drain the water in which they swim. The sea in which the Sicilian slave guerrillas swam was that of peasants and their villages. The moves of the anti-guerrilla forces are therefore directed to 'drain the water'. They devastate the countryside and storm the villages, loot them and set them on fire; force the inhabitants to deliver hostages and harvests; capture entire populations, killing all those caught with a weapon in their hands, selling these prisoners to the slave traders and the civilian populations, and violating the women. They face one small group of guerrillas after another; perform wide-ranging searches and systematic round-ups; and when they locate the enemy, they smoke him from his hiding places and slaughter him. They also set up various camps, but not far from each other, so that, if necessary, the soldiers of one can cover another. By operating in this way, the counter-insurgents can inflict severe blows on the guerrillas. Each time, however, the vanquished reorganize and resume fighting. It is as if Heracles was fighting again against the Hydra of Lerna, the mythological, multi-headed sea serpent. The guerrillas are dangerous every day, carrying out sudden attacks and ambushes, causing hunger and thirst, poisoning wells. They keep pricking the enemy, keeping him tied down.

King Antiochus accepted the suggestions of Achaios. He forbade the army from devastating the rural villages and isolated houses, harassing field workers, destroying agricultural tools and burning crops. He also ordered them to respect the sanctuary of Ceres in Henna, because Henna was the centre of the island's grain production and Ceres was its tutelary deity.

Chapter 9

King Antiochus' Army and its Commanders. Looting and Taking Cities. The Joining of Free Proletarians.

Achaios and plundering raids

The fugitive slaves divided themselves into small groups and – under command of Achaios – roamed the territory around the city on horseback. Lightly armed, with only scythes, sticks, axes or knifes, they needed to provide themselves with proper weapons of war, military equipment and horses as soon as possible. They aimed to take them from weapons depots and from the soldiers they would have captured and defeated, respectively. They spread over the fields, woods and mountains, attacking farms and hamlets, carrying out raids against owners of large estates, starting with the cruel masters of slaves, promoting their cause among their slaves, while avoiding the walled towns and cities. Their plundering raids had no strategy other than getting food, clothing and money and valuables to finance their cause. Central Sicily was a rich region, as were its inhabitants. Their cause was aided by them only targeting large estate owners and the bad masters of slaves, marking the raiders as different from the usual invaders. But when violence was unleashed it was easy for those with robbery in mind to turn into rapists and murderers. So the raiders often stole, killed and raped without check or mercy, spreading fear through their acts of bestial ferocity. The fugitive slaves thus behaved as free men would in the same circumstances, with equal violence, cruelty and ferocity. Every army during war in this age, in enemy territory, conformed to a kind of shared, customary law: it took the livelihoods it found in the theatre of war, depriving the civilian populations, raping, killing, and burning everything. Accumulating the loot of war was normal. Even those who suffered dispossession realised this, that they had merely been unlucky to find themselves on the route of an enemy army. When, however, the enemies were fugitive slaves, the victims felt more aggrieved, as from their perspective, these insurgents were not true warriors, and a slave revolt was not a war.[1]

News spread quickly through the countryside around Henna, raising the morale of slaves living there, who, in increasing numbers, rebelled against their masters, ransacked the farms and joined King Antiochus and his companions. The rebels' ranks thus increased from just 400 to around 6,000 within the short space of three days after the revolt began in Henna. Achaios became the undisputed commander of that army, beloved by his companions as he embodied their aspirations of freedom and independence. However, as we will see later, he was destined to not have the place he deserved with the kingdom's new rulers.

Kleon, the taking of Agrigentum and the fall of Morgantia

In this phase, there were no clashes with the territorial militia, because the provincial authorities were far away (in Syracusae and Lilybaeum) and were slow to react. The taking of Morgantia should be placed in this context. More or less contemporarily, a fugitive slave called Kleon gathered around him 5,000 other fugitive slaves, was recognized by them as their chief and then occupied Agrigentum.

Kleon[2] was a Cilician, born and raised somewhere in the Taurus mountains which separate the Mediterranean coastal region of Cilicia from the central Anatolian plateau (in modern south-eastern Turkey). He was captured and then sold in Sicily, together with his brother, Komanus. It is likely that he was sold at the slave market of Side, in Pamphylia. It is likely that he was a guardian of horses, perhaps also a brigand, before losing his freedom, and that, as a slave, he had the same kind of life he had in his homeland. Kleon and his followers asked and obtained to be welcomed into the Western Kingdom of the Syrians. Achaios and Kleon joined their forces and King Antiochus appointed Kleon as commander-in-chief of his army, perhaps even as viceroy. Probably one of the reasons for joining together was the hope that they could establish contacts with the Cilician pirates. Antiochus most likely wanted the Cilician pirates to transfer their predatory activity to the seas around Sicily, which would create major problems for the Romans. It would have been much more difficult for them to fight back against the Western Kingdom of the Syrians. The territory controlled by the new slave state now extended from the central area of Sicily to the southern coast, including the major cities of Henna, Morgantia and Agrigentum, with an army of 15,000 effectives.

Armed bands of free proletarians join the fugitive slaves

The success of the rebels brought further followers to the their cause, with thousands of individuals fleeing either from slavery or from conditions of life not dissimilar to those of slaves: mistreatment, too much hard work, solitude, malnutrition and being badly clothed. This point deserves to be stressed: the newcomers were in part new groups of slaves who had rebelled against their masters, and in part an unknown number of people of low social class. The latter were free citizens, but poor and living in squalor, with only basic food to eat and minimal to no income, sometimes supplemented by meagre sales of vegetables in the markets. They were all on the edge of having just enough to live, struggling to stay alive and hungry, often not having enough bread to fill their stomachs. They were also angry against the rich and the powerful, who marginalized and exploited them, usurped public lands and even deprived them of the air to breathe.[3] They wanted to join the fugitive slaves, sharing the same causes and seeing in the struggle a means of social redemption, driven by a revolutionary fervour.

The addition of free men to their number changed things. Previously the insurgents were all fugitive slaves. That they had regained their freedom and personal dignity by performing an act of strength and had become citizens of the Western Kingdom of the Syrians (although their masters and the Roman authorities did not acknowledge them this way) did not change the salient facts. But now not all the followers of King Antiochus were fugitive slaves, but included many free citizens. It is also important to note that they were volunteers, not conscripts or mercenaries. Moreover, since their plan was to seize the entire island, tearing it from the Romans, their reward would be the distribution of fertile lands, where they would live as free citizens, subjects of a kingdom, not mere veterans of war. Thanks to these new arrivals, Antiochus' army gradually became 15,000-strong.

King Antiochus' army

In part, the army were former first-generation slaves, who knew freedom before being deprived of it. But they were also free men familiar with weapons, or even ex-prisoners of war, expert in the use of weapons. The rest came from the most varied professions. There were people who worked their own land, former impoverished farmers, tenant farmers, day-labourers, shepherds, herders and beggars. Often, being involved in field work or grazing animals, they were robust, agile individuals. But all earnestly desired to take revenge on those who mistreated and oppressed them. However, they did not always match the courage or ability to fight of their new comrades who were former prisoners of war. They would have to learn how to use weapons and be trained in combat, but the command of Achaios would transform these individuals into a victorious army.

We have few details in this regard, but it seems likely that King Antiochus' army had an organized chain of command based on a well-planned fighting strategy, and was made up of units large and small, the former suitable for major clashes and the second fighting in open order. It also seems reasonable to assume that the larger units were organized in a Macedonian-style phalanx,[4] because most of it comprised former prisoners of war, who before being captured had fought in a Hellenistic army, and because lining up on the battlefield and fighting in this Greek manner was easier.

The phalanx was the means that allowed Philip II of Macedonia and his son Alexander the Great to achieve their conquests. This instrument, however, had changed over time. The armies used in the Wars of the Epigonoi ('Επίγονοι, 'Successors', better known as the Diadochi) were quite different from the glorious Macedonian army of the past, having gradually adopted new units and tactics, developed its warfare and improved its tactics, favouring numbers over quality and weight over manoeuvrability. They continued to base their strength on the phalanx, an infantry formation characterized by dense ranks of pikemen. The fighters, known as phalangites, were professional warriors, drilled in tactics, weapon use and formation. Certain reforms in the weight of phalangite equipment, and the conscription methods used, turned the phalanx from a manoeuvrable formation into a bulky, slow-moving steamroller, yet whose charge few enemies were able to withstand. As long as the phalanx remained on relatively level terrain and its flanks were kept secure, it was not beaten by any other formation. The role of the phalanx on the battlefield was to act as an anchor for the entire army, holding the enemy in place, pushing him back and exerting a heavy toll on enemy morale, while the cavalry struck the enemy flanks and delivered the fatal blow to cripple their opponents. In most battles it was used as the main weapon to achieve victory.

The phalangites' equipment included a helmet, ranging from simple, open-faced affairs to stylized Thracian models (complete with mask-like cheek protectors that often imitated a human face). Body armour ranged from a cuirass of hardened linen, that may or may not have been reinforced/ decorated with metal scales, to metallic (typically bronze) breastplates.

The primary weapon of the phalangite was the sarissa, a massive spear, up to 22ft long. The sarissa was largely useless in single combat, but a compact, forward-facing infantry formation employing it was almost impossible to overcome. The first five ranks of the phalanx would have their sarissai projecting horizontally to face the enemy, with the remaining ranks angling theirs in a serried fashion, often leaning against their fellows' backs. If front-rankers were killed, those behind would lower their spears and step forward to maintain a solid front. When this way of fighting was impractical, a variety of swords were used. The phalangite shield was round, with a diameter of about 60cm, and slightly concave. Metallic greaves were also in use. The primary drawback of the phalanx was its vulnerability to attacks from the rear and flanks. It also had a tendency to fracture when led across broken terrain for extended periods in close-ordered battle formation.

Chapter 10

Like a Fire Driven by an Impetuous Wind, the Rebellion Spreads

The ruinous defeat of L. Plautius Hypsaeus

A clan is a group of families that have a common ancestor. In Latin this concept is expressed trough the word *gens* (pl. *gentes*). Every Roman family belonged to a *gens*, due to descent or adoption. The most ancient and prestigious *gentes* were those of the families that had populated the nascent city of Rome and formed the 100 members of the primitive Senate, called *patres*, 'fathers', as the head of their respective family. These were the '100 primary *gentes*' and formed the noblest nucleus of the patriciate, called *nobilitas*. The Roman family of Hypsaeus was plebeian, but of noble descent, because more than one of its members had been a senator (in Rome, one became a senator after being elected as an *aedilis* or praetor). The Hypsaei were therefore enriched plebeians: economic operators, owners of private companies, who made their fortune after the Second Punic War through public procurement, and went on to swell the equestrian ranks. They were a class of businessmen and speculators, greedy and enterprising, eager to rise to the level of nobility, but did not have the blood nor, more importantly, the class. The neo-rich had risen to a higher economic and social condition without having acquired the manners appropriate to the new state. They tended to emulate the patricians, lacking the culture of the ruling class, which had its roots in the substratum of the values of Romanity, with special regard to the good habits that once informed the customs and lifestyles of the Roman people, based on parsimony and austerity. They did what patricians did not do, that is, show off their riches in order to distance themselves from the less fortunate members of their own class. Despite all their money, they remained separated from the patricians by an impassable ditch, as the distinction between patrician and plebeian was based on descent rather than wealth.

Like anyone in their economic condition, they kept away from the lower plebeians. Rather, they imitated patricians, but doing so in a nagging way.

The Hypsaei belonged to *gens* Plautia, or Plotia, which perhaps came to Rome from Privernum, in lower Latium. It seems that in the beginning this family was called Venox, or Venno, a hunter. It appears that Caius Plautius, censor in 312, received his nickname after discovering the springs that would later feed Rome's first aqueduct, the *Aqua Appia*. As often happened, the nickname later replaced the *cognomen*, the 'family name'. The *cognomen* Venox was later replaced by another *cognomen*, Hypsaeus, or Ypsaeus. Hypseus was the mytological king of the Lapiths. His daughter, Themisto, married Neptune, the Greek god of the sea, who presided over earthquakes and to whom horses were sacred. That couple generated a son, Leucon. The Lapiths were an Aeolian tribe, natives of Thessaly and linked to the Centaurs, legendary individuals who were half-man and half-horse. Perhaps the *cognomen* Venox changed to Hypsaeus to recall that the Hypsaei were involved with the origin of the Plautii, who claimed descent from Leucon. This happened with Caius Plautius Venox Hypsaeus, consul in 347 and 341. His descendants were no longer able to register their name in the *Fasti consulares*.[1] In 135 or 134,[2] however, one of them was a praetor, fuelling the prestige of his family.

A praetor was an elective magistrate of high rank, inferior only to the consul, and, like him, belonged to the restricted group of the magistrates with *imperium*, the right to oblige Roman citizens to perform their orders, if necessary by using force, as well as the power to conduct armies in war. These magistrates, when they appeared in public, were preceded or surrounded by six bodyguards, called lictors. The lictors carried the *fasces lictorii*, a bundle of thirty rods, from which (only when the praetor was outside Rome) the blade of an axe protrudes. In the beginning, there were two praetors, increasing to four in 227 and then six in 197 in consideration of the need to organize the new *provinciae* of Hispania Citerior and Hispania Ulterior. Two remained in Rome, while the others were assigned to the government of a province, to where they had to travel. At that time there were eight provinces: Hispania Citerior, Hispania Ulterior, Gallia Narbonensis, Sardinia and Corsica, Sicily, Macedonia, Achaia and Africa. Every year, before the elections, four were chosen by the Senate. The remainder went to the consuls, who chose them in agreement with the Senate. If circumstances required it, one or more provinces were assigned to a consul, rather than magistrates of praetorian rank.

The *praetura* was a magistracy born to do many things, but mainly to administer justice. Each judge, at the beginning of his mandate, issued an edict to establish the modalities to which he intended to abide in the exercising of his duties; during the mandate, other edicts would also be issued. The magistrates' sentences created jurisprudence. The magistrates based in Rome who received the highest number of votes were the Urban Praetor and the Pilgrim Praetor. The first decided on disputes between Roman citizens; the second on quarrels between Roman and foreign citizens, and those between foreigners. When one of them was out of town, the other exercised the functions of both in Rome. Of the two, the most important was the Urban Praetor. He was the one who had been elected with the highest number of votes. When the consuls absented themselves from Rome, they held the imperium and subrogated them for the convocation and presidency of meetings of the Senate, reception of foreign ambassadors and maintenance of public order. Because of the great importance of his office, he could be absent from the City for no more than ten days at a time.

Praetor Lucius Plautius Hypsaeus had just been appointed as governor of Sicily when, thirty days after the rebellion in Henna,[3] he landed in Sicily.[4] He knew that his primary task was to repress the great revolt of slaves on the island. But he also knew very well how the Senate and consuls coped with revolts of slaves. In their eyes, if one was a slave, then it was right that they remain so. A revolt of slaves was a rebellion of a handful of men who did not accept their servile condition and the related labours and harassment. The recalcitrant slaves, whether gathered in bands or not, were not people in search of a life worth living, but the most vile brigands – in short, *latrones* – and as such were scum, the most despicable and corrupt of men. Dealing with such a rebellion was felt to be simply a question of recapturing the fugitives and returning them to their respective owners. To Rome, it was not an important problem, rather a nuisance. As there was no honour in carrying out such a task, there was no glory, and above all no booty, so it was not worth wasting good soldiers for what was essentially a police action to clean up the territory. The best troops – real soldiers, well trained, efficient and brave – were sent elsewhere, where there was an enemy commonly considered their equal, courageous and fearsome; for instance to Spain, where the Celtiberians,[5] a group of native tribes around the Ebro valley (central-northern Spain), had been facing the Romans for decades.[6]

Thus, when he landed in Sicily, Hypsaeus was accompanied only by a small following and his six lictors. He had failed to form a army before leaving Rome. Nobody wanted to engage in a warlike enterprise that seemed incapable of conferring glory or procuring appreciable spoils of war; in case of defeat, moreover, they would have suffered the humiliation of having been beaten by the most despised category of men.

To face the insurgents, Hypsaeus recruited in Sicily 8,000 volunteers, mercenaries and conscripts made available to him by the cities. These were local men, not Roman soldiers, many only lightly armed. Hypsaeus trained them hastily and, with this improvised force, he challenged the insurgents, who agreed to fight him in the open field. Hypsaeus suffered a heavy defeat, his troops being overwhelmed and killed or put to flight. The disaster was complete, Hypsaeus and his staff fleeing the battlefield with the enemy at their heels. The number of victims in this clash is unknown, but many would have fallen on the battlefield, been wounded or taken prisoner. The insurgents stripped the bodies of weapons and armour, and also plundered the Roman camp, taking food, clothing and weapons.

Camps built by the Romans on campaign were rectangular in plan, subdivided in four sectors by two roads crossing each other, and defended with a palisade erected over a low embankment, which had a narrow and shallow ditch in front of it, through which a bridge was thrown at the four entrances. They were guarded by sentries and, when the troops were absent, by a few *centuriae* (formations of 100–150 troops), which, in the event of an attack, gave the alarm and engaged the enemy to slow them down. Perhaps on this occasion Hypsaeus' camp was attacked when it was almost empty, was not adequately manned or the sentries were not alert. The attackers eliminated the sentries and fell on the *centuriae* without giving them time to deploy, quickly overcoming them.

King Antiochus' army takes control of the territory, the lines of communication and supply

Antiochus' army had achieved a striking victory. This caused many others to join the rebel slaves, so their numbers grew still further. According to one estimate – probably exaggerated – the army by now had 200,000 fighters.[7] Its equipment and weaponry had also changed. To begin, their weapons were disparate and improper, including knives and kitchen skewers, hatchets, slingshots and clubs. The slaves and low-born freemen walked barefoot and dressed in simple tunics, tied at the waist with a piece of rope or a belt. Now they were true infantrymen and cavalry, armed with swords, spears, bows and arrows, daggers, ballistas, shields, helmets and armour, taken from the captured towns and cities and from enemy soldiers either killed or captured. Much equipment was also abandoned by fleeing Roman soldiers. The army's logistics had also improved. While in the beginning the army's nourishment was obtained by stealing supplies from the enemy, or hunting wild animals and raiding crops and food, it now had properly organized services. What was missing, though, were siege machines (towers, rams, catapults), ships and medical services, although the latter was not even had by the Romans. The sick and wounded were therefore not treated, with the most serious ones left to die.

The military strategy of King Antiochus consisted of taking control of territory and lines of communication and supply, especially from east to west, not in withdrawing into defensible sites as slave fugitives, nor simply plundering the province for short-term survival. The insurgents could not cut off access to Sicily from Italy across the sea, but they did control a large part of the island: they held the central area, the southern coast (at least Agrigentum and its surroundings) and the plain of Catania, which included some of Sicily's greatest grain-growing regions. They also controlled the main roads leading into the centre of eastern Sicily.[8] The territory that fell into their hands included three cities: Henna, Agrigentum and Morgantia. The first two of these were strongly fortified and controlled all overland communications through the centre of Sicily.[9] Henna, in particular, controlled movement across Sicily, as there were only two roads from the south coast to the north coast, and from the east to the west coasts, and they both passed either through or near the city. One was the road from Agrigentum to Thermae, the other that from Catana to Agrigentum. Agrigentum was located at the convergence of the roads from Panormus and Thermae and, together with Henna, controlled access to the west of the island. Morgantia and Centurĭpae also had strategic importance: the first lay on the 'grain road', which linked Campi Leontini to Thermae, one of the ports for shipments of grain bound for Rome; while the second controlled the plain of Catania. Later, another city fell in the hands of rebels – Centuripae.

Syracuse, Catana and Messana resist

Centurĭpae is about 730 metres above sea level, some 40km from Enna and about 30km from Catania. From that position it dominated the western slope of Etna, the Simeto valley and part of the plain of Catania. Its territory extended between the valleys of the Dittaino and Salso rivers and was predominantly mountainous. Many slaves worked there, mostly in the countryside. Between 135 and 132, they rebelled against their masters, took possession of the city and joined the army of King Antiochus. King Antiochus' army then moved towards the eastern coast, setting ablaze all that it touched. The insurgents incited the communities of citizens on the east coast – of which the most important were Syracusae, Catana, Tauromenium and Messana – to join them, and to show that they had a common cultural basis. These communities were of Greek language and descent, having originally been Greek colonies.

Undoubtedly the eastern origin of the fugitive slaves favoured the cohesion of their forces (both the rebels and the inhabitants of the cities spoke Greek), but that was not enough to establish an alliance. The urban elites admired the insurgents more than before their military victory over Hypsaeus, but to them they remained slaves and bandits. Neither among the free men, nor among the slaves themselves, was there anyone who questioned slavery as a social institution (Antiochus himself did not abolish slavery). Everyone in the eastern cities understood that slaves aspired to freedom and that those who had set themselves free had become brigands, but did not believe that slaves and bandits could form a state that claimed to be independent and sovereign, operating within another state, overthrowing the existing system, based on the exploitation of man over man, as had Antiochus and his followers. The cities of the eastern coast of Sicily had been the most wealthy and flourishing of the entire island in the past, and they continued to be successful under the Romans, while Henna, Centurĭpae and Morgantina, instead, had declined as settlements after the Roman conquest, essentially because they were inland. Therefore they were not sensitive to the propaganda of the insurgents that incited them to free themselves from the oppression of the foreign rulers in Rome; indeed Rome was by no means an enemy in their eyes. The horde that had devastated everything in its passage was regarded with suspicion by those to whom they offered friendship and alliance. The mainly educated and bilingual slaves of the Greek cities of the eastern coast felt they had little in common with those working on the large farms or the large estates. Moreover, they were better treated than those who were put to work in the rest of Sicily. Therefore, the cities refused to stand beside the insurgents, except perhaps Tauromenium.

The fall of Leontini and Tauromenium

However, the insurgents did not give up, trying to take by force what they failed to achieve through persuasion. They attacked Syracusae to cut off Rome from any major harbour on the east coast south of Messana, despite having no siege machines nor a navy. Fighting thus extended to south-eastern Sicily. They did not manage to conquer Syracusae, but took control of Leontini a little further north. Then they attacked Catana and Tauromenium, and while not managing to take the first, did take possession of the latter. Tauromenium was one of only two Sicilian *civitates liberae et foederatae*, the other being Messana, so, like Messana, had been treated very well by the Roman conquerors. It was surprising, then, that Tauromenium subdued spontaneously to the insurgents.

Large parts of Sicily were now in flames. Antiochus' army already controlled six major cities – Henna, Agrigentum, Leontini, Morgantia, Centurĭpae, and Tauromenium – and two of the three largest grain-growing regions, the central area and the plain of Catania. The cities and rural areas affected by fighting were plunge into terrible misfortunes. Many people suffered the worst afflictions. However, we have to distinguish between Antiochus' army and the bands of free proletarians. They were all volunteers, but their motivation and behaviour were far different.

King Antiochus' army did not fight for the looting, but to create and gradually expand a homeland for themeselves and their descendants. Their goal was to take possession of all of Sicily and drive away the Romans. In their case the spoils of war, with which the soldiers of any army are usually paid, in addition to the money, was the earth itself, the homeland they had chosen for themselves. Essentially, this was the reason why they repeatedly defeated the territorial militia.

Of course, there were also other reasons for their success. The territorial militia was inferior in number to their enemy and was not made up of professional soldiers who had chosen the profession of arms, nor of conscripted men enlisted to fight for the defence and greatness of their country. It thus did not have a strong motivation to fight. Its enemy was organized in a different way, applied different strategies and tactics, and was insidious, elusive and irreducible; they fought like furies, because they had nothing to lose and, if caught, could expect no mercy but would be condemned to death and crucified or thrown from a cliff. Antiochus' army also had the ability to choose the place to attack and could manifest themselves in places very distant from each other.

The armed bands of impoverished free men were not the avant-gardes of a social revolution. If they were so, they would be fierce against the rich, plundering their properties, prosecuting them and punishing them for having caused moral and material damage to the poor, in order to affirm the principle of social equality. At least they would steal from the rich and then distribute the spoils among the poor. None of this. Yet it is wrong to suggest that such bands were formed by free proletarians. It would be more appropriate to see them as gangs of criminals, murderers, adventurers and escaped convicts. This explains why the abuses committed by the insurgents were largely due to them.

They were autonomous from King Antiochus' army, so were not subject to the operational limitations to which the freed slaves held and did not distinguish between one objective and another. This made them feel free to roam the countryside and perform all sorts of robbery, arbitrary executions and acts of wickedness. They threw themselves on the villages and large estates, looted property and burned isolated villages and suburban villas. They commited serious crimes against people and property without favour, looting, assassinating, raping and setting everywhere ablaze. They shamelessly killed all those they came across, whether slaves or free, if they refused to join them, so as not to leave behind anyone to testify of their misdeeds.[10]

It is easy to suppose that these criminals and terrorists, which is all they were, tortured their victims in a horrible manner, hanging them or nailing them, naked and mutilated, to trees, burning them in houses to which they set fire, or by heading them, burning the bodies, dispersing the ashes and delivering their heads in a basket to their families, relatives and friends as a horrible warning. This is what, in the subsequent ages up to recent times, the Sicilian brigands and, more generally, the brigands of Southern Italy used to do to their victims.

PART III

THE ROMAN ARMY MOVES

Chapter 11

The Reasons of Rome

Why Rome cannot renounce Sicily

The Senate of Rome and the consuls received the news from Sicily with increasing alarm. No longer could they limit themselves to saying that a revolt of slaves was under way and judge it with the usual air of sufficiency. The facts were clear in their crudity. After the taking of Henna by a large group of insurgents, most of which were Syrians and former prisoners of war, they had established the Western Kingdom of the Syrians, which had a Hellenistic imprint, with its capital in Henna. The ruler of the kingdom was a former slave, the soothsayer Eunus, who had been elected by an assembly and had chosen for himself the royal name of Antiochus. He had an army of tens of thousands of men, far more numerous than the original group of insurgents, due to the fact that many other fugitive slaves and many free citizens had joined then. What had broken out in Sicily was not a mere revolt of slaves, but a war unleashed by the Western Syrians against Rome to take control of Sicily, yet still the Romans were not willing to call it that, but at most a slave war, emphasizing that – in their eyes – it was conducted against a handful of beggars, fugitive slaves and inferior beings. But what emerged – however you judge it, as a war or in any other way – was, by its scale, able to endanger Roman sovereignty in Sicily and considerably damage the export of grain from the island. The insurgents did not totally cut off the supply of grain provisioning Rome from Sicily, but caused a major reduction in the quantity exported, with the consequence that cereal was arriving at Rome in quantities inferior to what was required to satisfy the food needs of the population.

This was exceptionally serious for the Romans, because the failure or inadequate importation of wheat caused a famine, with inevitable consequences on public order. Indeed, the history of Rome had been marked by a succession of famines (due to natural causes, epidemics, wars, the incompetence of those responsible, corruption or speculative manoeuvres) and popular revolts, often violent.[1] The scarcity of wheat flour did not allow the production of enough bread to feed the population. The reduction in the quantity of wheat available on the market led to an upward trend in the price of cereals, which the massive sale of public grain at a subsidized price could not moderate. On the one hand, inflation favoured the greedy speculation of traders and black marketeers; on the other hand, it undermined and exasperated consumers, especially the less well-off. This caused bad feelings and anger towards political institutions, since Roman citizens believed that the regular provision of food was their sacred right and the first duty of government was to properly manage the food supply system. They accused the authorities of evading their responsibilities, of negligence or incapacity, of tolerating corruption and speculation, and of abuse and harassment of poor people, because they were involved personally. False information was disseminated, simulated operations performed or other artifices put in place to provoke a significant alteration of the price of wheat (known as rigging). In addition, the purchase and resale of large quantities of wheat was carried out in order to make a profit based on the difference between current and future prices (speculation). Protests often degenerated into violence, causing damage to property and injury. Attacks on the bakeries were increasingly frequent. Some families' mothers, by cunning or violence, striving to survive and feed their children, organized such acts spontaneously. They passed word around and went, equipped with escorts, to obtain what little bit of food they could. Babies were carried in their arms, and they used their older children to shield their actions. Sometimes the mothers were urged on by demagogues seeking to obtain the consensus of the masses, flattering their aspirations, especially economic, with promises that were difficult to achieve.

Those responsible for maintaining public order, the *aediles*, were unable to restore peace and ensure respect for laws and institutions, or to control social and political tensions. Ensuring public order meant dissolving the gatherings, preventing riots, repressing crimes against the state and public offices, prosecuting crimes against the person and property, identifying the perpetrators, arresting them, judging them and punishing them, all of which required the use of legalized force. However, there was no urban police body in Rome, and the army would only intervene if there was a very serious infringement. It was actually forbidden for the military to cross the *pomerium* (the religious boundary of every Roman city), under penalty of sanctions, except in strictly determined cases and under specific conditions. For public order the state could only count on three magistrates, who, escorted by public slaves, went at night into the most infamous areas of the city, with the power of arrest and even to deliver death sentences.

These magistrates were called the *tresviri capitales* or the *tresviri nocturni*. The solution to the problem of maintaining peace and security in the city was the removal of the cause of the discontent that caused the violation of public order laws. In short, the city's food supply system could not be allowed to fail to function perfectly, whatever the cost.

The need to return the flow of grain exports from Sicily to normal levels, to avoid repeating what had already happened in Rome in the past, when the city's food supply mechanism had broken, was one of the considerations that swirled in the minds of the Senate and the consuls made aware of events in Henna. The others were political, economic and strategic. Sicily was close to Rome, and Roman tradition did not allow that it negotiate with nearby and dangerous enemies. The island had become a Roman dominion at the cost of two wars – first against Syracuse and then against Carthage – which lasted without interruption for a quarter of a century and absorbed enormous resources. It was a vast territory, which guaranteed the treasury of Rome an important tax revenue. It also had great strategic importance for maritime trade, because its ports were crucial points for Mediterranean sea traffic, given the geographic centrality of the island. But alarm bell also sounded for the Senate and the consuls because of the risk of contagion from the slave revolt. When news of the revolt in Henna emerged from Sicily, there had also been movements by slaves in Italy and Greece. A conspiracy of 150 slaves had been discovered in Rome. Four hundred and fifty fugitive slaves had rebelled, been recaptured and crucified at Minturnum (Minturno), a city in Lower Lazio. A further 4,000 rebel slaves had been routed by Quintus Caecilius Metellus and Cnaeus Servilius Caepio at Sinuessa (Mondragone) in Campania.[2] Movements of thousands of slaves were also reported in the Attica region and the Aegean island of Delos.[3] A very serious situation had been created, which had to be tackled with decisiveness to avoid bread riots[4] by the Roman plebs adding to the social movements in Italy, Sicily and Greece.

The Senate and the consuls reflected on why the revolt had taken on such threatening proportions and concluded that this happened because its repression had been entrusted only to the praetors, who only had weak forces at their disposal. Leaving Sicily to its destiny was impractical for various reasons, each of which alone would motivate the need for action. The Senate and the consuls concluded that the only possible response that could be given to the insurgents was to slaughter them; the defeats and humiliation they had inflicted on the might of Rome for so long could not be allowed to go unpunished. The task of doing such work could not continue to burden the territorial militia: it must be entrusted to the Roman Army. The Army had lost some battles, even important ones, but had won all the wars, proving it was the best organized, trained, equipped and armed in the Mediterranean world, where no rivals could currently match it. However, the bulk of the legions were involved in the war in Spain, a very exhausting conflict where the enemy was valiant in battle, while the Roman commanders were often inept, as evidenced by recent defeats.[5] If it wanted to intervene militarily in Sicily, Rome had to raise a new army. There were difficulties in this, though, as insufficient conscripts and volunteers made it hard to form new legions.

The Roman Army

The Roman Army was both popular and temporary, reconstituting every time a war was declared through the enlistment of Roman citizens and being dissolved when hostilities ceased. Most of the soldiers were farmers or rural workers, since the Roman economy was essentially agricultural. When war broke out they left their work, home and family to go and fight, which had happened for longer and longer periods, in ever more distant theatres of war. If an experienced farmer was absent for many years, it would be difficult to find a suitable replacement to work the land efficiently. Thus, over time, the numerous recruitment drives began to endanger the economic strength of the entire country. This, together with the unsustainable concurrence of ever larger estates and larger quantities of slaves to work on them, had caused the collapse of small peasant properties. The combined effect of this was a sharp decrease in the flow of conscripts. Moreover, the duration of military service was endless (sixteen years in the infantry, ten years in the cavalry), it was hard and dangerous, military discipline was very strict and the chances of returning alive or uninjured from Spain were low, while those of returning with money were even slimmer. All this, as well as the horror stories told by veterans returning from Spain, frightened the sons of wealthy families and pushed them to avoid military service (the upper social classes had more opportunity to do so than the common people, and as they usually served in the cavalry, consequently that arm decreased even more). One of the effects of the Spanish War was thus the disaffection of Roman citizens with regard to compulsory military service. This phenomenon had grown rapidly after the failure of Marcus Fulvius Nobilior's offensive against Numantia in 153. The rising number of desertions, added to insufficient conscripts, therefore made it difficult to form new legions, and the Senate of Rome had to reduce by half the number of soldiers in Spain, from two legions in each province to one.

The chain of command

Rome's Republican army was formed of legions and relied especially on the infantry. The cavalry, not one of its strengths, was, besides combat, also used for reconnaissance, communication and escort duties. The legions included Roman citizens recruited by military conscription who were sent by the Senate for a single war. Their number was not fixed, but proportioned to the military need of the moment. Generally, there were two legions to each army, each composed of *manipula* (plural of *manipulum*, literally a 'handful' of soldiers), centuriae and *contubernia* (tents). Each maniple included two centuries, and each centuria consisted of ten tents. Each legion was under the orders of a *legatus legionis* (legate of the legion), who in turn commanded one *praefectus castrorum* (camp prefect), one *praefectus equitum* (cavalry prefect) and six *tribuni militum*. The *tribuni militum* (tribunes of the soldiers, military tribunes) controlled the centurions, each of whom led a centuria. The legates and all other officers were not professionals, and ultimately depended upon the centurions, all of whom were particularly capable veterans. Generally the legate was a relative, friend or political ally of the consul, chosen at his discretion. He was appointed to the Senate for a term of three or four years, sometimes longer. When a legion had its ongoing base in a province, the *legatus* served as governor of the province, regardless of whether there was only one legion there. Otherwise, all *legati* depended on the governor of the province, who, in turn, relied on the consul for military matters. The *praefectus castrorum* – a sort of vice-legate – as well as the commander of the first centurion, who was the most senior, both came from the ranks of the centurions. The military tribunes were partly elected by the people and partly the result of a highly personal appointment by the officer responsible for enlistments (the consul). Typically, equestrian families occupied the post, while older, distinguished senatorial families tended to ignore it.

Each legion was flanked by an *ala* made up of auxiliary troops, or *auxilia*, led by a Roman officer with the rank of prefect. The *auxilia* consisted of allies, conquered peoples and those from Roman and Latin colonies recruited from among provincial non-citizens: when discharged, they received Roman citizenship as a prize, to be handed down to their descendants.

The uniform of each legionary consisted of a tunic, cinched at the waist with a leather belt, and a cloak, usually fastened at the left shoulder with a metal brooch. His shoes, called *caligae*, resembled spiked boots that rose above the ankle, with leather straps tied around the calves. Footwear for everyone in ancient Rome consisted of sandals tied at the calf or ankle boots, of various types. Those of the legionary soldiers were particularly robust, with a heavy hobnailed sole and arch. *Caligae* were worn by all ranks up to and including centurions. The equipment was completed with a helmet, occasionally covered with leather or felt (a high domed pattern that protected the top of the head, but also had hinged cheek-pieces and a stubby nape-guard), a chain mail vest, reinforced leather armour, and a shield, rectangular and convex, made of wood and leather, with extra protection made of strips of metal. The officers and centurions wore a helmet with a feathered crest and full body armour, which, for senior officers, was made entirely of metal, with small bas-reliefs and friezes in silver or gold.

The consular army's battle formation and fighting technique. The irresistible impact of the legions

The consular army had a very regular battle formation and fighting technique. Each legion took a side of the battlefield in four parallel lines of 1,200 men each, except for the fourth row, which consisted of 600 men. The first line is made up of 1,200 *velites*, light-armed 'fast men'. The *velites* lacked any body armour, only being equipped with a helmet and a small shield, and armed with javelins and a sword. Behind the *velites* were the *hastati*, 'men with spears', organized in ten maniples of 120 men each. The *hastati* were armed with a large oval shield, helmet, greaves, breastplate, a long sword called a *gladius* (whose blade alone could measure 69cm), a dagger and two heavy javelins. Behind them were the *principes*, 'first men', armed in similar fashion to the *hastati*, again with ten maniples. The fourth row consisted of the *triarii*, the 'third men', with ten maniples of 60 men each. The *triarii* were armed like the *hastati* and *principes*, though they carried a thrusting spear instead of a javelin. The *velites* were the younger legionaries. The soldiers of the other lines were more mature, up to the *triarii*, the older veterans of proven value. The *hastati* were separated by gaps, but the *principles* were ready to close these spaces, while the *triarii* closed the gaps of the *principes*. Once the battle signal sounded, the legions advanced in tightly closed ranks, like a Macedonian phalanx. Just before impact with the enemy, they implemented a tactic different from that of the Greek hoplites, which was more mobile and characteristic of the Romans. The *velites* disengaged from the rest of the legion and fought scattered in the swarming, messy melee, sometimes accompanied by the cavalry. They projected forward, seeking head-to-head combat in order to prove their courage and valour, to satisfy their desire for personal glory and to stand out and earn decoration. In cases of necessity, they retreated into the spaces between the *manipula* behind them, passing on to the *hastati* the task of engaging the enemy; then they launched themselves forward again. In turn, the *hastati*, if pressed by the enemy, retreated between the maniples of the *principes*, who could move back through those of the *triarii*, which immediately closed the ranks. If the *triarii* were thus involved it meant the situation was critical, in which case the legion often took up a closed, compact, massive formation, which if successful, was able to advance.

The Roman Army was an extremely efficient and effective war machine. It was a compact array of infantry and cavalry squadrons, organized into legions and cavalry regiments, and reinforced by support troops on foot and on horseback. The soldiers were well-armed and equipped, having various types of weapons, for cutting and throwing, and, except the lightly armed infantrymen, wore full armour with their heads protected by a metallic cap-shaped helmet with feathers. They knew how to build bridges, fortified camps and fortification lines in a flash, assisted by service personnel. They were commanded by good centurions, and often also by good officers. They were endowed with a positive spirit, discipline and an unparalleled technical preparation. They trained continuously. Their combat tactics were based on the head-on collision between armies. In this the legions were very strong. War was their test bed, and, in war, Rome knew no half-measures. All who hinted at resisting its war machine were attacked with unstoppable violence. Any who insisted on opposing them were hit until annihilated. Roman soldiers sent to assault enemy cities were ordered to kill everyone, without exception, so after the taking of a city, there were corpses of men and animals and pieces of butchered bodies scattered in the streets and inside buildings. Prisoners were either executed or deported and then sold to slave traders, without distinguishing between the military and civilians, nor between men, women, the old and children. Cities that defied them were besieged, with assaults on the walls and missile attacks until they collapsed or the defenders surrendered. Once conquered, cities were looted, burned and systematically demolished, being razed to the ground. Only the most fortunate among the vanquished could be integrated in some way in the Roman State, provided they submit to its laws and conditions.[6]

Chapter 12

A Hole in Water

War breaks out

The consuls currently in office in 134 were Publius Cornelius Scipio Aemilianus and Caius Fulvius Flaccus.[1] Scipio Aemilianus, in agreement with the Senate of Rome and his colleague, commanded war operations against the Celtiberians, with the primary objective of breaking the resistance of their strongold, Numantia. He, since the Senate prevented him from carrying out a supplementary leverage of soldiers, recruited 5,000 volunteers from his clients to overcome the difficulty in recruiting sufficient resources for assembling legions.[2] Fulvius Flaccus would lead an army to Sicily to put an end to the 'slave war', restore order and security, and normalize grain exports. Unfortunately, he had to be content with what forces he found, with insufficient numbers and a low degree of discipline and training. He planned to add to his forces during the march south to Sicily, as was normal in urgent military interventions. In particular, he hoped to attract potential recruits with shining armour, helmets, insignia and weapons as his soldiers marched through the streets of cities and towns, with the air resounding to the sounds of horns, trumpets and drums, and the rattling of supply wagons, in the midst of a roar of applause, excitement and song.

Legions on the march

Flaccus reviewed his army, then gave the order to march. High-pitched trumpet blasts gave the signal, with drumming punctuating the rhythm. The ranks were arranged in columns of five and set off, parading between crowds that gathered to watch the show. Flaccus wore splendid armour and a helmet with a fiery red plume, which could be seen from a distance, and was surrounded by his personal guard – a squadron of cavalry – and officers of the general staff, also on horseback and dressed in flame-red uniforms. He proceeded on horseback, flanked by a praetor.[3] The group was preceded by the lictors of the consul, lined up in an orderly formation: twelve strong men, each of whom held a bundle of reeds tied with ribbons, symbolizing the power of command; outside the city, an axe would be inserted, signifying the power to put to death. There followed the legions, which advanced in columns of five, in blocks, with first the squadrons of cavalry. Then came the first century of the infantry, then the baggage (pack animals and carts drawn by oxen, with luggage and provisions), and finally the last centuries. The column left the city from Porta Capena, which opened in the Servian Walls in an area where the Celio, Palatine and Aventine hills met. At that point the Via Latina began, which after a short distance split into the Via Latina and Via Appia. At the junction, the army took the Via Appia, marching at a fast pace to Capua, and from there continued to the south, for the Via Popilia that passed through Nuceria Alphaterna (Nocera), Moranum (Morano Calabro), Consentia (Cosenza) and Hipponion (Vibo Valentia). The march south would last several weeks, with the setting up of an entrenched camp at each stop. A longer stop was made on the shore of the Strait of Messina, in a town located between Punta Pezzo and Cannitello, 18km before Rhegium (Reggio Calabria), as they waited to board ships for the short crossing to Sicily.

Crossing the Strait of Messina

The stretch of coast between Punta Pezzo and Porticello is the best point to cross the Strait, because here the distance between the two shores is reduced to just over 3km. You cannot say the same of Reggio Calabria, which is located on a stretch of the Calabrian coast where the Strait widens for those coming from the Tyrrhenian Sea towards the Ionian Sea. Punta Pezzo is a promontory called by the Greeks Cenide, from the river of the same name. It is located just across from Capo Peloro, the north-eastern extremity of Sicily. Cannitello was a rather large and populous town, able to accommodate the legions' passage and help ferry them to and from Sicily. Located between Punta Pezzo and Cannitello was a lighthouse, a source of drinking water, often used by sailors to resupply their ships, along with the Columna Rhegina and the Poseidonion. The Columna Rhegina was a tall tower with a large statue of the god Poseidon. It was located near the Poseidonion, a temple dedicated to Poseidon, the Greek god of the sea and earthquakes, called Neptune by the Romans. Poseidonion was at Porticello, a landing place for boats and sailors, sheltered from the storms, strong winds and currents of the Strait. The Greek colonists who founded Rhegion (the Greek name of Rhegium) included Porticello in the territory of the city and called it Abàlas, which meant 'without agitation', so was calm and quiet. Greek mythology located at Porticello the cavity of a rock, in which there was the sea monster Scylla.[4] Across from Porticello, on the Sicilian coast at Capo Peloro, the same mythology placed a similar cave, home to another sea monster, Charybdis. Scylla was described as a vastly tall beast, with a huge body and serpentine legs, and six dog heads, each of which had three rows of teeth. Charybdis was also huge: it was said to be almost half the size of Rome, or as big as the whole sea. It was said that it had a gigantic mouth full of concentric rows of teeth, like a lamprey, and that it sucked up and threw out the sea several times a day,[5] creating enormous vortexes which swallowed passing ships. It was said that Jason and the Argonauts, on their ship *Argo*, were sailing in these waters and escaped death only because they were guided by Thetis, a sea nymph and mother of Achilles. A similar adventure was had by Ulysses (Odysseus), king of Ithaca, a warrior in the Trojan War and architect of the wooden horse stratagem that took the city for the Greeks. It was said that he preferred to face Scylla, for fear of losing the ship passing near Charybdis (according to myths, ships passing through the Strait were forced to pass near one or the other cave), but that he lost his best rowers and almost ended up in the jaws of the monster. Legend had it that a blinding flash filled the air, the sails were shredded, the mast broke and fell, water began to pour in and the ship rolled over three times before being wrecked. The comrades of Ulysses were dragged into the waves and disappeared into the angry sea.[6]

Crossing the Strait here when the sea was totally quiet presented no difficulties, so long as the sea currents were taken into account, the effect of which is visible on the surface; and that the vortexes that formed along the opposite banks were avoided during the alternate flows and refluxes of the two seas, which generate low and high tides. The duration of the eddies is inversely proportional to the turbulence of the current that give rise to them. Seafarers must take care to avoid not only the small whirlpools, but above all the three main ones, on the outer edge of the San Raineri peninsula (which protects the harbour of Messina), at Punta Pezzo in Calabria and off the beach of Ganzirri on the Sicilian coast, between Messina and Capo Peloro. Abàlas/Porticello was the location of a ferry carrying people, animals and goods from Calabria to Sicily and back. There Flaccus commanded owners of boats, helmsmen, sailors, fishermen and port haulers to provide the necessary shipping to transport his army across the Strait. When everything was ready for the crossing, the consul gave the order of embarkation. The fleet that carried the army cleaved the waters of the Strait on a sunny day, the sea so calm that it was totally flat.

Roaring statements, but no result

When the army landed in Messana, the local Senate, the duumvirs and other authorities – decurions, quaestors and censors – crowded around the consul in the port and welcomed him with great pomp. For the Romans, Messana was a safe place to gather and coordinate the legions. Since Rome had liberated it from the Mamertines (at the beginning of the First Punic War), it had been the most faithful and supportive of its Sicilian cities, a precious ally without which Rome could hardly have kept Sicily in its power. The behaviour of the city was rewarded by the Senate of Rome with the status of *civitas libera et foederata*, 'free city and allied'. Messana has not joined in the whirlwind of the First Sicilian Slave War for two good reasons: it was defended by large military forces, and it and the surrounding territory contained few slaves. Most slaves working here in the countryside were owned by small businessmen, with others employed in maritime trade and services. They were usually treated humanely, giving them no reason to want to escape and join the insurgents.

Flaccus moved along the coast on the Ionian side of the Peloritani Mountains, with the sea on his left and hills, carved by rivers and streams, on his right. He crossed the torrent of Giampilieri, reached the head of Capo Scaletta, passed the Capo d'Alì and then crossed Fiumedinisi, Pagliara, Savoca and Agrò, resisting the temptation to climb the bed of the River Fiumedinisi, deeply cut and rich in argentiferous galena,[7] and then to ascend from the plain of Margi to Mount Scuderi (1,253 metres), in whose bowels, according to a legend, a large treasure was hidden. It was said that the treasure was guarded by a young princess, the victim of a spell, and consisted of piles of gold, silver and copper, baskets of precious stones, necklaces and bracelets, and also a hen with twenty-one golden chicks. Crossing the Agrò stream, he reached its head, a steep promontory of whitish rock, surrounded by small rocks, called by the Greeks *Argennon akron*, 'Cape Silver'. He crossed another torrent, the Letojanni, and reached a beach, from where he continued to Capo Sant' Andrea, at the base of which were sea caves. Capo Sant' Andrea opens into the bay of Isola Bella. A little further on is Capo Taormina, from which you can see Mount Etna and the coast below it. From there to Capo Schisò, and therefore to Naxos, is a short step. Flaccus avoided climbing to Tauromenium. Instead he continued to Catana. He then entered the interior, leaving Etna behind. He crossed the plain of Catania, with its wide spaces of cereals and pastures, dotted with farms. He crossed the Simeto river and passed along Lake Lentini. He passed through the sacred source of the '*fratres Palici*', to whom a sanctuary was dedicated, and to the site of the ancient city of Menai, founded in the fifth century by Ducetius, king of the Sicels, with its remains of megalithic walls and tombs. Flaccus also passed through Leontini, or rather what remained of it after the devastation of war, as well as the city of Hydra, a Greek colony. Finally he reached the foot of the mountain on top of which was the city of Henna.

Flaccus arrived in central Sicily in the first warm days of 133, when in Rome the echo of his roaring statements about the punishment he would inflict on the insurgents had not yet been extinguished: 'I will be so strict with them – he said before leaving – that anyone else who wants to follow their example, will have to think about it more than once.' Only when he arrived at the foot of the mountain of Henna, which rises on the undulating plain like a natural fortress, did he realize its height and strength. In addition, the city at its summit was powerfully fortified and seemed impregnable. He was reminded that it was only by treason that the tyrant of Syracuse, Dionysius I the Great, had been able to seize the city after a siege from 404–01. The Romans themselves had labelled Henna as '*urbs inexpugnabilis*' ('impregnable city'), from the experience in 212 of the consul Marcus Claudius Marcellus. Flaccus convinced himself that the enterprise to conquer Henna was daunting, even impossible. He attempted to take the city, but no matter what efforts he made, they yielded no result, so he returned to Rome without achieving anything.[8] His successor in the consular office was Lucius Calpurnius Piso Frugi, a son of Caius, consul in 180, who died after being poisoned.

Chapter 13

Chasing the Final Victory

A new army lands in Sicily

Poisonings were frequent in the Roman world, especially in upper-class families.[1] Many matrons were involved in scandals in which one or more lovers appeared. Poison was a means used to get rid of an unwanted spouse: Marcus Porcius Cato, the Censor, had drawn inspiration to say 'every adulteress is also a poisoner'.[2] For this reason, fear of being a victim of poisoning was extraordinarily widespread among Romans, and anyone who felt sick after eating could think that they had been poisoned and accuse someone of their family, household or neighbourhood. However, accusations that someone had been poisoned were difficult to prove because of insufficient medical knowledge. It is possible that Caius Calpurnius Piso Frugi, consul in 180 and father of Lucius Calpurnius Piso Frugi, died because he had poisoned by his wife, Quarta Ostilia.[3]

He was the first member of his family to cross the milestone of the consulate. His family was plebeian. His fortune began to improve around 210, when a Lucius Calpurnius Piso Frugi, a magistrate, was appointed as a *magister equitum* by the dictator Quintus Fulvius Flaccus in Capua.[4] Previously none of his parents or relatives had been elevated to a position of such high responsibility. Between 180 and 133, three other Pisones became consul: Lucius, nicknamed *cesoninus* (148), Cnaeus (139) and Quintus (135).

It is interesting to note that both the consuls of 180 and 148 had as a colleague a Postumius; respectively, Aulus Postumius Albinus and Spurius Postumius Albinus Magnus. It should also be noted that a Calpurnius Piso Cesoninus was a magistrate in 154, the year of the consuls Lucius Postumius Albinus and Quintus Opimius. It is evident that there was a link between the Calpurnii Pisones – enriched plebeians – and the Postumii, patricians; and that this bond replaced the friendship that linked the Calpurnii Pisones to the Claudii Fulvii Flacci before 180.[5]

Lucius Calpurnius Piso Frugi, son of the consul of 180, was born a little before or just after the tragic death of his father. He too became consul, in 133. His collegue was Publius Mucius Scaevola, a famous jurist and legal consultant. He was an ultraconservative, so was openly and tenaciously opposed to the Greek contamination of Latin culture, and nostalgic for the good old days. His ideas in this regard was reflected in *Annales*, a work in seven books which he wrote. *Annales* told the history of Rome from its origins to current times, with an emphasis on the honesty of the Romans of the past, compared with the corruption of the present, allegedly imported from Greece. It was therefore a historical work, but also, in a certain sense, moralistic.[6] The works of Quintus Fabius Pictor and other Roman historians aimed to counter the partisan interpretations given to the Punic Wars by the Carthaginian historians. In particular, it is located next to the works of Lucius Cassius Hemina[7] and Cnaeus Gellius,[8] which reflected a strong moral tension in relation to the ongoing evolutionary processes concerning Roman customs and culture. Pictor, Hemina, Gellius and Piso Frugi no longer felt the need to resort to Greek as a language of communication. They wrote in Latin: this reveals the greater diffusion in the second century of the language of Rome, and demonstrates the intention to speak with citizens about current issues and to reread the past of Rome for internal purposes. Piso Frugi was nicknamed *censorinus*, 'little censor'. This was given to him when, in 149, he was a tribune of the plebeians and supported the fight against corruption. At that time he promoted and led the approval of a bill containing rules in defence of Roman citzens who complained of having been victims of abuses committed by provincial magistrates in the exercise of their functions. The intervention contrasted with the spread of a worrying phenomenon: provincial magistrates often took advantage of favourable circumstances to recover the expenses they had incurred for their election.

When we speak of favourable conditions we refer to the position of supremacy of the magistrates themselves, a source of almost absolute power, as well as the exercising of the charge far away from Rome and the absence of checks. These magistrates, abusing their powers, sometimes commited illicit acts which turned to their advantage: forcing or violently threatening someone to do or not do something in order to derive an unjust profit (extortion); claiming or accepting the undue payment to oneself or to a third party of a utility, even of a non–pecuniary nature, to perform acts (corruption); making illegal use of public funds or assets administered on behalf of others; or dividing the loot accumulated in fraudulent way or taking possession of unspent cash funds (embezzlement). Before 149, those who demanded justice for damages suffered by one or more of such acts had to bring a civil action against the latter and be represented in court by Roman citizens chosen by senators; the decision of the dispute was up to the praetor peregrinus (a magistrate who judged disputes between foreigners and Roman citizens, and offences committed by foreigners). The abuses of the magistrates were therefore considered by law as a private dispute, censurable as such by the application of a civil law institute. The situation had improved somewhat in 171, when, in order to protect Roman citizens living in the Hispanic provinces of Rome from the abuses committed by five magistrates, a commission was set up to judge the defendants and they were forced to return the stolen goods. In 149, the tribune of the plebeians, Lucius Calpurnius Piso Frugi, promoted – and succeeded in having approved, despite the opposition of the nobility – the *lex Calpurnia de pecuniis repetundis*.

The intervention, in the wake of that of 171, established that judicial proceedings of an accusatory nature, activated against provincial magistrates accused of having committed abuses in the exercise of their functions to the detriment of Roman citizens, were to be exclusively heard by a specially established permanent court, the *quaestio perpetua de repetundis*. The judicial body of this tribunal was not the praetor peregrinus who presided over it, but a jury of thirty-two members, all of senatorial extraction, all drawn from a public list, renewed annually. It deliberated by a majority and the verdict was binding on the magistrate, who was responsible for issuing the sentence.[9] Furthermore, the *lex Calpurnia de pecuniis repetundis* had amended the penalty connected with the sentence, in the sense of replacing the return of stolen goods, with the imposition of payment as compensation for an amount equal to the asset value of the unlawful enrichment achieved.

The Battle of Messana

In 134, King Antiochus' army spread through Sicily, with no force apparently able to stop it. The Senate of Rome had already sent one army after another to the island to repress it, without success, as forces under the praetor Lucius Hypsaeus, then fellow praetor Manlius, an army under the guidance of Lentulus and another led by the consul Flaccus were all defeated. The latest expedition sent by the Senate and the consuls was led by Lucius Calpurnius Piso Frugi Censorinus, who had already been in Sicily, in 136, as governor of the *provincia*. His campaign in 134 proved to be very difficult from the beginning. He could not recruit enough soldiers owing to the collapse of the peasants owning small properties, which were once the backbone of the army, and to increasing disaffection among Roman citizens with regard to compulsory military service. The listlessness and indiscipline of recruits also made them unsuitable for carrying out their duties. However, by resorting to drastic measures Censorinus succeeded in both forming an army and improving its discipline, and they set off for Sicily.

The column was formed of two full legions, which meant that was about a quarter of the entire Roman army at this time. It took the usual route, along the Via Appia to Capua and then continuing south until they reached the Calabrian shore of the Strait of Messina. The army stopped *at fretum ad statuam*, between Punta Pezzo and Cannitello, then crossed the Strait and landed in Sicily. Upon arrival of the army in the port of Messana, it was warmly welcomed. The festive atmosphere was increased by the consul bringing to the city's authorities a much-appreciated gift, a decree from the Roman Senate which exempted the city from the payment of any tax or levy imposed on the province, with the following, flattering justification:[10]

'While a great and frightful war subjugated Sicily with a multitude of fierce conspirators, with an array of forces (rebels), with power and vastness – and this first had disorientated the Roman praetors and then had put to flight also the consuls – Messana treated the slaves sagaciously and kept them in peace, returning them to the consul Quintus Calpurnius Piso. The city removed such a scourge from the inhabitants of Sicily, every torment from the Republic, and from itself an equal future risk, therefore it escaped from the vile condition of slavery for the sake of precious freedom.'

Censorinus was overwhelmed by Sicilian hospitality. But he had not taken his army to Sicily just to reward Messana; it was to make war against Eunus and his companions, whom he considered had defied the authority of Rome for too long.

His first clash with them took place at Kurkourakis (Curcuraci), near Messana, where a clash had taken place in 264 as part of the Battle of Messana during the First Punic War. Now, in 133, the legionnaires overwhelmed the ranks of the army of King Antiochus at Kurkourakis, whose survivors retreated and left 8,000 fallen on the field. Censorinus' great victory at

Curcuraci avenged the earlier defeats inflicted by Eunus on the Romans. Those taken prisoner were hung by Censorinus,[11] who then rewarded his son for valour shown in battle[12] before descending on the east coast of Sicily.

The unsuccessful siege of Tauromenium

Arriving at Naxos, Censorinus and his army climbed the muletrack to Tauromenium and besieged the city. It was defended by a large contingent, commanded by Komanus, Kleon's brother. The defenders felt safe because Tauromenium was reputed to be an impregnable stronghold. Roman efforts to take the city were indeed in vain, and admitting defeat, Censorinus lifted the siege and first headed south-east, then moved west up the gorge cut by the river Alcantara in the lava around Etna.

The reconquest of Morgantia and a new attempt to take Henna

Censorinus next reconquered Morgantia, which fell after a siege,[13] and crucified the rebel garrison, said to be 8,000 men, then struck at Henna. He concentrated his troops at the foot of the hill, in the wide flat area under the Rocca di Cerere – a place known by the locals as Cozzumpisu or Cozzo di Piso – and from there launched repeated attacks against the city, using heavy slingshots.[14] However, he failed to take Henna, and one of his cavalry units, commanded by the prefect Caius Titius, surrendered to the enemy when surrounded, losing many men, horses and weapons. Furious at such a loss, Censorinus punished Titius for surrendering.[15] The punishment consisted of an extraordinary humiliation, more psychological than physical. Titius was forced to wear a toga 'cut into tatters', to forgo bathing and to stand on guard barefoot outside Piso's headquarters for all the time that Piso himself was still on the island. His men were turned into a unit of slingers, the lowest level of the Roman Army. When, at the end of 133, Censorinus returned to Rome, he admitted before the Senate that his repressive action against the Sicilian *latrones* did not achieve the desired result. He reported some successes in the clashes, but had not achieved a final victory.

The assassination of T. Sempronius Gracchus

While Piso was fighting in Sicily, the tribune of the plebeians, Tiberius Sempronius Gracchus, maintained his promise to promote an agrarian reform.

His project aimed to revitalize peasants with small properties, defusing the 'social bomb' represented by the concentration of a large mass of poor people in the city and increasing the flow of conscripts to meet the needs of the army. Because this was harmful to the interests of the great landowners, which included many senators, it was opposed by the Senate. Publius Cornelius Scipio Aemilianus, the destroyer of Carthage and Numantia, cousin and brother-in-law of Gracchus, led the opposition. A cousin of Scipio Aemilianus, Publius Cornelius Scipio Nasica Serapio, who was the *pontifex maximus* (chief high priest) and a great landowner, led an excitable crowd of senators, clients, freedmen and slaves in an outpouring of violence in which 300 Roman citizens were killed, including Gracchus. The bodies of the victims were left unburied. The Senate tried to deal with the problem of how to legitimize the aggression perpetrated against Gracchus. Using strong judgements of the authoritative jurist, legal expert and law teacher Publius Mucius Scaevola, it attacked the character of Gracchus in order to criminalize him and eradicate his memory. It tried to solve the problem by inventing a scenario whereby the state had to react with force to an attempt by Gracchus and his supporters (the Graccani) to violently overthrow the political institutions and re-establish the monarchy. The Senate claimed that Gracchus had plotted and practised violence first, which they reacted to, and thus he became, through his great ambition and desire to be made king, the cause of his own death and that of so many of his supporters. However, this accusation was false. Gracchus never thought to make himself king, and the Graccani had not started any violence before being attacked by the frenzied crowd headed by Nasica Serapio. It was falsely said that the night before they had held a secret meeting to negotiate a putsch of the following day. They were actually unarmed, and only when attacked did they arm themselves with any objects they could find to defend themselves.[16] By decree of the Senate, a special commission of inquiry with judicial powers was established to judge the followers of the deceased tribune, who were charged with complicity in their leader's attempt to carry out a coup. Members of the committee were appointed by the consuls in office – Publius Popilius Laenas and Publius Rupilius – as well as Caius Lelius, the Sapiens, a close friend of Scipio Aemilianus. The judges sentenced hundreds of defendants to death at the same time that news arrived in Rome of the latest events in Spain and the Sicilian Slave War.

Chapter 14

The Turning Point

Determined to win

The Roman Army was not the terror of its enemies because it was invincible, as it wasn't: it could lose a battle (even more than one), but it won all the wars. This happened because, after every defeat, however terrible this may have been, the legions were reorganized and sooner or later returned to the attack, striking the enemy like a hammer, over and over again, until they broke their resistance and were victorious. This was eventually the case in the wars in Spain, where the Romans sent against their enemies – the Celtiberians and Lusitanians – one army after another, using all the means at their disposal, including deception and corruption. The Celtiberians resisted until 134, when the Senate sent against them yet another army, under the command of Publius Cornelius Scipio Aemilianus, who had sworn to end the many failures of his predecessors, from Quintus Cecilius Metellus onwards. When Scipio Aemilianus reached Numantia, the defenders came out of the city ready for battle. But Scipio refused to fight. He had in mind a different strategy, which required patience, holding the city in a stranglehold, suffocating it little by little. He asked for and received reinforcements from his Hispanic allies, and ended up with 60,000 men, including legionaries, volunteers and auxiliaries. He distributed his troops in various entrenched camps, building seven forts around the city and joining them with a moat and fence. He also built two forts on opposite banks of the Douro and obstructed navigation so that Numantia could not be supplied by the river. He then dug a second moat and erected a wall, or embankment, reinforced by towers every 30 metres, and established a communications system for the immediate signalling of enemy attacks, so that he or his brother, Quintus Fabius Maximus Aemilianus, could promptly intervene to rescue the threatened sectors.

The fortified walls of Numantia were 4km long, but the wall that surrounded the city was more than twice as long. Scipio distributed 30,000 men along the encircling walls, and 20,000 in a position to the rear, with another 10,000 as a mobile reserve. The Numantians performed various sorties, attacking the walls at different points, but were repulsed each time. They then asked to negotiate a peace, but Scipio Aemilianus refused; with ruthless resolve, he demanded that the city surrender unconditionally. The siege continued for another fifteen months. The Numantians, exhausted through hunger and disease, were reduced to eating human flesh. When they were no longer able to resist, many laid down their arms and filed out of the city, emaciated and crying. Others preferred to die rather than choose an inglorious freedom, either through poison, stabbing themselves or leaping to their death from their homes.

The entry into the city took place in an atmosphere of unreal calm. The signs of the long siege were visible everywhere, with destruction and devastation. Numerous bodies, abandoned to wild animals, lay scattered about. Only a few survived. Scipio Aemilianus razed Numantia to the ground in imitation of what he himself and Lucius Mummius Achaicus had done at Corinth in 146, to create a constant warning to the vanquished not to challenge the wrath of Rome again. All the prisoners were sold to slave traders, save fifty whom Scipio Aemilianus saved for himself.

Back in Rome, Scipio Aemilianus celebrated a triumph for the second time (his first was for having conquered Carthage). Following the celebrations for the victory, the heroes of the war were rewarded. One was Jugurtha, whom Scipio Aemilianus identified as a future king of Numidia. He adopted Jugurtha, giving him equal rights to those of his natural and legitimate children.

Meanwhile, the Senate was not discouraged by news of the setback encountered by the other consul, Caius Fulvius Flaccus, against the slaves in Sicily. In 133 it sent to Sicily the praetor Marcus Perperna, who remained on the island in 132 as a propraetor. Perperna eventually managed to secure an important success, defeating part of the army of King Antiochus near Henna after besieging it in its camp.[1] The besieged forces surrendered after being starved and hit by the plague. The prisoners were all crucified, and Perperna returned to Rome victorious, celebrating an *ovatio*[2] for his success against the slaves. Perperna's success was partial not definitive. Henna had not been taken and Eunus was steadfast in the command; the bulk of his army was intact and clung to him. The insulting capacity of the rebels had been affected only a little. In confirmation of this, shortly after the celebration of Perperna's triumph, the news arrived in Rome that King Antiochus' army had attacked Messana and seized part of the city. While the population had fled to the safety of the city walls, they lost control of the fortress that protected the harbour; the attackers took possession of the structure and barricaded it, and at night pulled a chain across the mouth of the harbour to block access. Messana, Rome's main ally and stronghold in Sicily, was thus in real jeopardy.

P. Rupilius

By the autumn of 132, the Western Kingdom of the Syrians held the cities of Henna, Agrigentum, Morgantia, Centuripae, Leontini and Tauromenium, and controlled much of Sicily, from the southern coast through the central area to the east coast. It had routed all the Roman armies sent against it and cut off the hands and arms of those it took prisoner.[3] Now it had also taken possession of the port of Messana, Rome's faithful ally. The reaction of the Roman Senate to this latest news was vigorous and immediate. They urged the consuls to wipe out the 'Syrian *latrones*' and their supporters once and for all and to reconquer Sicily, starting with Messana. Taking the initiative would be the consul Publius Rupilius, in agreement with his consular colleague, Publius Popilius Laenas. Rupilius was a former tax-clerk, and thus an *eques*, while Laenas belonged to a senatorial family of enriched plebeians, well known in Rome for their cruelty and arrogance. Rupilius and Laenas were two of the three members of the commission of inquiry with judicial powers which had recently sent hundreds of followers of Tiberius Sempronius Gracchus to their death, the third member being the chairman of the commission, Caius Lelius the Sapiens. The successful completion of the commission's work accelerated Rupilius' career. His election to the consulate – as well as that of Laenas – can be seen as a reward from the senatorial oligarchy for the excellent work done on that occasion. The special command that was conferred on him allowed him to close the circle on the slave revolt and procured him great glory. Rupilius demonstrated once more his skill, enlisting the necessary troops and urgently mobilizing another Roman army to march south again.

The reconquest of Messana

At the news of the arrival of Rupilius' legions on the Calabrian shore of the Strait of Messina, King Antiochus' army deployed along the coast north of Messana. The Romans had this time come by sea, as the *via Popilia* was not yet completed. Publius Popilius Laenas was in the process of building it[4] to facilitate the movement of the legions from Capua to Rhegium (Roma and Capua being linked by the *via Appia* and *via Latina*).[5] When finished, this road would be the most important in southern Italy. The Romans crossed the Strait, but did not disembark at Messana. Their ships concentrated in Paradise Bay, a large natural inlet, protected from winds and waves, where ships could lay at anchor safely. Paradise Bay is north of Messina, above the Torrente Annunziata, along the coastal arc between Messana and Capo Peloro (the latter is 10.5km from the city). It is the first of three suburbs along the coast which bore names suggestive of their beauty: Paradiso, Contemplazione, Pace (Paradise, Contemplation, Peace). The Roman ships moved in groups from Paradise Bay, attacking the harbour of Messana in waves. The attacks continued for days, from dawn to dusk, without rest, putting a great strain on the defenders' resistance. Rupilius observed the battle from his ship, recognizable by its red sail, moored in Paradise Bay, rotating slowly, pushed by the rowers so as not to let it be cast adrift, pushed by the current, sometimes putting the bow towards the centre of the Strait. The battle to regain control of all of Messana turned into a bloody massacre. It ended with the storming of the port fortress and the landing of Roman troops in the harbour of Messana, with a final butcher's bill of 8,000 dead. Rupilius emerged victorious when his legions completed their occupation of the city. His ship then approached the quay and he sealed Rome's revenge with a new orgy of blood-letting, a mass martyrdom. Among the prisoners taken, those who were fugitive slaves, and there were thousands, were crucified along the entire coastline between Messana and Capo Peloro. The whole coast of white sandy beaches was dotted with crosses in a horrendous show of Roman power.[6]

Chapter 15

A Bloodbath

The slaughter of Tauromenium

Rupilius continued his campaign, moving down the Sicilian coast, along the Ionian side of the Peloritani, to Naxos, and from there climbed to Tauromenium, which was defended by walls and a garrison commanded by Komanus, the brother of Kleon. As the city refused to yield, Rupilius besieged it. The consul used hunger to reduce the defenders and the population to despair with a sharp and close siege. The besieged, running desperately short of food, sent ambassadors to Rupilius asking him on what conditions he was willing to grant peace. The only answer of the consul was a demand for unconditional surrender. The besieged, however, preferred to die rather than surrender; at least they would die as free men, and would not suffer the indecorous death that the Romans commonly reserved for fugitive slaves guilty of blood crimes (crucifixion, precipitation from a cliff). As the situation worsened there were outbreaks of cannibalism: '[The besieged] – it is reported – begin by eating their children, then they pass to the bodies of their women, eventually they eat each other.' An act of betrayal by a fugitive slave named Sarapion, which suggests a Graeco-Egyptian origin (however, it was reported that he was a Syrian),[1] allowed the Romans to circumvent the defences.

Rupilius, before the final attack, exhorted the legionaries to prepare, then ordered them to assault the walls, protecting themselves with their shields, while the archers and slingers fired at the enemy from a distance. When the Romans broke into the city, Komanus, realizing all was lost, committed suicide after a fruitless attempt to break out of the encirclement. Covering his face with a flap of his cloak, he passed a chain around his neck and squeezed it to strangle himself with his own hands. Others also took their lives to avoid capture. The survivors, emaciated and filthy, marched out of the city and laid down their weapons. Once again, Rupilius' vengeance was tremendous. The prisoners were first tortured and then pushed from the edge of the high rock walls in the middle of which the city was built.[2]

The Battle of Henna

Rupilius, after having bloodily conquered the bastion of Tauromenium, advanced towards Catana, but diverted inland before reaching the city and moved on Henna, the sole surviving stronghold of King Antiochus, with a garrison commanded by Kleon. Antiochus and his bodyguard were also present. Rupilius embarked on a bitter, long and bloody siege of Henna. The besieged were afflicted by plague and reduced to starvation, but fought on. An act of treason once again caused the stronghold to fall. There was no final assault on the walls, one of the besieged (the name of the betrayer is unknown) either opening the gates to the Romans or revealing a way into the city. The Romans burst in, taking the defenders by surprise. Kleon died in the fighting; his body, covered in wounds, displayed before the city walls. His soldiers fought to the bitter end, with almost every man killed (many by a companion to avoid being taken prisoner) or captured and put in chains.[3]

The capture and death of King Antiochus

King Antiochus fled with a bodyguard of 1,000 men 'in unmanly fashion' into the mountains. However, those who remained with him, with Rupilius hastening towards them and realizing that every escape route was blocked, refused to fight and die for Antiochus, accusing him of cowardice. They preferred death, each being beheaded by a companion until the last committed suicide, throwing himself on his own sword.

Such dramatic acts were not unique. Previous fighters had abandoned their Hellenistic leaders because of their perceived flaws, and faced with a choice of dying fighting for them and death by their own hands, had chosen the latter. An example of a cowardly king, with whom others would not serve, was King Perseus of Macedonia. Seeing the tide of battle turn during the Battle of Pydna in 168, he fled with the cavalry, abandoning his army, which was routed by the Romans. It is uncertain if this happened at the start of the battle,[4] or through injury late in the battle.[5] According to some historians, Perseus' cavalry had yet to engage, and both the king and his horsemen were accused of cowardice by the surviving infantry. Other historians claim that the king was injured by enemy missiles and was taken to the city of Pydna at the start of the battle.

King Antiochus was captured by the Romans in a remote cave, where it was said he fled for refuge with four attendants: a cook, a baker, a masseuse and a drinking-party entertainer (a man who had been accustomed, throughout their drinking bouts, to beguiling him). Thus, apparently, at the moment of his arrest, Antiochus was in the company of a group of degenerates who symbolized the life of luxury he had chosen to lead. The behaviour of King Antiochus in the final hours of his reign was the polar opposite of what the Greeks expected from a king. Rather than fighting at the head of his men, he fled, abandoning them to their fate and passing his last hours in the company of those with whom he indulged in luxury and gluttony.[6] It is unclear whether events actually unfolded in such a way or whether such stories were motivated by prejudice against a slave who had become king. It must also be considered that Eunus was no longer young at the time of his fall, and probably unable to take part in combat. With hindsight, it is possible to see that he could have felt he had no choice but to flee the battle.

After the fall of Henna, 20,000 prisoners were put to death. The former king of the Western Syrians was placed in chains and moved to Morgantia, which since its reconquest by Piso had been used as a military base. He was held in custody, waiting for Rupilius to decide his fate, but died in prison shortly thereafter from a disease in which his flesh was said to be eaten by lice (maybe scabies).[7]

The scene recalls a similar episode, of which the protagonist was another Antiochus. Antiochus IV Epiphanes (215–164), king of the Seleucid Empire from 175 until his death, was described as dying in a similar fashion, albeit infested with worms. So perhaps the account of the later Antiochus' death was a biased historical reconstruction to discredit the demise of a man hated by Romans.

Rupilius moved throughout Sicily to clear the island of rebels more quickly than any could have expected. So ended the first act of the Sicilian Secession War. As we will see, this tragedy was to have a second and final act.

Lex Rupilia

Rupilius remained in Sicily until 130 as proconsul and provincial governor to consolidate his victory. Ten legates, appointed by the Senate of Rome, assisted him in the task of reviewing the judicial order of the province, with particular reference to dealing with disputes between Sicilians of the same city, Sicilians of different cities, and Sicilians and Romans, including the appointment of jurors: this was known as the *lex Rupilia*.[8] The Sicilian cities that had been compromised in the revolt of Eunus were, after the reorganization by Publius Rupilius, reinstated to their legal status under pressure from pro-Roman factions. Other centres of the island obtained autonomy, including Netum (Noto), which was detached from Acrae (Palazzolo Acreide).

Once the urban connective tissue was re-established, Sicily recorded an increase in the immigration of Latins and Italics; for example Publius Clornius, a rich *eques*, owner of an estate with eighty slaves.

Meanwhile, it was prohibited to arm slaves, an attempt to prevent further mass rebellions. Yet this did not put an end to banditry being practised by slaves. This was proved by the fact that, around 131, a Gorgus of Morgantia, surnamed Cambalus, a rich man and a local official, was caught outside the city by a band of robbers and killed when attempting to flee.[9]

PART IV

THE REVOLT OF SALVIUS

Chapter 16

Twenty-Eight Years Later

Facing the Germanic threat

The Senate and the consuls began preparations for a new war in 107. This time Rome was not fighting in the East, but in the West, to protect its own territory. This area became a Roman *provincia* in 124 after the success of consul Fulvius Flaccus against the Transalpine Ligurians and Celts and the Allobroges. It had been called Narbonensis after its major centre, Narbo Martius (Narbona). The area was threatened by a multitude of Germanic, Celtic and Helvetic migrants/invaders, 800,000 men, women and children, of which at least 300,000 were armed and able to fight. The imposing mass had grown from a nucleus of 600,000, formed by the Germanic Cimbrians and Teutones and the Celto-Germanic Ambrones.

They migrated in 120 from the western coast of Denmark and adjacent North Sea regions because of a series of natural disasters, which had made these lands uninhabitable, searching for a better new home. They filled waggons with their goods, burnt their houses and started a long march, on horseback or foot, or on carts drawn by oxen, bringing with them their flocks and herds. They initially wandered in central and central-eastern Europe, being rejected first by the Celtic Boii, then by the Celtic Scordisci. Later they looted Noricum (modern southern Austria and western Slovenia) and – in 113 – clashed with a Roman army commanded by the consul Caius Papirius Carbo. Carbo was acting under orders from the Senate of Rome, at the request of the Norics, who, in 115, had become friends and allies of the Romans. He gave battle at Noreia (likely near Klagenfurt, Austria), but was forced to retreat, leaving many fallen on the field. The Romans feared that the barbarians would cross the Carnic Alps and invade northern Italy. In that case, the first to suffer would have been the populous and prosperous city of Aquileia in Lower Friuli. Instead, the multitude circumvented the Alps to the north, crossed the Swiss plateau from east to west and entered France around Lake Geneva. It was then that they were joined by some 200,000 people of the Swiss tribe of the Tigurins. Descending the Rhone

Valley, their progress was difficult, sinking in snow half a metre deep. With the exception of a few individuals who wore furs, they were only lightly clothed, despite the bitter cold. Most had only a tunic tightened at the waist by a wide belt, muddy boots and maybe a cloak. In the mass, the druids and warriors stood out. The druids were the priests of the traditional Celtic religion, wearing white robes and having flowing beards. The latter were big men with long blond hair, blue eyes and strong muscles. They were armed with bows and arrows, short spears, swords, knives and battle axes. Some rode small horses bareback, clanging from their weapons, helmet and shield. In 107, the migrants/invaders penetrated the Roman territory of Gallia Narbonensis and demanded permission to settle. In response, the Senate of Rome sent to Gallia Narbonensis an army commanded by the consul Marcus Junius Silanus to reject them.

The loss of three Roman armies

Silanus crossed northern Italy from east to west, then the western Alps, and, after a month's journey, reached the middle of the Rhone Valley. He proceeded with caution in the wooded landscape dotted with meadows, swamps and ponds to discourage the enemy from attacking. Scouts reported that the Germani were nearby, concentrating in an open area, with the evident intention of fighting. Silanus halted his army and chose a place for a camp to be set up. The barbarians then attacked the Romans and their allies when they were in an unfavourable position and could not fully exploit their tactical and technological superiority, overwhelming and annihilating them. Silanus ordered a retreat, and what remained of his army began to fall back, leaving on the field some 5,000 bodies and a large amount of weapons, equipment, means of transport and horses. The enemy then fell on the camp of Silanus, abandoned and deserted, taking food and wine in large quantities, blankets, tents, pack animals, weapons, furnishings, mirrors of polished bronze, precious fabrics, cups and silver plates. Many of the Romans were taken prisoner, with large numbers missing. Thereafter the Cimbrians, Teutones and Ambrones forged an alliance with the Tigurini and prepared to invade Italy.

At the news of the disaster, the Senate of Rome launched another military expedition against the invaders, sending six legions and 6,000 mounted knights, commanded by the consul Lucius Cassius Longinus, to Gallia Narbonensis. Other commanders of the Roman army were Lucius Caesoninus and Caius Popillius Laenas. Longinus was not naive. In 111, when he was a praetor, he had successfully carried out a delicate mission. During the Jugurthine War, he went to North Africa on behalf of the Senate of Rome and managed to convince Jugurtha, king of Numidia, to go to Rome under the protection of safe conduct to publicly reveal the names of the Romans he had corrupted. However, he was probably a better diplomat than a military commander. The Tigurini, under the command of Divico, ambushed him at Aginnum (Agen), on the River Garonne, where he was routed, and killed him and the most of his troops at the Battle of Burdigala. If Longinus had taken greater care, events may have turned out differently for him and the many soldiers who lost their lives from his actions. The survivors, gathered by the highest ranking officer, Caius Popilius Laenas, under his command, to save their lives, had to agree to surrender most of the army's supplies to the enemy and to pass under the yoke.

In 105, the multitude destroyed a third Roman army, led by the consul Cnaeus Manlius Maximus and the proconsul Quintus Servilius Caepio. This latest military catastrophe took place at Arausium (Orange, in France) and was more serious than the previous ones, indeed of unheard-of proportions. It was the worst defeat in the military history of Rome,[1] caused by the irresponsible conduct of Maximus and Caepio. Because of a quarrel between their commanders (the proconsul was supposed to obey the orders of the consul but he did not, for reasons of social discrimination – he was a noble, while the consul was a plebeian) the legions were overwhelmed one by one by the barbarians, who attacked them in unstoppable waves, with immense slaughter. The bodies of 80,000 legionaries were left on the ground after the fighting, while to these must be added the losses suffered by the support troops (auxilia), some 40,000. There were also many prisoners and missing. Afterwards, the battlefield was filled by the contrasting sound of the opposing forces; on the one hand there was the despair of the vanquished, while on the other the jubilation of the victors.

However, while the Romans could lose one or more battles, they never gave up. They were able to send one army after another against the enemy and continue fighting until they won the war. With this spirit, the Senate of Rome prepared its revenge. They urgently needed to recruit and send a new army to the front to prevent the Germani from reaching the Roman *provinciae* in Hispania, as it seemed they intended to do, or in case they opted to switch their target and attack Massalia (Marseille in southern France) and its eastern colonies, which were friends and allies of Rome, and then continue towards Italy. The consuls in charge were Caius Marius and Caius Flavius Fimbria. They were to take over on 1 January 104, after the celebration of the triumph of Marius for his victories over Jugurtha, king of Numidia, in the Jugurthine War (113–105). Marius had already been a consul in 107, and was elected to his second consulate due to the widespread conviction there was no one better than him to repel the barbarians. Exceptionally, a law was approved in order to authorize the presentation of his candidacy both *ex officio* – by virtue of his being a military commander fighting abroad – and *in absentia*, 'in his absence'. Otherwise he could not have been a candidate for a series of reasons: the law did not allow him to do so before a couple of years had passed after his previous office; and as he was still in North Africa due to the aftermath of the war there, the law prohibited him being a candidate because he could not present himself personally to the polling station in Rome. Therefore Marius did not campaign and was not in Rome on the day of the vote, but he was still elected.

Recruitment difficulties

To form an army larger than that which had just returned from North Africa, Marius enlisted more volunteers than had ever been recruited for war and sent emissaries to the allies to obtain support troops. One such ally, Nicomedes III, king of Bithynia, replied that he was unable to help because the young people of his country, for the most part, were 'kidnapped by publicans' and 'currently held as slaves in the Roman provinces'. The Senate of Rome[2] was dismayed by this, but it's hard to believe it was in the dark over the situation. The companies of publicans, to which many senators belonged, had been involved in the slave trade since the time of Marcus Porcius Cato the Censor (234–149), who was himself a slave merchant.

The companies of publicans were groupings of a public nature operating in the field of public tenders, for both the execution of works (construction and maintenance of buildings, roads, bridges, aqueducts, barracks, etc.) and the supply of goods and services, for example of foodstuffs, military equipment and weapons of war, the management of the system of supply and distribution of public wheat, the collection of duties and taxes. They were each based in Rome, with an administrator, who remained in office for a year, and a variable number of employees, including local agents. One of their most lucrative activities was the management of the tax collection service. This service was periodically contracted by the Senate of Rome (in the future, after the approval of the *lex Sempronia de provincia Asiae*, it would be contracted by the censors). The single contract created a perverse mechanism. Because the auction prices were so high, and the participants in the tenders, to get the contract, pushed the award price even higher, the contractor, to recover the costs incurred and earn a profit, made extensive use of the *pignoris capio*, a form of execution on the defaulting debtor's assets. The *pignoris capio* was the act of the creditor who took possession of one or more things of the defaulting debtor to satisfy his credit. The institute could only be used for advertising credits. It could be applied without the need of a precedent and even in the absence of the defaulting debtor. Moreover, it did not require the presence of a magistrate, therefore the application could take place even outside the court, and on days in which the competent magistrates refrained from administering justice. The attached asset did not necessarily have the same value as the claimed credit, since the function of the attachment was not to settle the debt, but to put pressure on the creditor to pay. If the debtor continued not to pay, the creditor would become the owner of the attached asset, so he could sell it. With this system, the companies of publicans leaned hard on the tax payers of the sums advanced to the State, consequently attracting contempt and hatred.[3]

The capital of the publican companies was held by a variable number of shareholders, who shared the profits in proportion to the amount paid by each. A portion of the profits was invested in other profitable assets, such as interest rate loans at very high rates (up to 48 per cent per annum); wholesale, mainly maritime, trade; the extraction of minerals from the ground and salt from the sea; the purchase of rustic funds, dwellings and extra-urban villas; and the purchase of slaves and luxury items. Usually, the members of the companies of publicans were wealthy businessmen enrolled in the '3rd class of income', that of the *equites*: principally skilled financiers, coin dealers and pledged lenders (*argentarii*). However, it was not uncommon for senators to participate in the capital of the companies of publicans. It is impossible to say how frequent this was, because participation in capital could also be hidden. In some cases, the companies of publicans acted as nominees for companies that were 100 per cent financed by senators. The senators preferred not to appear and to stay behind the scenes: they did not act directly, but through a freedman, a figurehead acting on their behalf. The companies of publicans therefore carried out economic activities that were instrumental in the further enrichment of already very rich families. The companies of publicans, while enriching their members, also made richer those able to facilitate them in business, through the payment of bribes and other forms of corruption, such as the granting of loans at very low rates.

The companies of publicans were able to organize large companies, make big deals, contract a large number of taxes and lend money to individuals and entire communities, even to city-states. They had interests in various provinces, dealing with politicians, military commanders, magistrates in office (who were organs of the state), princes and kings, to whom they lent huge sums of money. Since the ignition of a loan implied the establishment of a relationship of subordination between the creditor and the debtor, their members, individually and collectively, were able to exert great influence on the functioning of the Roman state, its internal politics, and thus on the wars of Rome, on city-states, principalities and foreign kingdoms. The companies of publicans operated mainly in Asia Minor.[4] In Sicily, their field of intervention was more limited: they collected taxes on public pastures and on maritime transport.[5]

In 104, the Senate of Rome ruled that no citizen of a friendly state or ally of the Roman people could be forced to serve as a slave in a Roman province; the provincial governors must therefore restore freedom to those born free in allied cities, then enslaved in their provinces.[6] From this we can see that the Senate of Rome did not always act to protect its interests (slaves were often used in large estates, and the largest landowners were the senators).

The Revolt of Vettius

In the second half of 105, recruitment operations were underway in Rome when thirty slaves rebelled in Nuceria Alphaterna (Nocera) and 200 in Capua. The revolts broke out in rapid succession, but were both repressed easily. The rebels who resisted capture were overwhelmed and killed on the spot, with very few managing to escape. Those that were taken prisoner were crucified. Soon after, a similar episode occurred, again in Capua, but larger than the previous one. At the root of this revolt was a tale of love and madness. In 104, Titus Minucius Vettius, son of a very rich man, an *eques*, fell in love with a slave of another man. He strongly desired to make her his own and committed himself to redeem her for a huge sum – seven Attic talents, to be paid within a certain period – and to live with her. When the deadline expired, Vettius was not able to pay the agreed sum. He was allowed to delay the payment for thirty days, but even then could not respect the terms. He asked for and got a second extension, but still unable to pay, he went out of his mind, or pretended to be crazy. He freed the slaves of the area, armed them and channelled their fury against the great landowners, who had many slaves and treated them like animals. The revolt spread, initially involving 400 fugitive slaves, then 700 and eventually

3,500. The rebel slaves who worked in the camps in Campania were mostly Greeks. Vettius was now at the head of an army of slaves, armed and ready for anything, which he organized into centuries in an entrenched camp on a hill. In the euphoria of the moment, Vettius proclaimed himself king, acquired a crown for himself, dressed in purple and other insignia of power, and had a 500-strong bodyguard. He also beheaded several debt collectors.

The great landowners of Campania asked for help from Rome and the Senate instructed Lucius Licinius Lucullus to re-establish security and public order by any means. Licinius Lucullus was the pilgrim praetor, who dealt with quarrels between Romans and foreign citizens. He had 600 men with him – not enough to give battle – so resorted to other means, corrupting the commander of the slaves, Apollonius. He promised him money, gifts and impunity, in exchange for betraying Vettius. Betrayal was a formidable weapon of war, often used by the Romans when the enemy was stronger or proved elusive in pinning down. For example, Viriathus, commander-in-chief of the Lusitans, was killed while he was sleeping in his tent in 138 by people in whom he had confidence, who had been bribed by the consul Quintus Servilius Caepio; afterwards, when Viriathus' assassins asked Servilius Caepio for their payment, he answered that 'Rome does not pay traitors who kill their chief'. Apollonius betrayed Vettius, who committed suicide to avoid capture. Lucullus exterminated the rebels and crucified the prisoners, all except Apollonius. Then he returned to Rome, received the praise of the Senate and returned to his duties as pilgrim praetor. Later, when he was a consul, he would again have to counter a slave revolt, this time a much larger one.

Chapter 17

The Rebirth of the Phoenix Arab

A new revolt of slaves in Sicily

It is uncertain if, when the revolt of Vettius broke out, the Senate of Rome had already ordered the provincial governors to ascertain whether there were individuals in the territories who were kidnapped and sold as slaves despite being free citizens of allied states, and to free those who were. If the order had been given, the slow pace of the Romans in implementing the edict could explain the enthusiastic response of so many slaves to the appeal of Vettius. In execution of that edict, Publius Licinius Nerva, governor of Sicily, concluded that many slaves were illegally withheld their freedom, and freed 800 of them. This caused discontent among many great Sicilian landowners, who pressed the governor not to liberate other slaves who were entitled to it. Nerva gave in to their request and turned a deaf ear to the protests of slaves who have not been released despite having the right to be so. These then rebelled: in Syracusae, a large group of fugitive slaves took refuge in the sacred wood of the Palici, being joined by fugitive slaves from other areas who had killed their masters. Nerva failed to act decisively, proving unable to cope with the situation. He eventually dispatched against the rebels 600 Roman soldiers, based in Henna, together with some outlaws to whom he had offered immunity for their crimes. One of those criminals was Caius Titinius, nicknamed Gadaeus. He has been operating on the island as a bandit, sparing slaves and killing only free people, in contrast to Kleon because his actions had some kind of social character. He had been sentenced to death in 106, but had fled into the hills to escape execution. This was not the first time that a bandit had been officially recognized by the authorities, or given *defacto* control of the area in which he operated. The fact that the Roman government of Sicily, in order to ensure public order and security, had to use criminals to carry out their work, revealed the maladministration of the *provincia*, and was further confirmation that in Sicily it was sometimes difficult to distinguish between guards and thieves, or good and bad. Gadaeus joined the rebels together with others, and was elected as their leader. He quickly facilitated the entry of the Roman troops into the rebel camp. Most of the rebels were killed on the spot, the survivors abandoning their weapons and fleeing. Some were killed during their flight, while others were captured and crucified.

It is often said that if an outbreak of fire is extinguished, another one immediately flares up elsewhere. The revolt was only beginning and it reignited near Eraclea Minoa, where some eighty slaves rose against their owner, Publius Clonius, a Roman *eques*, cut his throat and gathered on Mount Capriano. Nerva, being ill-advised, had disbanded most of his army, but marched out against the rebels with the troops he retained. The delay gave time for the rebels to strengthen themselves. As soon as the praetor passed the River Alba, though, he turned away from the rebels and went to Heraclea. He was accused of cowardice and many slaves were encouraged to join the revolt. The number of the rebels greatly increased in just a few days, growing from 800 to 2,000. Nerva sent the garrison from Henna, under the command of Marcus Titinius, against the rebels. Titinius, disadvantaged by the ground and his lesser numbers, was defeated and lost many men, the survivors only escaping by throwing away their weapons and fleeing. The rebels collected the weapons of their slain enemies, greatly increasing their armament, and were more determined than ever to continue the uprising. All the slaves in the area were now ready to rebel.[1] As more slaves joined the revolt every day, the number of rebels increased to 6,000.[2] Like the slave war that had inflamed Sicily decades before, the new uprising grew rapidly and spread like wildfire. After starting as small bands that acted autonomously, an organized movement was quickly born. It is interesting to note that a significant number of female slaves also participated in the revolt.

The rebels called an assembly, held a debate and chose a king called Salvius, an interesting character. It was said he was an Italic (but this may not be true) and not even a slave.[3] He was reputed to be a fortune-teller, who played the flute dementedly in mystic orgies of women. The skill of Salvius was divination, as was that of Eunus. It seems that the slaves were sensitive to the suggestions of the supernatural and followed those who interpreted them. But the recurrence of this aspect in the Sicilian Slave Wars leads to the suspicion that by the Romans reputing that he had access to an expressly female religious rite, Salvius' own masculinity could be questioned.[4] Another hypothesis is that he had been sold to slave traders for having participated in an alleged conspiracy, perhaps one repressed by the Senate of Rome to avert the threat to the security of the State that was represented by the worshippers of Bacchus, many of whom were arrested and convicted of political subversion in relation to their participation in the *bacchanalia*, the orgiastic rites in honour of Bacchus.

King Salvius divided his army into three bodies, appointing a general for each of them and ordering them to make inroads up and down the country, then at a certain time and place join together again in one body. By these depredations the rebels provided themselves so well with horses and other animals, that in a short time they had more than 2,000 mounts. In the meantime their number increased further, reaching at least 22,000, of whom 20,000 were foot-soldiers and 2,000 horsemen, although they were very raw and inexperienced in warfare. Among other raids, they attacked Morgantia, a strong and well-fortified city. The rebels attacked it with great fury and made fierce, repeated assaults. Nerva embarked on a night march with about 10,000 men recruited in Italy and Sicily, with the intention of liberating the city. He surprised the rebels by the suddenness of his assault while they were busily employed in the siege. He broke into their camp, which was lightly guarded, releasing many prisoners and grabbing abundant plunder. He then marched towards Morgantia.[5] But the rebels hit back with great fury, and, having the advantage of the higher ground, routed him and his army to flee. Some six hundred Roman troops were killed, many fled and 4,000 were taken prisoner. Salvius ruled that the rebels should kill none of those who had thrown down their arms. He recovered what he had lost in his camp, gaining a great victory and much booty. The victory owed as much to Salvius' cunning as to the cowardice of Nerva's men.[6] Afterwards, many went flocking to join Salvius, the rebels' numbers swelling to 30,000.[7] Having made himself absolute master of the countryside, Salvius again besieged Morgantia. The rebels called for help from all the slaves in the city, promising them liberty. But their masters promised the same to the slaves if they would remain faithful and join with them in the defence of the city. The slaves chose to accept what was offered by their masters, fighting so resolutely that they forced the enemy to raise their siege. However, the praetor Nerva went on to revoke the promise of liberty for the slaves, which caused many of them to run away and join the rebels.[8]

Athenion of Cilicia

While Salvius next raided as far as the Campi Leontini, the figure of another slave chief, Athenion, emerged in western Sicily. Athenion was a character no less interesting than Salvius. He was born in Cilicia (south-eastern

Anatolia) as a free man. He became a slave after being captured and sold to slave merchants. In Sicily, he administered the properties of two very rich brothers. A man of superior culture and uncommon education, he was a famed astrologer, who claimed that through the stars the gods foretold that he should become king of all Sicily (as it emerges with evidence later – see page 159 – as already in the case of Eunus, it is not a boast but a prophecy). He therefore refrained from laying waste to the country or destroying cattle and crops, believing they belonged to him. Unfortunately, nothing else is known about Athenion. We don't know by whom, where, how and why he was captured and sold into slavery. If we did know, we would understand what he was or did in Cilicia. Maybe Athenion had been a victim of the pirates, or was even a pirate himself. It is understood, however, that he excelled in courage and had the ability to command men in war. He had a military attitude and experience, and his troops trusted him. He led 200 slaves in the countryside around Segesta, then recruited more followers and gathered 1,000 fighters.[9]

He immediately proclaimed his divine right to the island and besieged Lilybaeum. During the siege the harbour was entered by some ships transporting a contingent of Mauretanian auxiliaries, sent by Rome to help Lilybaeum. These fighters, commanded by Gomon, an otherwise unknown individual, attacked Athenion and his men at night and inflicted many casualties on them, both dead and wounded.[10] Athenion, pretending he was commanded to do so by the gods, withdrew with his men to concentrate at Mount Capriano, also known as Rifesi, between Bivona and Burgio, 4km from Calamonaci (in south-western Sicily, between Agrigento and Enna), the location of an important crossroads. Nerva, in Lilybaeum, sent an army to Mount Capriano, led by Titinius. But Titinius and his men, because of the roughness of the battlefield, their infidelity and the audacity of the enemy, would not face the rebels, instead throwing down their weapons and fleeing. The rebels gathered the abandoned weapons and equipment, ensuring from now on they would be better armed and equipped. By this time they had grown in number to 6,000. Another Roman army, with Nerva at its head, moved from Lilybaeum to face the rebels. It crossed the River Albus (Magazolo), about 15km from Eraclea Minoa, and entered this city. Nerva then managed to take the stronghold of Mount Capriano through treason, the rebels withdrawing after being heavily defeated.[11] Athenion was beaten, but not broken. He joined Salvius together with 3,000 men, leaving his remaining 7,000 followers under other leaders. Meanwhile, Salvius and his men have moved to Palikè (Rocchicella), a basaltic buttress close to the valley of the

Margi, in the plain of Catania, near the city of Menaeum (Mineo). Menaeum was the Roman name of Palikèn Nea, a city founded in 453 by Ducetius as the capital of the Kingdom of the Sicels which he had established.

Salvius, the fluteplayer, becomes King Tryphon

A famous sanctuary was located at Palikè, set on a series of terraces descending from a grotto towards a small lake, called Naphtia, and dedicated to the Palikoi (in Latin, *fratres Palici*) – henceforth Palici – two indigenous Sicilian deities living in the subterranean world. The Palici were sons of Adranus, or Adranòs (Hadranus or Hatranus for the Latins), the Sicel god of war, linked to water and fire, and assimilated partly to Hephaestus, the Greek blacksmith god. The monumental layout of the sanctuary included two *stoai* and a *hestiatorion*. The *stoas* and the *hestiatoria* were typical buildings in Greek architecture. The former was a covered walkway or portico, where merchants could sell their goods, artists could display their work and religious gatherings could take place. The most ancient examples were open at the entrance with columns, usually of the Doric order, lining the side of the building, creating a safe, enveloping, protective atmosphere. Later examples were built on two storeys, and incorporated inner colonnades, this time usually Ionic, where shops or sometimes offices were located. The *stoai* of the sanctuary of Paliké were buildings with a series of rooms and a shared colonnade. Due to the holy character of the site, they were used for religious purposes. A *hestiatorion* was a building where the meat of animals sacrificed on the altar was consumed during ritual ceremonies. They included a series of square rooms that opened around a courtyard, with beds (*klinai*), made of stone or brick, similar to a Greek *symposion*. Usually there were seven *klinai* in each room, placed along the walls. The *hestatorion* of Paliké had a rectangular plan and a wooden structure with a pavilion roof with terracotta tiles, and contained two blocks of rooms opposite each other (four lateral rooms, each with a square plan, roughly 5 metres along each side, and three smaller rooms, roughly 3 metres along each side) arranged around a central space, which was open to form a monumental entrance along the southern side. People entered the central space through a *propylaeum* of four columns. A frieze of triglyphs and metopes ran along the architrave of the *propylaeum* itself. In each of the larger rooms, the banqueters reclined on dining couches (these were seven per room). The smaller rooms were most likely service quarters.[12]

Inside the sanctuary the priests revealed prophesies and obscure rituals were practised. In this sacred enclosure, runaway slaves had a refuge where they could stay until they negotiated with their masters for more humane treatment. The agreements were guaranteed by oaths at the Palici. Anyone who had taken the oath then submitted himself to divine judgment, to demonstrate his good faith. The penalty for perjury was death or blinding, so no one dared to lie. Thus an expression was born for Sicilians, who when they had to swear something said: 'May I be deprived of the sight of my eyes', that is 'May I be blinded if I say a lie.' The sanctuary itself was dedicated to the Palici because the nearby lake Naphtia was of volcanic origin. It was a double lake, and while neither was big, there were many deep chasms, from the bottom of which flowed springs and sulphur vapours rose with dome-shaped jets.[13]

When Salvius arrived at Paliké, first he offered a ritual sacrifice to the Palici and dedicated to them a richly ornamented robe in gratitude for his victories. His followers then made him king and placed a crown upon his head.[14] Salvius chose as his royal name King Tryphon,[15] and made a number of the most prudent men his counsellors. In all things he both prepared and adorned himself as a king. Whenever he was conducting business, he put on a toga, edged with royal purple, and a wide-bordered chiton. He also appointed lictors with rods and axes to go before him, and took great care that all the other emblems and trappings of royalty were observed.[16]

The royal name chosen by Salvius for himself was allusive to Diodotus Tryphon, usurper of the Seleucid throne from 142–138. From 161–138, in a succession of very tangled situations, the Seleucid kingdom of Syria had been ruled by five kings: Demetrius I Soter (161–150), Alexander I Balas (150–145), Antiochus VI Dionysus (145–140), Diodotus Tryphon and Demetrius II Nicator (145–138). Diodotus[17] was a general of Demetrius I Soter, but he defected to the usurper Alexander I Balas, who had revolted in 152 and became king in 150. He had ensured that Alexander could capture the capital, Antioch. When, in 145 or 144, Alexander was killed after having been defeated by Demetrius II Nicator, son of Demetrius I Soter, Diodotus became the legal guardian of his successor, Antiochus VI Dionysus, a child of only three years, son of Alexander I Balas. As such, he held the imperial throne of the Seleucids. Later he continued the struggle against Demetrius, who was supported by Jonathan, king of the Maccabees. The Maccabees were a group of Jewish rebel warriors who in 167 had taken control of the Kingdom of Judea (at the time part of the Seleucid Empire), founded the Hasmonean dynasty, reasserted the Jewish religion, expanded the boundaries of Judea by conquest and reduced the influence of Hellenism and Hellenistic Judaism. In 143–142 Diodotus executed Jonathan after kidnapping him and started to invade Judaea, but had to withdraw due to a series of adverse circumstances. In 142, Demetrius had recognized Simon Maccabee as high priest in Jerusalem. Meanwhile, the Parthian king Mithridates I the Great had invaded the Seleucid Empire and conquered the satrapies of Media and Babylonia. In 141 or 140, Diodotus killed Antiochus VI and usurped the kingship, calling himself Diodotus Tryphon, 'the Magnificent', but was not recognized by Rome. In 139, Mithridates continued his conquest of the Seleucid Empire, occupying the regions of Susa and Elam. In 138, Demetrius was taken captive by the Parthians. The same year, Antiochus VII Sidetes, Demetrius' brother, supported by several allies, attacked Diodotus Tryphon and besieged him at Dor, a city in Phoenicia. Tryphon escaped, then committed suicide in Apamea.

Salvius' choice of this royal name provided him with a connecting link with the realm of Eunus/King Antiochus, who had founded the Kingdom of the Western Syrians in 136, which lasted until his death in 132. Salvius revived it twenty-eight years later. Eunus had chosen to be called Antiochus, alluding to Antiochus VI Dionysus, while Salvius had named himself after the first successor of Antiochus VI Dionysus (without being discouraged by the fact that Diodotus Tryphon was a usurper).[18] All this shows that Salvius saw himself as the successor of Eunus; the kingdom of King Tryphon was the same Kingdom of the Western Syrians established by King Antiochus. There are further links between the reigns of King Antiochus and King Tryphon. One is that Diodotus Tryphon was born in Casiana, a dependent town of the city of Apamea, and had died in Apamea, which was Eunus' home town. In the case of King Tryphon, however, the insignia of sovereignty were different. Like King Antiochus, King Tryphon also wore a crown, but publicly he appeared as a Roman magistrate – a consul or at least a praetor – since he wore both a broad-bordered chiton and a purple-edged toga (the *toga praetexta*, the same as Roman senators), and was preceded by lictors bearing rods and an axe. The crown, associated with the purple cloak, created a mixture of Roman and Greek signs of power. Essentially, the differences compared to the previous model consisted in the *toga praetexta* and the lictors. Likely they reflected their different geographic and cultural origins. Perhaps it was because King Tryphon was an Italic, and as such dressed in Roman fashion, while King Antiochus was a Syrian, born and raised in a Hellenistic environment. However, these external differences did not alter the effective continuity of the two kingdoms. An additional link was the common goal of tearing Sicily from the Romans to replace them in the rule of the island, with the involvement of the Sicilians. As for this, however, there was also a difference, dictated by a strategic choice of King Tryphon, based on the experience of King Antiochus: the failure of Eunus to involve the urban communities of Greek descent and culture. Tryphon attempted to involve the Sicels and Sicans in place of the Siceliotes (Greeks of Sicily).

Triokala and the imprisonment of Athenion

King Tryphon moved from Palikè with 40,000 men, and, after avoiding the cities, considering them a cause of inertia and negativity,[19] located his headquarters at Triokala (Sant' Anna, near Caltabellotta),[20] between Agrigentum and Selinus, some 15km from the coast, making it the capital of his kingdom. Triokala was in an impregnable position, built upon a high and inaccessible rock, called Kratas, from where it controlled a large territory. The site was also characterized by springs of fresh water, vineyards, olive plantations and cultivated fields.[21] It was occupied first in the Bronze Age. The acropolis was originally placed on top of the nearby Mount Gulèa. In about the thirteenth century BC, the seat of the chief was transferred to another close-by rock, called Camycus (Gogàla), from the name of a tribal king, the legendary Kokalos, who kindly received Daedalus on his flight from Crete. Minos, king of Crete, ordered Kokalos to hand over the fugitive, and, having received a refusal, led an army to Camycus in pursuit of him. According to others, Minos was killed by the daughters of Kokalos and his body was buried in a mausoleum in Eraclea, which, from that moment was called Eraclea Minoa. During Proto history, a settlement which had formed on Mount Gulèa extended first to the adjacent terrace of S. Benedetto, then incorporated some nearby settlements, creating Inycon, a city of the Sicans. Later, Inycon developed, flourishing in the sixth century. At that time, due to its Hellenization, it changed its name in Triokala, which means 'three beautiful things', a reference to the abundance of fresh water, richness of cultivable soil and defensibility from enemy attaks. In 258, during the First Punic War, Triokala was a Carthaginian stronghold and was destroyed by the Romans. Its inhabitants refounded it nearby (close to the modern village of S. Anna, in Contrada Troccoli), changing its name to Triokalis (New Triokala). Henceforth, we will continue to say Triokala, to be understood as the area of Triokala.

King Tryphon occupied the terrace of S. Benedetto and the Gogàla cliff with 40,000 men, and, in order to make it the capital of his kingdom, built a stately palace and agora.[22] He strengthened the fortress of Triokala, which was already imposing, surrounding it with a wall of 8 stades (equivalent to about 1,600 metres) and a deep trench. Athenion had followed King Tryphon to Triokala, but the choice of this as his capital gave rise to discussions in which they supported opposing theses. King Tryphon had withdrawn from the most productive grain regions of Sicily, located in the south-east and far west of the island, to the mountainous parts of the south-west. Athenion was 'obedient to Tryphon as a general obeys a king'. However, Tryphon distrusted Athenion, perhaps because of their difference in opinion over strategy,[23] or due to the fact that Salvius feared that Athenion was plotting to overthrow him. When Athenion sent his men away to plunder the countryside for supplies and persuade other slaves to join the revolt, in the absence of any apparent Roman threat to their movements, [24] King Tryphon put him in chains.[25]

Chapter 18

Disorder, Famine, Death

Looting, assassinations, rape and fire

A spiral of violence – with villages burnt, devastation, looting and killing – had created a situation where inhabitants of walled cities and the rural populations, who in panic had poured into the cities, felt that all their property outside the walls was lost to the outlaws. The army of Athenion, indeed, had been acting in a wider area than ever. The main victims of the violence were the rural people, who had usually been indifferent to those who governed in the country, because, whoever they were, their social and economic status remained the same.

The unsustainable situation of the Sicilian walled cities

The situation inside the walled cities worsened, due to overwhelming crowding, disastrous sanitary conditions, riots and rebellion by slaves. The riots were often caused by troublemakers, by ancient social hatred or resentment, with those who had nothing clashing with those with plenty, demanding money, kidnapping for ransom and damaging property. At other times the violence was due to tremendous and uncontrollable hatred between families. However, the main reason for the upheavals was famine, there no longer being enough food for the population, the countryside being abandoned and deserted, no longer bearing fruit. With no one to keep the law and punish the criminals, the urban communities plunged into anarchy, the entire island descending into chaos through hunger and disease.

Rome is hungry

Two quaestors supervised the regular functioning of the system of food supply in Rome. One was based in the port of Puteolis (the *quaestor puteolensis*), the other in the port of Ostia (*quaestor ostiensis*). These magistrates oversaw the consignments and distribution of wheat, controlling its quantity and quality. They also paid suppliers, controlled the selling price of cereals and liaised with the traders involved.[1] When the blocking of grain exports plunged the system of food supply in Rome into crisis, the Senate blamed the inertia or inability of the *quaestor ostiensis*, Lucius Apuleius Saturninus, and deprived him of his functions, instead attributing these to a commission of the Senate itself, directed by its most authoritative member: the *princeps senatus*, Marcus Aemilius Scaurus. However, the wheat crisis continued, with further market manipulation, speculation on retail prices and assaults on the ovens. There was widespread concern that public order would end up hampering domestic trade and the whole economy. The good reputation of Saturninus had been ruined; not only him, but his family suffered unfairly due to a groundless accusation. Saturninus reacted with a burst of pride. He made himself a candidate for the tribunate of the plebeians with the intention of using this magistracy to take revenge, exploiting it for personal gain, and was elected. His first legislative initiative consisted of promoting the approval of two coordinated bills: the first redefined the crime of high treason, the second established a special court to pursue it. Furthermore, he publicly accused Quintus Servilius Caepio of being the instigator of the Toulouse gold scandal (in which thousands of gold bars went missing after he captured them and shipped them back to Rome, reputedly stolen by bandits hired by Caepio), and Caepio and Manlius Maximus of being responsible for high treason as having caused, through their personal differences, the military catastrophe of Arausium. A trial in Rome ended with the acquittal of Caepio from the first indictment, despite much evidence against him, and with the exile of both defendants for the second indictment. The fate of Maximus was deserved because, due to insubordination with Caepio, he lost not only the battle, but also two sons, fallen in combat. It is not known where he went into exiled and his fate there. Caepio, meanwhile, was exiled to Smyrna, a city on the Aegean coast of Asia Minor, where he intended to enjoy the Gold of Toulouse (he was the one to rob it, having deceived the judges). An immense fortune was deposited in his name in a bank of that city. However, Caepio did not have time to put his plan into practice, as he died shortly after his arrival; we do not know how or why.

War on several fronts

In the meantime, Rome was also facing the multitude of Germani who had invaded Transalpine Gaul. This war was being directed by the consul Caius Marius, who, after returning to Rome from North Africa, had strengthened his army by recruiting a large number of soldiers, then led them to the mouth of the Rhone. There he entrenched his forces and awaited a clash with the Germani, trying to increase the army's efficiency and effectiveness. It was now that the Roman Army, that had until then been based on income, became a professional army and opened the doors to the poorer classes. This innovation allowed the Roman state to enlist larger armies, provide employment to citizens who were without work and create a closer relationship between the soldiers and their commander.[2] The legion system changed, with the maniples replaced by cohorts, resulting in more compact formations. The light infantry and the differences among the three different types of heavy infantry were abolished. All the legionaries from now on would be armed and equipped in the same way: with two heavy javelins, a short sword, chain mail, a helmet and a rectangular shield. In addition, the cavalry formed by Roman citizens would change their role, and in combat would be largely replaced by auxiliary cavalry.

Chapter 19

Lucullus' Reverse

A new Roman army intervenes in Sicily

The Senate of Rome, in December 102, met Lucius Licinius Nerva, outgoing governor of Sicily, to hear an account of his activity there. Nerva had to admit, in spite of himself, that he had not been able to guarantee the expected levels of grain exports from the island because of the new revolt, no less extensive and violent than the previous one over twenty years ago. He also told the Senate public order on Sicily was compromised, with armed bands roaming the countryside and the cities full of refugees, with serious problems of public health and civil coexistence; some cities had even fallen into the hands of the rebels. He said that, in his opinion, it would not be easy to bring the situation under control. Nerva argued in his defence that the blame for the situation was not only his, and he made great efforts not to say all that he would like to say about it. The Senate was aware of the outbreak of the revolt, and understood that Nerva was biting his tongue out of respect for them. It had reacted slowly so far, neglected to send the best troops to the island, for the usual reason that fighting fugitive slaves did not bring prestige, nor war booty or other prizes. Senators realized they needed to change their attitude. The Senate thus appointed the propraetor Lucius Licinius Lucullus as successor to Nerva in the office of governor of Sicily, assigning him the priority task of repressing the revolt by any means. Moreover, it provided Lucullus with adequate means to do so, unlike his precedessors. He could use 14,000 men, Romans and Italic allies, accompanied by 2,000 other auxilia, including Bithynians, Thessalians and Arcananians. In essence, he received three extra legions.

Lucullus, in 103, was 41 years old. He had been a pilgrim praetor in 104, and during his praetorship had successfully put down a slave revolt led by Titus Minucius Vettius in Campania. He belonged to a wealthy and influential plebeian family, but senatorial and therefore noble, which composed the *gens* Licinia together with the families Varus, Crassus and Mucianus. The Luculli became a consular family in 152–151, when the father of Lucullus, also named Lucullus, became consul. Lucius Licinius Lucullus married Caecilia Metella Calva, sister of Quintus Caecilius Metellus Numidicus and Lucius Caecilius Metellus Dalmaticus. This made him a relative of a very wealthy and powerful Roman family, closely linked to other high-ranking families through bonds of friendship or marriage. The Caecilii Metelli had permanently occupied the upper echelons of political life and traditional Roman religion for over 200 years. Handed down from father to son were public and religious offices, senatorial seats, the patronage of a great many clientele and vast agricultural lands, pastures and woodlands, town and country houses, means of transport and numbers of livestock and slaves. Their real estate assets were mostly made up of large farms, villas, vineyards, gardens and livestock. They were very large landowners and held much public land. The males of the Metelli were all called Caius, Lucius, Marcus or Quintus, while the females were invariably called Caecilia. As if they shared a common destiny, the men became senators, consuls, censors, provincial governors, auguries and popes, while the women were protagonists in marriages between families of high lineage. The Metelli were strenuous and irreducible defenders of the ideology of the Roman nobility, despite being of plebeian origin. They belonged to a plebeian family clan – the *gens* Caecilia – who came to Rome after the Gallic sack of Rome in 387, attracted by job opportunities related to the reconstruction of the city, perhaps from the area of Praeneste (Palestrina), a small town on a branch of Monti Prenestini dominating the Campagna Romana.

The Battle of Scirthaea

In 103, after landing in Sicily, Lucullus increased his forces to 25,000. He then marched towards Triokala, boasting that he intended to besiege it, take it by storm, and crucify all the slaves who fell into his hands. At the news of Lucullus' arrival, King Tryphon was alarmed. He had no less than 40,000 men available, so his army was superior to that of the Romans, at least numerically, but he was not a natural fighter, and therefore was anxious. He looked around and asked who he could lean on: the name of Athenion spontaneously sprang to mind. Athenion was a fighter, he was a prisoner of war when he became a slave and later gave a good account of himself as a military commander during the slave revolt led by Salvius, before he and his 5,000 men were merged into the latter's army and he was arrested. Tryphon freed Athenion and consulted with him on how to organize their resistance. A difference of opinion emerged over how to conduct the war.

Tryphon preferred to wait for the enemy at Triokala, under the protection of its walls and the harshness of its surroundings, while Athenion wanted to go in search of battle in the open field, ending the war with a single big clash rather than enduring a siege. The latter seemed their best option, and Salvius followed the advice of Athenion with no less than 40,000 men leaving Triokala under their joint command. The army marched north and entrenched at Scirthaea (possibly Àcristia, between San Carlo and Burgio, north of Caltabellotta), where it awaited the Romans.[1] When Lucullus arrived, he encamped at 12 stades from the enemy (just over 2.2km). Being so close to each other, they indulged in daily light skirmishes before engaging in battle. The clash was ferocious, its outcome remaining undecided while many fighters were killed on both sides. Athenion fought alongside a formation of 200 knights and killed many Romans, whose bodies lay scattered around him. He was injured in both knees, then suffered a third wound and was unable to continue fighting. King Tryphon saw Athenion fall and, thinking he was dead, became discouraged and abandoned the fight with 20,000 survivors, leaving Lucullus in command of the battlefield.

The Battle of Triokala

King Tryphon and his army withdrew towards Triokala. They were so disheartened that, along the way, they discussed the possibility of returning to their masters and submitting themselves totally to them. However, they opted to resist until the last breath, based on the consideration that if they surrendered, Roman revenge would be merciless. However, their defeat had been ruinous and the slave army was now more than halved.

Meanwhile, Athenion, pretending to be dead until evening, escaped from the battlefield. Wounded and in pain, he nevertheless managed to reach Tryphon at Triokala.

The Romans celebrated their victory, which was the turning point of the war. However, Lucullus acted cautiously. He refrained from immediately pursuing the retreating enemy and annihilating them, remaining in place for several days to cremate and bury the fallen. The Romans eventually reached Triokala after a march of nine days, but in the meantime the enemy had barricaded themselves in the citadel. The Romans besieged Triokala but could not take it, despite strenuous efforts. There was then another great and bloody battle, just outside the stronghold and in view of the fortifications. The entire strength of both armies was brought to bear, and this time victory went to the rebels. After much slaughter on both sides, the

Romans were overwhelmed and fled, their camp was captured and looted, and Lucullus withdrew towards Syracusae.[2]

News of the reverse suffered by Lucullus in Sicily reached the Senate in Rome at the same time as reports of a great victory in the north. The consul Caius Marius and proconsul Quintus Lutatius Catulus, assisted by Lucius Cornelius Sulla, commander of the cavalry of Lutatius Catulus and the Italic allies, had destroyed the mass of German migrants/invaders in two great battles. The Teutones and the Ambrones had been annihilated at Aquae Sextiae, in Gallia Narbonensis (in Transalpine Gaul, now southern France). The Cimbri, who had invaded Italy through the eastern Alps, were also destroyed at Campi Raudii in Cisalpine Gaul (northern Italy), despite having greater numbers and their warriors fighting as if obsessed, incited by their women, who faced them and even killed them if they retired. Contemporaneously, the Senate of Rome received a third piece of good news: the Swiss Tigurins, at the news of the military catastrophe that had befallen their allies, decided not to invade Italy through the eastern Alps, as they had threatened to do, and returned to their homes on the Swiss plateau.

L. Licinius Lucullus' lucid revenge

Praetor Caius Servilius the Augur strongly aspired to become governor of Sicily. Supported by the Supreme Pontiff, Cnaeus Domitius Ahenobarbus, he took advantage of the difficulties of Lucullus in the struggle against the rebels in Sicily to accuse him of conducting military operations without the necessary determination and insinuated that he was trying to deliberately prolong the war for the sole purpose of getting confirmed in command. Slandering Lucullus, Servilius the Augur succeeded in delegitimizing him and harming his credibility. The Senate was convinced of the inadequacy of Lucullus and replaced him with Servilius. Lucullus stoically accepted the news that his *imperium* would not be extended. He appeared a noble man who wanted to preserve a detached attitude. To his friends, his behaviour was very elegant; yet his detractors felt it came from an inflated ego, which made him feel superior to everything and everyone. Those critics felt Lucullus was a susceptible, rancorous, passionate and frantic person. Although he did not let it show, Lucullus was shocked by the news that Servilius, after having defamed him, was about to take his place and be allowed to end with little effort the work he started and carried out with great difficulty. He thus decided to prepare an unwelcome surprise.

Before the expiry of his mandate, he deleted all traces of his own work to prevent Servilius from benefitting from it. He demolished or burned down any siege works that had been built by his soldiers in Triokala (mobile tower, canopies, barricades, etc.), including a *ballista*, with which he filled a ravine. He destroyed siege engines (rams, catapults) and a large amount of war materiel that was contained in his camp. He even burned down the camp and incinerated any documents referring to his administration held at his Syracusae headquarters. He blamed and fined the Sicilians for having subjected his predecessor (Nerva) to excessive tensions, then used some of the income from the fines, which should have gone to Servilus, to hire a fleet to take the army home. He divided among 17,000 legionaries (all Roman citizens) and auxilia, Italics, Bithynians, Greeks, Thessalians and Macedonians all the loot of war accumulated and all the money left in the treasury, before dismissing them on the beach of Agrigentum, with the excuse that Servilius the Augur had not asked to keep them on duty.

As the troops were boarding, Lucullus got on his ship and left for Rome, resigned and ready to answer in court the accusation of having deliberately destroyed public property. He proposed to say in his defence that he wanted to leave the island as he had found it, foreseeing that the new governor wanted to do things his own way, so he had done him a favour. Arriving in Rome, Lucullus first of all sheltered his family from the property consequences of any conviction against him, transferring all his assets to his eldest son, Lucius, and giving his younger son, Marcus, in adoption to Marcus Terentius Varro, a wealthy patrician and friend. The adopted son thus became Marcus Terentius Varro Lucullus.[3] In Sicily, after the departure of Lucullus and his soldiers, Caius Servilius the Augur took over from his predecessor in the operations against the rebels, but achieved nothing of note. In the meantime, Tryphon died and Athenion was elected king of all the remaining rebels, including slaves and freedmen.

Chapter 20

Meanwhile in Rome …

Blood in the political elections

In October 102 the elections for the renewal of the magistracies for 101 were soiled with blood. Appius Nunnius, a candidate who had beaten Lucius Apuleius Saturninus in the race for election as a tribune of the plebeians, had been barbarously killed just after the proclamation of the elected. Saturninus had received the next most votes, so took the place that became vacant due to the death of Nunnius, as he strongly desired. There were rumours that Saturninus had instigated Nunnius' murder, but there was no evidence and nobody dared to talk about it openly.

The same round of elections had seen Mario confirmed as consul. Mario was a candidate in partnership with Manius Aquillius, who was a close collaborator of his, so the pair took office on 1 January 101. Mario had been consul four times before – in 107, 104, 103 and 102 – and furthermore, he was now consul for the fourth year in a row.

A secret agreement

In the second half of 101, Mario returned to Rome and celebrated his triumph together with Catulus for their victory in the Cimbrian War. This was the second triumph for Mario, who had celebrated his first in 104 after victory in the Jugurthine War. The festive atmosphere, however, was marred by heated controversy. Marius, on the occasion of the building of a temple to *Honos et Virtus*, had tried to take all the credit for the victory at Campi Raudii, failing to recognize the contributions of Catulus and Sulla, which had been even superior to his own. This was typical of Mario, who had behaved this way before when he disavowed the fundamental contribution to the victorious conclusion of the Jugurthine War given by Sulla with the capture of Jugurtha. Predictably, Mario's gesture had offended Sulla. While Sulla had continued to collaborate loyally with Marius in southern France, their reciprocal relationship was no longer the same. When opposing the invasion of the Cimbri, Sulla had been charged by Mario to assist Catulus in his tactical and strategic choices, given that Catulus, while commanding an army, was totally devoid of military capabilities. Sulla fought alongside Catulus against the Cimbri, and while they failed to stop the barbarians' advance in northern Italy, they collaborated well. The same could not be said for Mario and Sulla. Mario and Sulla understood each other professionally, militarily and when it came to drinking and having fun, but they were very different individuals. They differed very much in terms of character, personality, sensitivity, behaviour and interests. Sulla was rational, reflective, educated and cultured, Philhellene and bisexual (as such, closer to Catulus, who was a gentle soul and strongly attracted by male beauty); Marius instead was instinctive, impetuous, poorly educated, devoid of cultural interests, strictly heterosexual and homophobic.

Catulus reacted to the provocation of Mario with ill-concealed indignation. He publicly announced that he would publish his memoirs of the war, to deliver the truth about his contribution to the victory, and promised the citizens of Rome that he would enrich the city by building a temple and a splendid colonnaded portico. Sulla could not react in turn due to his subordinate position, stuck, as it were, in the middle between Marius and Catulus. His revenge would be taken in the future. Mario's attitude in provoking others was the real reason for the personal contrast between Mario and Sulla, which influenced the political scene and gave rise to a fight between factions (Mario was the chief of the populares; Sulla acted with the support of the optimates, who were the majority in the Senate) that developed into a civil war.

In the meantime Mario had made a secret pact with Saturninus in order to keep the promise he had made to the recruits of his army at the time of their enrollment: after the final victory, he had vowed, the Roman state would assign to his war veterans an agricultural fund as a reward for their services. On the keeping of such a promise depended Mario's credibility as a military commander to his soldiers, so he took great care to try to do so. Mario supported Saturninus' re-election as a tribune of the plebeians, putting at his disposal money and a bodyguard formed of hundreds of young people. In return, Saturninus, if elected, would exercise the power of legislative initiative proper to the tribunes of the plebeians to propose and have approved a bill that aimed to make real the commitment given by Mario to his soldiers.

Q. Caecilius Metellus' condemnation to exile

One of the first things which Saturninus did after his election was promoting a frumentary law, which was unsuccessful, then he promoted and brought into being a colonial law, for the purpose that he had agreed with Mario. The application of this law would lead to the establishment of several colonies in North Africa, including one in the Kerkenna islands. The war veterans of Mario and their families obtained for themselves and their families plots of arable land in the territory of those colonies. Meanwhile, Saturninus, strengthened by the support of Mario, dominated Rome. He used his bodyguards to terrorize his political opponents and ensure the approval of his bills. The strongest of the opponents was Quintus Caecilius Metellus Numidicus.

Metellus Numidicus was an old enemy of Mario, from when Metellus was consul and directed the Jugurthine War and Mario was one of his legion commanders. Metellus had opposed Mario running for the consulate, while Mario orchestrated a campaign against his superior.

Saturninus successfully conspired with Mario against Metellus. In agreement with Mario, he forced the senators to swear that they would observe a law promoted by him and approved through threats of violence, under penalty of exile. Metellus, who was against the law, fell into a trap set by Mario, refused to swear and was exiled. He was sent to Rhodes, where he stayed for several years before being officially recalled thanks to the insistence of his son, Quintus Caecilius Metellus Pius, and pressure from the Senate and public opinion.

In the summer of 100 another candidate was killed in the elections for the renewal of the Roman magistracies: Caius Memmius.

A mass lynching

Caius Memmius was a very active politician and a fierce critic of the vices of the nobility. He was known in the city as a great orator. When, in 111, he was a tribune of the plebeians, he had publicly urged the plebs not to oppose the nobility with violence, but with legal actions. He had ensured that Jugurtha, king of Numidia, against whom Rome was at war, went to Rome with the guarantee of safe conduct to give the names of the senators he had corrupted. Memmius had also promoted and brought to approval a bill that aimed to create the legal prerequisites for the prosecution of corrupt military commanders, who had acted against the national interest. This law later allowed the indictment of Lucius Cornelius Bestia and others, who were found guilty and largely convicted. Memmius accused Marcus Aemilius Scaurus, the *princeps senatus*, of having been bribed by Jugurtha. Scaurus – a well-known and very powerful character – was tried and acquitted after having defended himself, simply asking the public if they believed him or his accuser; the response had been a plebiscite in his favour.

In 106, Memmius opposed the draft law of Quintus Servilius Caepio which aimed to reinstate the Senate in the jury of the judicial organ of the court of the corrupt. He was later an urban praetor (104), then a proconsul of Macedonia (103). Returning to Rome, he was charged with extortion by Scaurus, the *princeps senatus*. If the accuser had not had valid evidence, no one would have been surprised. It was a well-established practice that former provincial magistrates were accused of having committed abuses against individuals and entire communities in the exercise of their functions and that the accuser was a tribune of the plebeians, who aimed to involve in the accusation the whole nobility. It was a way like any other to feed the political discourse, stirring up the issues of social conflict, and even to get publicity, when the action was promoted by young judiciary speakers who sought attention at the start of their career as magistrates. The judicial action against Memmius, however, did not reflect a demagogic and populist intent, nor a propaganda purpose, but was motivated by the desire for revenge. Scaurus sought revenge against Memmius. However, the trial against Memmius ended with his acquittal.

In 100, when the serving consuls were Lucius Valerius Flaccus and Caius Marius (the latter covering the consulate for the sixth time), the competition for the consulate was between Antonius the Orator, Caius Memmius, Aulus Postumius Albinus and Quintus Servilius Glaucia. Post-umius Albinus had earlier been delegated by his brother Spurius, outgoing consul, to command the army in North Africa, awaiting the arrival of the consul Quintus Caecilius Metellus; he launched an offensive against Jugurtha and was defeated at Suthul.

Glaucia was a tribune of the plebeians and a strong pretender. As tribune of the plebeians he promoted a bill aimed at obtaining a reduction in the selling price of public wheat, and had brought to approval a law that excluded senators from the jury of the tribunal of the corrupt.

Mario did not re-run: there were no more conditions that in recent years had allowed him to be elected to the consulate without asking for it, without an electoral campaign and without attending the vote. The restoration of normality implied the return to full observance of the *lex Villia annalis*, which he had derogated in his favour several times, before the Jugurthine War and then the Cimbrian War.

Antonius the Orator was the champion of the optimates, and therefore was preferred to his direct competitor, Albinus. For Glaucia, however, the opponent to beat was Memmius, who started well and increased his advantage as every day passed. On the eve of the vote, the victory of Memmius was clearly expected, but Glaucia plotted with Saturninus to prevent it, and during the voting operations Memmius was beaten to death by Publius Mettius, a commoner.

The horrific attack took place in the enclosure where voters were waiting to cast their vote, in Campo Marzio, just outside the city on the banks of the Tiber. The killer smashed his victim's head with a stick, then continued to attack his lifeless body, tearing it to pieces with his fingernails and teeth. This happened in the presence of many witnesses, who, at the sight of the blood, scattered in all directions, invoking help. Attracted by the screams, many others rushed to the scene. The murder weapon lay on the ground, bloody and encrusted with hair and fragments of the victim's muscles, skin and skull. The news of the incident passed among those waiting to vote. Shocked, the crowd in the enclosure swayed dangerously, causing a crush and leaving many feeling suffocated, creating panic as some fell and were trampled. The ordered and quiet gathering suddenly became disordered and violent. Voting was suspended until the return of calm, when it resumed and ended with the proclamation of the elected representatives: Antonius the Orator and Postumius Albinus.

The sense of what had happened was clear to everyone: first Nunnius, and then Memmius. Saturninus and his close friend Glaucia had introduced into public life the method of violent struggle, which had led to explosions of savage ferocity, repeated with dramatic frequency, conditioning the free choices of the electorate and creating problems for security and public order. The assassination of Memmius had come about at the instigation of Saturninus and Glaucia, with the complicity of Mario, who had guaranteed Saturninus support.

Mario himself was worried about the ugly turn taken by events. The tribune he trusted had turned out to be an imprudent and impulsive man, escaping his control and taking autonomous initiatives, which took on the appearance of an attempt at political subversion.

All the evidence suggests Saturninus was a seditious tribune. Once again, after the Gracchi and Mario, the tribunate of the plebeians was confirmed in the eyes of the senatorial oligarchy as a magistracy 'born of sedition for sedition'. The Senate of Rome accused Saturninus of aspiring to tyranny, of wanting to become king. Mario as consul could not escape the will of the Senate to intervene against his ally Saturninus, who, after a bitter fight, surrendered and was detained in the Senate, awaiting trial, together with a number of his supporters. In the night, a mercenary hired by Quintus Caecilius Metellus Pius climbed on the roof of the Senate, dismantled part of it and threw heavy masonry and tiles onto the arrested men from above, killing them all. Saturninus' legislation was later removed.

Chapter 21

The End of the Story

Further war operations

King Athenion, after reorganizing his army, re-establishing a positive mood among his fighters, encouraging and exciting them, attempted unsuccessfully to take possession of Lilybaeum. He devastated the countryside, the rebels sowing terror, killing, robbing and looting. Then they enlarged the theatre of operations and gained control of large new areas, unopposed by the Romans. A section of the island much larger than that during the revolt of Eunus had fallen into his hands. The slaves in the cities became the terror of their masters. Athenion also commanded operations in the plain of Lentini, between Syracuse and Catania, and around Palermo,[1] but did not manage to take any city.[2] However he had control of the countryside, making the roads impassable, and added to the main base of Triokala the stronghold of Makella (Montagnola di Marineo).[3] The latter is in the valley of the River Eleuterio, 30km from Palermo, on a hill (about 620 metres above sea level) of an almost conical shape, surrounded by steep slopes and walls on the northern slope. The valley of the Eleuterio was a crucial hub in communications between the southern and northern coasts, and the intense relationship between 'indigenous' centres, the Greek colonial world and the Punic cities. Strategically placed in control of the valley, Makella was the most important settlement of the entire valley itself, by position, extension and duration. Habitation of the site had started in the sixth century. There had followed a consistent occupation in the Archaic period and a period of great prosperity of the city between the middle of the fourth and the first half of the third century. The Romans besieged Makella in vain between 263 and 262,[4] and took it in 260, while from Segesta they headed towards Thermae.[5] The city had fallen into crisis after the Roman conquest. In 211 it rebelled against the Romans, who then captured it.[6]

The year 102 saw the annihilation of the army of Servilius the Augur in Sicily, by the rebels led by Athenion, who consequently became masters of Sicily. In 101, Lucullus was tried, found guilty of embezzlement and sentenced to exile and to the usual accessory penalties (deprivation of Roman citizenship, confiscation of the family patrimony, expulsion from the Senate). He went to Herakleia, a city located in Basilicata (southern Italy), where he remained until his death. As soon as they could, his sons – Lucius Licinius Lucullus the Younger and Marcus Terentius Varro Lucullus – promoted a judicial action against Servilius the Augur, arguing that he stole from the state.[7] When Servilius the Augur was replaced by Manius Aquillius, the collegue of Marius in the consulate of 101, matters finally changed.

The irresistible advance of legions

For two years (101–99) Aquillius led a successful war without quarter against Athenion. The revolt of Salvius had its tragic epilogue when slaves from all over Sicily gathered in Triokala, choosing this sacred and inaccessible place as their stronghold. The slaves barricaded themselves there when Aquillius led his troops against them. Once again, the Roman soldiers penetrated the defences thanks to the betrayal of a condemned man who had escaped and given himself to brigandage. The traitor opened the gates of the fortress, the Romans burst in and they went on the rampage, killing all they met, burning and destroying the whole city.

A war of extermination

All armed rebels were killed on the spot and Triokala was destroyed.[8] Many other rebels committed suicide to evade capture. Any survivors were pursued and hunted down by Aquillius until they all gave up. The last battle was fought on the banks of the River Alba (Verdura), near Triokala (Caltabellotta). It was a hard-fought clash, starting with Athenion facing Aquillius in single combat. Although the rebel leader inflicted a serious head injury on Aquillius, he was killed.[9] In the ancient world, single combat was a fight on equal terms between two contenders, within the framework of a broader battle. It was not generally part of the Roman tradition, being more commonly associated with their barbarian foes. However, some Roman soldiers did have a tendency to engage in such clashes, maybe the desire for fame inspiring them to perform heroic gestures, or because they were forced to do so by the habits and challenges of the Celts, or perhaps because we do not as yet fully understand the duel's importance to the Romans during the Republic. But a single combat could decide an entire battle.[10]

The companions of Athenion, seeing him fall, elected a new leader, Satyr, but the Romans renewed their tireless assaults and finally prevailed. The rebels were wiped out, being killed in their thousands.

Game over

Aquillius sent 1,000 prisoners to Rome, where the Senate condemned them *ad bestias*. This was a form of Roman capital punishment in which the condemned were killed and eaten by wild animals to entertain the public in the circus, and was applied to the worst criminals, as the runaway slaves were considered. The animals included lions, bears, leopards, Caspian tigers and black panthers. The spectacle was combined with gladiatorial combat and took place in the Forum or the Circus Maximus. The encounter with the beasts in the arena could only end in one possible way, the condemned having no arms or armour. The first mention of such a punishment refers to 167: after the victory over Perseus, king of Macedonia, in the Third Macedonian War, Lucius Aemilius Paullus, who was later called *Macedonicus*, condemned the deserting allies of the Roman army to be crushed by elephants. Rather than being thrown to the beasts to amuse the crowds, however, the prisoners of Aquillius preferred to kill each other. Satyr was the last to die, turning his sword on himself. Thus died the last survivors of the slave uprisings of Salvius and Athenion.[11]

Conclusions

In search of a definition for what happened

Agira is a town of about 8,000 inhabitants located in central Sicily, about 35km from Enna. It is in the valley of the River Salso, some 650 metres above sea level. Its origins are very old. In the Classical Age, when it was called Agyrion and was the main centre of central Sicily after Enna, it was ruled by tyrants, one of whom was called Agyris. Under the Romans, it became Agyrium. Diodorus of Sicily (90–30), a Greek-speaking Sicilian aristocrat, lived there. He was a historian and wrote a universal history entitled *Bibliotheca Historica*, a monumental work, of which much survives.[1] In books 34 and 35 of the *Bibliotheca Historica* Diodorus dealt with slave movements that took place in Sicily in the second half of the second century. Unfortunately, those books have not survived, but they are known through Phothius' summary, dated from AD 855, supplemented with a few passages which a Byzantine excerptor made in the tenth century AD for the emperor Constantine VII Porphyrogenitus (Diod. 34/35, 2; 8–11).

As Diodorus was a Sicilian, he had access to local traditions and knew the theatre of fighting. Probably, with regard to the Salvius revolt, his account is based on that contained in *Histories*, a historical work in fifty-two books, written by Posidonius of Rhodes (*c.* 135–151), a stoic philosopher, geographer, and historian, close to the Roman aristocracy. *Histories* offered a narration from 144–85. Unfortunately, the original manuscript of *Histories* is also lost. But Posidonius' observations can still be found in Diodorus' work (book 36 of *Bibliotheca Historica*), as well as those of Athenaeus of Naucratis (late 2nd and early 3rd century AD) and Strabo of Amasea (64/63 BC – *c.* 24 AD). The other literary sources available for Rome's Sicilian Slave Wars are mostly epitomes relying on Livy (the *Periochae*, Orosius, Obsequens, Floras), some short passages of Valerius Maximus and of Frontinus, and a few *obiter dicta* of Cicero. The only archaeological sources are three issues of coinage (perhaps also a fourth), found in various parts of Sicily, and some inscribed sling pellets found in the vicinity of Enna.

The account of Diodorus is important, but omits most of the wars and is affected by partiality, to the disfavour of the slaves who rebelled. It is full of prejudices and ironies about the slaves who were protagonists. In this respect Diodorus, as a Sicilian Greek, lived in a Hellenistic context and was fully integrated into the local ruling elite who, no different to the Romans, despised slaves as mere talking animals. It thus requires careful discernment from the scholar, in order not to be too influenced by a vision that is partisan, not objective.

Diodorus Siculus calls the social movements in question the Revolt of Eunus and the Revolt of Salvius, after their leaders, despite the latter also being headed by Athenion after Salvius' death. Even today the great Sicilian slave revolts are commonly known as the Revolt of Eunus and the Revolt of Salvius, or alternatively the Sicilian Slave Wars. What definitions should be used is an old question, posed even by Roman historians, given that they could not agree whether the revolts of slaves should be considered as an external war or a civil war, or even as a war. Such prejudice is reflected in the words of Lucius Annaeus Floras, who lived in the first and second century BC and was a historian and rhetor. Concerning the Rebellion of Spartacus, which happened a few decades after the Revolt of Salvius, he writes: 'one could nevertheless also endure the dishonour of fighting against them, since, constituting, so to speak, a second species of human being, they can participate in our freedom.' He is unable to define such a movement, since 'the soldiers were slaves and the commanders were gladiators, the men of the lowest condition, the others of the worst, the latter increased the disaster of Rome with disgrace'.[2]

Modern scholarship considers the terms 'slave revolt' and 'slave war' essentially interchangeable: so a slave war is the same as a slave rebellion or slave revolt. In German, this concept is expressed with the word '*Sklavenaufstande*', and in Italian with '*Guerra Servile*'. Recently, the term revolt has been substituted by 'insurgency' (see Strauss, B., 2010, 'Slave wars of Greece and Rome', in Hanson, V.D. (ed.), *Makers of ancient strategy*, Oxford, p.201). This presupposes the idea that you are talking about a condition of revolt against a government that is less than an organized revolution and is not recognized as belligerency (see Merriam-Webster Dictionary, *cfr.* v. insurgency). One of the modern scholars who have recently studied this topic is Peter Morton, lately lecturer at the University of Manchester. Morton argues that 'the so-called Sicilian Slave Wars are best understood as two differing instances of civic disquiet, social disorder and provincial revolt in Sicily, rather than as slave wars. Both events are reconnected to their Sicilian context geographically, politically and socially, and shown to have arisen from those contexts.'[3]

As for the Revolt of Eunus, the Revolt of Salvius and the Sicilian Slave Wars, however, the terms revolt, war and insurgency are particularly difficult to place, for at least two reasons: 1) both the movements were less improvised and much wider and better organized than previous similar episodes; 2) they were born as a slave revolt, but later became a war and changed their objectives (no more only freedom from slavery, as in the beginning, but also political self-determination). Indeed, it is difficult for any expression to define completely the complex series of events in Sicily, because there had never been movements of slaves so great and so ruthless in the whole Ancient World. Perhaps the expression 'war of secession' could be used, in the sense of an attempt at political secession brought into being through armed struggle.

A secession war

I consider the Sicilian Slave Wars as an attempt at political secession in Roman Sicily. I want to explain why. The wars were fought in two stages, about a quarter of a century apart. The contenders were the Western Kingdom of the Syrians – established by Eunus and his fellow Syrians in Roman Sicily – and the Roman *res publica*. At stake was control of the territory. The Western Syrians could have achieved that result only by driving away the Romans from Sicily. And that was what they wanted to do. The insurgents stormed the city of Enna. They regained their freedom through the force of weapons, then elected a king, organized an army and took possession of a territory of increasing size within Sicily. We point out in this regard that a man called Eunus, who was a Syrian of origin, led the insurgents. He was elected by the insurgents as an absolute king and chose for himself the royal name of Antiochus: the same as one of the dynasts of the Seleucid Empire.[4] So the plan of the insurgents was to take control of the entire island, drive away the Romans and rule in their place. A number of fierce clashes between the Syrian army and the military forces of the Roman governor followed the conquest of Enna. As the latter was repeatedly defeated and the prevailing chaos in Sicily damaged the export of wheat, the Senate of Rome sent the legions into Sicily, but had to repeat the intervention three times before securing victory. After fluctuating events, lasting at least five years, the Romans stormed the capital of the insurgents, Henna, and conquered it with immense massacre. After being the cradle of the revolt (in spite of itself), Henna was also the theatre of its tragic epilogue. Eunus/King Antiochus was captured and died in prison. All his companions fell in battle or were taken prisoner and then crucified or thrown into the void from a cliff. Rome regained possession of the lost territories and hostilities ceased in 131; but only for the moment.

The bloody drama which had started with the Revolt of Eunus had a second act a little more than twenty-five years later, which in turn lasted several years. A new revolt of slaves brought to power a flute player called Salvius. He too was elected king, picked up both the political heritage and the strategic plan of the late King Antiochus, and resumed the war against the Romans to replace them in control of the island. The second stage of the war also ended with a blood bath after Athenion of Cilicia had substituted on the throne King Tryphon (Salvius). The Syrians were eventually eradicated. The prisoners, judged as fugitive slaves who had practised violence against both their masters and the Roman state, were precipitated from cliffs or crucified.

It is interesting to note that Salvius assumed for himself the royal name of Tryphon, that of a contemporary Syrian king. So, also in this case, a sovereign of Sicily referred to the contemporary, tangled political events of the Kingdom of Syria (the Eastern one) and the Seleucid dynasty. The political events of Syria did not affect the political events of Sicily, but among the actors who trod the scene of the Sicilian theatre, the main protagonist reconnected himself to facts and characters from contemporary Syria, and in this sense tied the two countries together.

This proved that King Tryphon wanted to place himself in continuity with King Antiochus, and considered his kingdom as a re-edition of the Western Kingdom of the Syrians, its resurrection, brought back to life after more than two decades. Notwithstanding that only Eunus/King Antiochus was of Syrian origin, while Salvius/King Tryphon was reportedly originally from the Italic territories, nothing prevents us from thinking of Salvius as being Syrian too.

Of course, King Antiochus and King Tryphon were not a dynasty, the latter not being a parent nor a relative of the former, but it is quite evident that the latter was the successor of the former because King Tryphon's plan of action was the same as that of Eunus: driving the Romans out of Sicily, triggering a secession war rather than an insurrection. So the war of these kings was the same war, which suggests that this was indeed a secession war.

A war of liberation

King Antiochus did not realize the impact of one aspect of his actions, which would prove a strategic error. He asked for help from the Greek cities of Sicily despite giving to his monarchy a national connotation – the Syrian one – which was completely foreign to Sicilian reality, in its double aspects (Greek and indigenous), even if he himself chose to follow the model of Hellenistic monarchy. He was able to find common cause with the low-born freemen of the island, and aimed for a general uprising of Sicilians, but he didn't consider the point of view of the urban elite, who were linked to the Romans, and therefore he didn't manage to obtain their support. Another strategic error of King Antiochus consisted in not having thought of integrating in his constitution the diverse elements that made up the variegated Sicilian ethnic and cultural framework: Siceliots (Greeks of Sicily), Sicans, Sicels and Helymians. King Antiochus and his Syrians, not having done this, ended up appearing in the eyes of the Sicilians as the Galatians[5] had appeared to the Frigians: as a warlike foreign aristocracy, which wanted to impose itself on the native populations, from whom it demanded payment of taxes. The difference was that the interlocutors of the Galatians were weak populations of shepherds and peasants, while Eunus addressed the Greeks of Sicily, communities of citizens of ancient traditions, the best organized and most prosperous in Sicily, proud of both their past and their present, loyal to Rome, who had in common with the insurgents only their Hellenistic culture.

King Tryphon wanted to use King Antiochus as his example, to be his successor and to continue his work, but he avoided the errors of his predecessor. For this reason, some elements distinctive of the second stage of the secession war suggest a connotation of liberation war, fought by the indigenous components of the demographic framework of Sicily – Sicels, Sicani and Helymians – against the Romans, who were seen as foreign rulers. This clearly emerges in the location at Palikè of the consecration of Salvius as king. Salvius was invested with sovereign signs in that sanctuary, holy to all the Sicilians. That place was located close to the ruins of the ancient capital of Ducetius, who died in 440. Ducetius had been a Hellenized leader of the Sicels, and founder of a united Sicilian state and numerous cities. He was a symbol of the last resistance of the natives to the Greek invasion. Salvius/King Tryphon did not neglect in particular the Sicani. In fact he chose as his residence the city of Triokala, which stood on the site of the ancient city of Kamikos, which had been the capital of the Sicanian king

Kokalos. This showed that Salvius/King Tryphon proposed to unite under his sceptre both the Syrians and the native peoples of Sicily, excluding the Greeks, in a common struggle against the Romans. The kingdom of Tryphon was Syrian from the point of view of its origins, and Hellenistic under the profile of the cultural setting, but it was also Sicilian. In this sense it could be appropriate to consider the war started by King Antiochus and continued under King Thryphon as a war of secession, and that under Salvius it became a war of liberation from the Romans fought by an alliance of Western Syrians and Sicilian natives.

The result of such a war was bankruptcy: the fighters were largely killed, the survivors killed each other to escape their torment, and the memory of the events in which they were protagonists was insulted. The anxiety for freedom led the rebels to a catastrophe without their deaths being used to change things in matters of slavery and the relationship between masters and slaves. Sicily – both the countryside and the cities – was devastated, but did later recover as the communities struggled to return to normal life.

Not a slave war, but a war fought by free men for self-determination

Ancient writers say that the enemies of the Romans in this war were fugitive slaves, who had nothing to lose except their chains. This is misleading and is the result of a corruption of the truth by hostile sources, which aimed to accredit a version of convenience. The facts show that some runaway slaves regained their freedom and political independence, first rebelling against their masters, then establishing a Hellenistic kingdom, fighting first to extend their control in the island, then to defend themselves against the Roman legions. They were slaves before the foundation of the Kingdom of the Western Syrians. After that, they were former slaves, individuals who had taken their freedom through an armed struggle, becoming citizens of free status and members of a national community, governed by a central power, provided with a territory and defended by an army. Therefore it is wrong talking of kings of slaves, a kingdom of slaves or an army of slaves, regarding Rome's so-called Sicilian Slave Wars. The enemies of the Romans, in these circumstances, were citizens of free status, who, together with the armed bands of proletarians, were fighting in order to defend their political independence, in an attempt to affirm *ante litteram* the principle of self-determination.

We are talking of the largest and longest-lasting challenge to the power of Rome that had ever risen within the Roman world. This is also the reason why it is not appropriate to link this war with the rebellion of Spartacus as if they were similar episodes. Spartacus and his companions did not establish a new state, nor tear a territory from the Romans to settle in their place. Their struggle took place in different parts of the Italian Peninsula (Central, South), which they reached by moving continuously. Perhaps they would have stopped in Sicily if their attempt to disembark to the island had not failed, due to the betrayal of the pirate fleet that was supposed to ferry them across the Strait of Messina and the inclement weather conditions which prevented their rafts from being able to reach the Sicilian coast. Barry Strauss, author of *The Spartacus War* (Simon & Schuster, New York, 2009), however, says it clearly: Spartacus and his family did not want to stay in Italy. Their intent was not to conquer with arms an Italian land where they would settle, but to go home, wherever that was: to Gaul, Germany or Thrace.

Appendix

The Rebellion of Spartacus

Capua

A war took place in Sicily in the second half of the second century, in two stages, separated by an interval of twenty-eight years. It was born as a localized uprising of a few hundred slaves and developed into a large-scale uprising in just about the whole island. The insurgents first fought for freedom from slavery, then for political independence from Rome. On both occasions the Senate and its consuls spent years mobilizing and dispatching large resources of men and means. The insurgents were finally exterminated by the Roman legions, with all the survivors captured and executed. After that, the Roman governors of Sicily forbade slaves from having weapons; these had usually been held by slave-shepherds, and it was they who had started the war. However, the Roman government underestimated a particular form of servitude, that of the gladiators. In such an environment in 73 exploded the Rebellion of Spartacus, the most famous – or infamous – of the slave wars. It erupted a little over thirty years after the secession war fought in Sicily, and the scenario was different: no longer in Sicily, but the southern Italian peninsula, starting at Capua (Santa Maria Capua Vetere) in Campania. Capua was a large city, based on agricultural, handicraft and trade. It was in a wide, fertile plain, the *Campania Felix* ('happy Campania'), scattered with cities, towns, villages, isolated villas, rural houses and farms. The most important centre of that area was Capua. It suffered serious hardships due to its defection from Rome during the war with Hannibal. Later, however, it recovered: economically, socially and culturally. The lands that had been confiscated and had become *ager publicus populi romanorum*, 'soil owned by the Roman people', were put up for sale and bought by private individuals and put to good use. This was the driving force behind the local economy, whose flowering was also due to the diversification of production activities. The growth and development of the city was helped by two main factors: its topographic position in relation to the Via Appia and Via Latina, which connected Capua to Rome; and the concentration in the territory of dynamic entrepreneurs, who projected their activity beyond the local area, even outside Italy, for example in the Aegean. Capua became the main city of Campania and the only city in Italy able to compete with Rome in size, number of inhabitants and economic prosperity. It was considered a second Rome and compared to Carthage and Corinth before their destruction. The slaughterhouses of Capua supplied Rome with pork and lamb. The craft workshops of Capua produced a variety of products: metal tools and weapons, worked bronzes, fabrics, perfumes, ceramics, ornments, etc. Capua was also famous for its large, beautiful and fragrant roses, as well as for its school of gladiators, frequently visited by impresarios from Rome in search of talent for the Forum and circuses.

The break out

The gladiator school trained young, fit slaves of various origins and back-grounds to perform in mortal duels for the enjoyment of an audience of bloodthirsty spectators. A rebellion broke out there, headed by Spartacus, a former prisoner of war belonging to the Maidi tribe of south-western Thrace (modern European Turkey), in an area close to the Macedonian border. They were known as men 'endowed with extraordinary strength and courage'.[1] Spartacus, after fighting with the Romans, defected but was then captured and sold to slave traders, ending up at the gladiator school in Capua. One day in 73, he and about seventy other gladiators rebelled and escaped from the school. The fugitive slaves took to the slopes of Vesuvius and practised brigandage. Many other fugitive slaves joined Spartacus, as well as free men, mostly farmers. The rebels who gathered around Spartacus grew in number to 70,000, all armed and all organized along paramilitary lines. The original small act of rebellion had become a war against Rome.

A gang of fugitive slaves keeps the Roman legions in check for years

The Roman legions faced tens of thousands of rebels, many of whom were former prisoners of war, and thus free-born. The intention of the rebels was merely to make themselves free from slavery, or to free themselves from the work of the fields. They fought desperately, as they had nothing to lose and knew that, if captured, there would be no pardon for them. First the praetor Publius Varinius, then the praetor Publius Valerius, tried in vain to intercept and overcome the rebels, and Varinius narrowly escaped being taken prisoner. The success in battle of Spartacus and his companions was so great that at one point they threatened Rome directly. The Senate sent against them both the consuls in office – Caius Aurelius Cotta and Lucius Octavius – each with one legion. Cotta faced Crissus, Spartacus' vice-commander, on the Gargano promontory (on the Adriatic coast of central Italy). Crissus was defeated and killed, along with two-thirds of his forces. Cotta then confronted Spartacus, but was defeated, as was Octavius. Later, after having sacrificed 300 legionaries he had taken prisoner, Spartacus headed for Rome, along with the mass of his followers, who by now were some 120,000 strong. The consuls tried to stop Spartacus in a great battle in the Picenum (Marche), but were defeated. At that point Spartacus halted, at least for the moment, his march on Rome and camped in the mountains around Thurii, a former Greek colony in Basilicata (Southern Italy). Five years later, in 70, the Senate instructed the consul Lucius Licinius Crassus, a fellow of Lucius Cornelius Sulla in the Civil War, to end the revolt of Spartacus by any means, providing him with a major army. This proved the turning point of the war.

The final repression

Licinius Crassus marched against Spartacus at the head of six legions. Once in the area of operations, he punished the legions for being defeated so many times: one legionary in ten was put to death. Crassus then confronted Spartacus and killed two-thirds of the 10,000 who were with him. Spartacus fled, intending to embark for Sicily, but Crassus cut ahead of him. The rebel column moved towards Sannio, a region of central-southern Italy, but Crassus set off in pursuit and slaughtered another 12,000 rebels in battle. The Senate, as Spartacus continued his guerrilla actions, decided to support Crassus with his consular colleague Cnaeus Pompeius Magnus, who had fought victoriously in Spain against Quintus Sertorius, a relative, political follower and military commander of Mario, veteran of the Jugurthine and Cimbrian wars. After fighting in the Civil War between Mario and Sulla and their followers, Sertorius was elected to the *praetura* and ruled the Roman province of Hispania Ulterior until he was driven out by an army sent against him by Sulla, the winner of the civil war, who had become a life dictator. Sertorius then became the head of a mercenary army in Mauritania, then leader of the Lusitanian rebels in Hispania, and was confronted, militarily, with various vicissitudes, by the army of Cnaeus Pompeius Magnus and Quintus Caecilius Metellus, sent by Sulla. Spartacus offered peace, but his messengers were rejected. Shortly afterwards, informed of the forthcoming landing at Brundisium (Brindisi) of Lucius Licinius Lucullus – a famous commander and veteran of the Mithridathic Wars, whose father had fought in Spain against the Celtiberians and later against King Antiochus' army in Sicily – Spartacus decided to give battle. In the ensuing bloody clash, Spartacus fell in combat with many of his men, the rest of his army fleeing in disorder. The Romans lost 1,000 men, but their losses were dwarved by those of the rebels. The fallen were so numerous that the Romans gave up counting them. The surviving rebels took refuge in the mountains, but were pursued and hunted down, 6,000 eventually surrendering. Crassus crucifed them all along the Appian Way between Capua and Rome. This brought to an end end the third great slave war of Late Republican Rome.

Historians have long wondered who Spartacus was, what his aims were, and how, starting with only a handful of fellow adventurers, he was able to form a large and powerful army, able to confront the formidable Roman legions and to keep them in check for three years. It has been said that the rebel slaves fought for freedom for all and social justice, but it seems probable that the truth lays elsewhere. Spartacus did not have a political programme; he did not want to alter the existing social and economic system, nor abolish slavery or create a classless society founded on equality. He just wanted to go home, in his case to Thrace.[2]

Chronology

Revolt of Eunus (First Sicilian Slave War)

136, the year of the consuls Lucius Furius Filo and Sextus Atilius Serranus

135, the year of the consuls Quintus Calpurnius Piso and Servius Fulvius Flaccus

134, the year of the consuls Caius Fulvius Flaccus and Publius Cornelius Scipio Aemilianus

133, the year of the consuls Lucius Calpurnius Piso Frugi and Publius Mucius Scaevola

132, the year of the consuls Marcus Popilius Laenas and Publius Rupilius

131, the year of the consuls Lucius Valerius Flaccus and Publius Licinius Crassus Dives Mucianus

Revolt of Salvius (Second Sicilian Slave War)

106, the year of the consuls Quintus Servilius Caepio and Caius Atilius Serranus

105, the year of the consuls Cnaeus Maximus and Publius Rutilius Rufus

104, the year of the consuls Caius Flavius Fimbria and Caius Marius (II)

103, the year of the consuls Lucius Aurelius Orestis and Caius Marius (III)

102, the year of the consuls Quintus Lutatius Catulus and Caius Marius (IV)

101, the year of the consuls Caius Marius (V) and Manius Aquillius

Abbreviations and Notes

Below is a list of the full titles of the ancient works referenced and their modern short codes.

Aug. Civ.	–	Augustine of Hippo, *Civitate Dei*
Cic. Leg.	–	Cicero, *On Laws*
Cic. Nat. D.	–	Cicero, *On the Nature of the Gods*
Cic. Verr.	–	Cicero, *Against Verres*
D.S.	–	Diodorus Siculus, *Library of History*
Flor.	–	Florus, *Epitome of Roman History*
Hom. Od.	–	Homer, *Odyssey*
Liv.	–	Livy, *History of Rome*
Obseq.	–	Iulius Obsequens, *Book of Prodigies*
Oros.	–	Orosius, *Seven Books against the Pagans*
Ov., *Metamorphōseōn librī*	–	Ovid, *Metamorphoses*
Plb.	–	Polybius, *Histories*
Strab.	–	Strabo, *Geography*
Thuc.	–	Thucydides, *The Peloponnesian War*

Latin inscriptions

CIL, *Corpus Inscriptionum Latinarum*

ILLREP, *Inscriptiones Latinae Liberae Res Publicae*

ILS, *Inscriptiones Latinae Selectae*

Greek Inscriptions

IG, *Inscriptiones Grecae*

Notes

Preface

1. So called from the Latin noun *socius*, "ally", and the plural *socii*.

Chapter 1: The Slave Trade

1. Str. XIV, 5, 2. Strabo says that the exportation of slaves was most profitable, inducing many people to engage in their 'evil business'; not only because the victims of this trade were easily captured, but also because the market, large and rich, was not far away. He refers to Delos, where, he says, 'they could both admit and send away ten thousand slaves on the same day; whence arose the proverb, "Merchant, sail in, unload your ship, everything has been sold."'

2. Andreau, J. and Descat, R., 2009, *Gli schiavi nel mondo greco e romano*, Il Mulino, Bologna, p.84 (tit. or. *Esclave en Grèce et a Rome*, Paris, Hachette, 2006).

3. Side, soon after its foundation, entered the orbit of Lydia. When, in 333, it was occupied by Alexander the Great, it was a Persian possession. After the disintegration of the Macedonian Empire, it became part of the dominions of the Ptolomeians, then passed under the Seleucids. The Peace of Apamea, in putting an end to the Roman-Syriac War, made Antiochus III yield to the victors (Rome, Pergamon and Rhodes) Anatolia west of the Taurus. At that time Pamphylia was included among the provinces annexed by the Romans to the dominions of Eumenes of Pergamum. Afterwards Side became the chief centre and slave mart of the Pamphylian pirates.

4. Plb. IV, 38.

5. Str. X, 2, 2.

6. 1 stade = on average 157.7 metres (172.5 yards); 60 stades = 9,462 metres (10,347.77 yards).

7. Str. V, 1, 8, 3-4.

8. A second century inscription, found near the ancient city of Bodrum, Turkey (ancient Halikarnassòs, Caria), speaks of two women kidnapped together with their children by pirates and sold as slaves to Delos. The buyer was an inhabitant of the place, who later released them and ensured an education for their children.

9. Dio, 36, 20, 1, says that pirates always used to harass sailors and those who dwelled on land, and comments that this had always been and always would be, because human nature is what it is, and does not change.

10. Hom., *Od.*, XIV, vv. 1–530.
11. The Strait of the Dardanelles is the 1,250-metres wide and 10km long arm of the sea that joins the Aegean Sea to the Sea of Màrmara. It is the physical border between Europe and Asia, together with the Bosphorus Strait. Along the coasts of that bottleneck arise several cities. On the European shore: Eleunte, Maidos, Sestòs and Lysimácheia. On the Asian bank: Troy/Ilion (Ilium, Hissarlik), Dardania (Çanakkale), Abydos (Nara Burnu), etc..
12. Plut. *Cimon*, 8.3 reports that the inhabitants of Scyros (Skyros) have practiced piracy on the high seas since ancient times, and do not even spare foreigners who land in the ports of the island and trade with them: for example, they have plundered and imprisoned a group of merchants coming from Thessaly, while they were at anchor off the coast of Ctesium.
13. Hdt. VI, 138, 1, records that the Pelasgians, dwelling in Lemnos and desiring vengeance on the Athenians, acquired fifty-oared ships, captured many Athenian women celebrating the festival of Artemis at Brauron, and brought them to Lemnos to make them their concubines.
14. D. S. XX, 82, 5.
15. In the twenty-first century there were no pirates in the Mediterranean, fortunately.
16. Plb. II, 3. 8 says that Teuta gave letters of marque to privateers to pillage any ships they met. A letter of marque is a commission authorising privately owned ships (known as privateers) to capture enemy merchant ships.
17. Ptolemy I Soter, after Alexander's death (323), took possession of the area, and from then Korakesion was under the control of the Ptolemaian dynasty. With the passage of time the port became a refuge for Cilician pirates. It resisted the Seleucid Antiochus III the Great, king of Anatolia, Syria, Mesopotamia and Persia, in 199, but afterwards was loyal to Diodotus Tryphon when he usurped the Seleucid crown (142–138). Diodotus began work to reinforce the fortress and the port that his rival Antiochus VII Sidetes had completed in 137.
18. The Cilician piracy also managed to interfere in the main conflicts within Italy, between the last decades of the second century and the beginning of the following century, always in support of the enemies of Rome. Cilicians like Kleon and Athenion appeared alongside the rebels in the Sicilian Slave Wars. The Romans also fought against the Cilician pirates in 102, with Marcus Antonius the Orator. During the

Social War (91–89), the Cilician chief-pirate Agamemnon forced the naval blockade that had been established by the navy of Rome before the coast of Italy. In 84, Lucius Licinius Murena reported victories against pirates. In 81 and later, other Cilician pirates operated in support of Quintus Sertorius from the naval base of Dianio in Spain. However, the Romans, despite their victories over the pirates, had failed to eradicate this malady. This aligns in the east as in the west of the Mediterranean, and was a phenomenon that was extremely damaging to the interests of Rome.

19. G. Wolf, 2014, *Rome, history of an empire*, Einaudi, Turin, p.99, remembers how: 'Already at the beginning of the 2nd century, thanks to the Balkan wars, Rome found itself in possession of numerous slave labour. The agreement between the Romans and their allies of the time, the Aetolians is well known: to these the last cities and conquered territories would have gone, while the Romans would have had the booty and the population taken captive. From then on, prisoners of war remained one of the main items of booty in the most important military campaigns.' Wolf refers to IG X 2.1.141, in which J. Bartels, 2008, *Städtische Eliten im römischen Makedonien: Untersuchungen zur Formierung und Struktur*, Berlin, pp.207–212, recognized an *invitatio ad munera* which presented a revised text. See also Chaniotis, A., Corsten, T., Papazarkadas, N. and Tybout, R.A., *SEG* 60–659. *Thessalonike. Invitatio ad munera, ca. 226–229 AD*, in *'Supplementum Epigraphicum Graecum'*, Current editors A. T. N. R.A. Chaniotis Corsten Papazarkadas Tybout. http://dx.doi.org/10.1163/1874-6772_seg_a60_659

20. Plb. XXX, 15.1. / Str. VII.7.3 / Liv. XLV, 34.

Chapter 2: First Uprisings

1. *Magna Graecia* is what the Greeks called *Megàle Hellàs*. The expression was first used by Timaeus (third century) to signify that the whole of the territories colonized by the Greeks in Italy far exceeded the small and overcrowded homeland. Polybius (second century), however, believed that the expression identified the distribution area of Pythagoreanism, the philosophical current that, at the end of the fourth century, had exalted the cultural and mercantile grandeur of some Italiote foundations. This influenced the idea that the Romans had of *Megàle Hellàs*. In fact, for the Romans, the expression *Magna Graecia* did not include Sicily and Puglia. Even Pliny (first century AD) meant only the stretch of coast from Metaponto to Locri. Servius (fourth

century AD), however, extended the meaning of the term to all the coast of southern Italy between Taranto and Cuma.

2. Oros., IV, 7, 12, says that 3,000 slaves and 4,000 '*navalium sociorum*' had planned a massacre in Rome, and that if the conspiracy had not been discovered, the city would have perished.

3. Zon. VIII, 11, 6–7; VIII, 11, 8–9; VIII, 11, 7–12.

4. Liv. XXII, 33, reports that a Carthaginian spy, who had worked secretly for two years, had his hands cut off and that twenty-five slaves were crucified for having conspired in Campo Marzio, and that the informer was granted freedom and 20,000 acres as further reward. Vd. Anche Zon. IX, 1, 1.

5. Capozza M., 1967, *Movimenti servili nel mondo romano in età repubblicana, I. Dal 501 al 184 a. Cr.*, L'Erma di Bretschneider, Roma, pp.95–100.

6. Setia, Norba and Circeii are all located in the province of Latina, in the region of Lazio. Each of them was a colony of Latin law, formed by Romans and Latins, and an autonomous community. The colonists lost their original citizenship and became citizens of the new foundation. When, in 338, Rome established its domination over Lazio, it maintained for seven of the old colonies (Circeii, Ardea, Nepet, Norba, Setia, Signia and Sutrium) the title and status of Latin colonies, communities technically non-Roman, but strictly linked to Rome.

7. Liv. XXXII, 26 (see later note 31). Vd. Anche Zon. IX, 16, 6.

8. For the actions of the two servants and the intervention of the praetor: Liv. XXXII, 26, 9–13. See also Liv. XXXII, 32, 26, 14, and Liv. XXXII, 32, 26, 16.

9. According to Zon. IX, 16.6, Setia was to be conquered, with great slaughter of its inhabitants by the Carthaginian hostages, their servants and slaves, ex-prisoners of war.

10. Str. V, 3, 11. It was in one of the tunnels cited that Marius the Younger perished, when he was besieged by Sulla during the Civil War.

11. Both the episodes are reported in Liv. XXXII, 26.

12. Liv. XXXIII, 36,1–3.

13. Liv. XXXIX, 29, 8–10 reports that the praetor Lucius Postumius intervened militarily in the province of Taranto to repress a serious conspiration of slave-shepherds. About 7,000 people had been condemned and many executed. Others escaped. See also Liv. XLI, 6–7.

14. The primary sources on the repression of the Bacchanalia scandal are: Liv. XXV.1, Liv. XXXIX.8–19 e XLI, Liv. XL.19, Cic. *Leg.*, 2, 37 and Aug. *Civ.*, 6, 9. For the competence of the Senate of Rome to intervene

in all crimes committed in Italy that required a public inquiry, such as treason, conspiracy, poisoning or wilful murder: Plb. 6, 13.

15. Cic. *Nat. D.*, II, 62.
16. Commonly known as the 'repression of Bacchanalia', the episode is reported with ample details in Liv. XXXIX, 14–18. A copy of the decree of the Senate of Rome with which Bacchanalia was banned throughout Italy was found in 1640 AD in Tiriolo, in the province of Catanzaro: *senatus consultum de bacchanalibus* – CIL, I (2), 581=IL, 18=*Inscriptiones Latinae Liberae rei publicae*, 511.
17. Finley M. I., 1981, *Economy and Society in Ancient Greece*, Chatto and Windus, London, ch. 5.
18. Andreau J. and Descat R., 2011, *The Slave in Greece and Rome*, The University of Wisconsin Press, Madison (originally published in France as *Esclave en Grèce et à Rome*, Hachette Littératures, 2006), p.145.

Chapter 3: A Large Triangle-Shaped Island

1. Ephorus of Cyme in Fr. 135 Kakoby. The perimeter of the island measures 1,152km. Str. VI, 2, 1 says 4,400 stadiums. He wrote in Greek, and in Greece the Roman *stadium*, of which the length was 185 metres, corresponded to the Attic *stadion*, which measured an average of 177 metres (this measure changed according to the city-state, but remained between 150 and 300 metres). 4,400 Roman stadiums are equivalent to 814km. But the esteemed Strabo is wrong, the exact perimeter of Sicily being greater at 1,152km. The surface of the island is 25,708km².
2. The Greeks called Sicily Trinacria because of its shape (in Greek, *thrìa* means three and *akrōn* extremity). They modified this name as 'Trinachia' (Str. VI, 2, 1). Sometimes Trinacria is confused with *Triquetra*. It is good to clarify that these names are not synonymous. Triquetra, in fact, is not a Greek toponym, but a Celtic symbol. It derives from the Latin adjective *triquetrus*, 'three-cornered'. This symbol is similar to another, *triskelion*, or *triskele*. A triskelion is the head of a Gorgon, whose hair is snakes, from which three legs are spread, bent at the knee. This symbol was introduced in Sicily by Greeks, and identified Sicily at the institutional political level. It is one of the constituent elements of the emblem of the Sicilian region: a triskelion is placed in the middle of the yellow and red flag of Sicily.
3. Pindar, *Pythian Ode* 1, 19–25. English translation (Perseus Project): http://www.perseus.tufts.edu/hopper/text.jsp?doc=Perseus:text:

1999.01.0162:book=P. Greek text of Pythian Ode 1 with word-by-word translation (Perseus Project): http://www.perseus.tufts.edu/hopper/text.jsp?doc=Perseus:text:1999.01.0161:book=P.

4. Str. VI, 2, 3.

5. A number of small archipelagos – Aeolian, Aegadian, Pelagian – and single islands – Ustica, Pantelleria – surround Sicily. Except the Aegadians, their origin is volcanic, therefore dark and arid. The Egadians, instead, are calcareous, tuffaceous or sedimentary, with abundant spring water, so they are white.

6. The description of Sicily from here refers to the second half of the second century.

7. D. S. V, 2, 1. The island in ancient times was called, after its shape, Trinacria, then Sicania after the Sicani who were established there, and finally was given the name Sicily after the Sicels, who came from Italy.

8. The Sicani emigrated to Sicily because the Umbrian and Sabine tribes had driven them out of Central Italy.

9. Eighteen years before the Trojan War, the Ligurians of King Siculus arrived in Sicily, having been driven out of their land by the Umbrians and the Pelasgians, and from that moment Sicily was so called.

10. According to Thucydides, the Greek historian who lived in the fifth century, the place of origin of the Elymians was Troy, the Anatolian city described by Homer in his *Illiad*. Some Trojans fleeing from their burning city landed on Sicily, where they built two cities – Eryx and Egesta – and mixed with the Sicans, founding the *ethnos* of the Elymians. Hellanicus, another Greek historian from the fifth century, reports instead that the Elymians came from mainland Italy. These traditions are complementary, since one navigational route from the East to Sicily has always been the 'northern one', stopping off on the Italian coast.

11. The Hellenistic world extended east up to Central Asia and south as far as Egypt and the Libyan coast.

Chapter 4: From the Phoenicians to the Romans

1. D. S. V, 35, 1–5. The Phoenicians were the first to exploit metals in Iberia. They obtained great riches by bringing silver to Greece, Asia and other lands. As they had practised these businesses for a long time, they were enriched and founded numerous colonies, some in Sicily in the neighbouring islands, others in Libya, Sardinia and the Iberian peninsula.

2. Tucid. VI, 2, 6.The Phoenicians occupied the coastal promontories all around Sicily and the small islands near the coast to promote their trade with the Sicels. When the Greeks began to arrive in large numbers by sea, they left the majority of their positions, gathered together and occupied Mtw, Zyz and Kfr, all near the Elymians, because they had confidence in the Elymians and Sicily was near to Carthage.

3. D. S. XXII, 10.

4. D. S., V, 9, 1–3. Cnidus and Rhodes, to escape the heavy yoke imposed by the kings of Asia, decided to send a colony overseas at the time of the fiftieth Olympiad. They chose as their chief Pentathlus of Cnidus. Pentathlus and his men sailed to the vicinity of Capo Lilibeo in Sicily. They found that the inhabitants of Segesta and Selinus were at war with each other, and allied with the Selinuntines. They lost many men in a battle, including Pentathlus.

5. The Greek historian Thucydides dedicated two chapters of his *Peloponnesian War* to the Sicilian Expedition of Athens in Sicily.

6. The foreign policy of Rome was marked by territorial expansion, so it was imperialistic. The Senate and the consuls believed that a continuous expansion of the Roman state and the domination of Rome over other peoples were a priority objective, to be pursued by any means and at any price, if necessary curbing the rights of others and even eliminating physically anyone who opposed it to defend their rights. Historically, this policy had been justified in several ways. In the beginning, it was a response to the need to defend itself from hostile neighbours, therefore as a result was imposed on the government regardless of its will – perhaps even against its will – and was dictated by the concomitant and converging action of many factors. Soon it had turned into a deliberately aggressive and predatory policy, and a strategy of preventive war, to eliminate or subdue those neighbours who represented a danger or could represent it; perhaps, in some cases, to justify some achievements already made for economic, political or military reasons. Finally, it had led to the conviction that the boundary of the security of the state should always be moved further, due to the impact of economic factors on political choices, with particular reference to the pressure exerted on the governing bodies by financial groups and their supporters, in direction of an expansionist policy that considered war an instrument of exploitation and accumulation of wealth. To justify the 'just wars' of Rome, 'defensive' reasons had

been adduced, which in fact masked the economic reasons behind the conflicts. Undoubtedly Roman imperialism had arisen from the insatiable appetite of wealthy patricians and plebeians, who, in order to increase their already conspicuous wealth, did not hesitate to resort to war even when it was not strictly necessary. It was therefore functional to the further enrichment of the more affluent Romans.

7. Plb. I, 15, 1–9. Polybius cites Philinus, who reports that the Carthaginians and Syracusans were besieging Messene, when the Romans, coming from the sea, marched out against the Syracusans. The Romans were severely handled and returned to Messene. Later, the Romans attacked the Carthaginians, but were worsted and lost a considerable number of prisoners. Hiero, after the fighting, ordered the burning of his camp and fled to Syracuse, and withdrew his garrisons from all the forts which menaced the territory of Messene. The Carthaginians, after the battle, quit their camp and distributed themselves among the towns. The Romans followed up the enemy, laid waste the territory of the Carthaginians and Syracusans, and besieged Syracuse. According to Polybius, this account is full of inconsistencies and he explains why.

8. Plb I, 15, 10. But the latter is true; for as a fact the Carthaginians and Syracusans abandoned the open country, and the Romans at once began to lay siege to Syracuse and, as he says, even to Echetla too, which lies between the Syracusan and Carthaginian provinces.

9. D. S. XXIII, 3. / D.S. XXIII, 1.

10. During and after the Second Punic War (218–202), Rome confiscated many lands of entire communities in the territories of the Latins and those of the Italics to punish them for having betrayed it and joining Hannibal. Moreover, over the next fifty years, Rome had fought and won many other wars, both inside and outside the Italian peninsula, gradually increasing its territorial possessions. This meant that the *ager publicus* would grow enormously. In the second half of the second century it covered about 55,000km^2, of which about 37,000 was located in Italy. The surface of Italy is about 302,000km^2, so the *ager publicus* was about 8 per cent of this. The *ager publicus* in Sicily was very extensive, and was managed in the same way as that in Italy, North Africa, Spain, Istria, Dalmatia and Greece. A part of it was, for example, represented by a large part of the territory already owned by individual citizens and by the community of Leontinoi, a Greek city north of Syracuse.

Chapter 5: A Vibrant Urban Life

1. Plin. *Nat. Hist.* III, 14 [In this island there are five colonies and sixty-three cities or states.]. Pliny the Elder (23–79 AD) wrote the passage we have just reported over 100 years after the First Sicilian Slave War, but the general situation could not have changed much in the meantime.

2. As for place names, as we noted already, the name indicated first is the original. The names in brackets are those attributed subsequently to the same place, including the modern one.

3. Greek archaeologists discovered jewellery, dozens of coins and remnants of a housing settlement close to the village of Chiliomodi in Greece's southern Peloponnese region. These affirmed the location of the ancient city of Tenea, thought to have been founded in the twelfth or thirteenth century by Trojans who were taken prisoner by Agamemnon, king of nearby Mycenae.

4. The story of Ducetius was told by the Greek historian Diodorus Siculus in the first century, who drew on the work of Timaeus.

5. The Latin adjective *punicus* derives from the Latin *poenus*, in the plural *poeni*, the term with which the Romans collectively called the Carthaginians.

6. The River Platani (ancient Halykos) flows into the Strait of Sicily, near Capo Bianco, between Agrigento (ancient Akragas) and Cattolica Eraclea (Eraclea Minoa).

7. Herod. VI, 156.

8. Thucid. VI, 75, 1.

9. Plb. 7, 6. The city of Leontini faces north. In a flat valley there were the government offices, the courts and the agora. The valley is flanked on either side by a ridge, above which was a plateau full of houses and temples. The city had two gateways, which open towards Syracuse and the *Piana di Catania*. Below a ridge that borders the valley on the west side flows the River Lissus, and parallel to it, just below the rocky wall, was a row of houses.

10. D. S. XIV, 58.1.

11. It has been lapped several times by lava flows over the centuries.

12. In this case, and in similar cases cited later, the first name is that of the indigenous settlement, previous to the arrival of the Greek colonists, while the third is that of the Roman city. The indigenous settlement of Messina was Sicel.

13. Str. VI, 3.

14. On the basis of what the lawmaker Diocles of Syracuse reported, Diodorus Siculus narrates the episode as follows: 1. It remains for us to speak of the death of Charondas, in connection with which a peculiar and unexpected thing happened to him. He had set out to the country carrying a dagger because of the robbers, and on his return the Assembly was in session and the commons in an uproar, whereupon he approached it because he was curious about the matter in dispute. 2. But he had made a law that no man should enter the Assembly carrying a weapon, and since he had forgotten he was carrying the dagger at his side, he provided certain of his enemies with an occasion to bring an accusation against him. And when one of them said, 'You have annulled your own law,' he replied, 'Not so, by Zeus, I will uphold it,' and drawing the dagger he slew himself. Some historians, however, attribute this act to Diocles, the lawgiver of the Syracusans. (D.S. XII, 19) It is interesting to note that Diodorus Siculus reports a similar death of the Locrian lawmaker. D. S. XIII, 33, 2 [2. After the termination of the war Diocles set up the laws for the Syracusans, and it came to pass that this man experienced a strange reversal of fortune. For having become implacable in fixing penalties and severe in punishing offenders, he wrote in the laws that, if any man should appear in the market-place carrying a weapon, the punishment should be death, and he made no allowance for either ignorance or any other circumstance. 3. And when word had been received that enemies were in the land, he set forth carrying a sword; but since sudden civil strife had arisen and there was uproar in the market-place, he thoughtlessly entered the market-place with the sword. And when one of the ordinary citizens, noticing this, said that he himself was annulling his own laws, he cried out, 'Not so, by Zeus, I will even uphold them.' And drawing the sword he slew himself.]

15. The Romans set up at Naxos a station for changing horses on the route between Messana and Syracuse. It is likely this happened after the events narrated in this book. Strabo (60 BC–AD 21/24) says that in his time the city had disappeared, as well as Megara Hyblaea: Str. VI, 2, 97–99 (The cities along the Sicilian side of the Strait are, first, Messene, and then Tauromenium, Catana, and Syracuse; Naxus and Megara, which were between Catana and Syracuse, have disappeared; on this coast have their mouth, with good harbours, the Symaethus and all rivers that flow down from Aetna.)

16. Paternò I., Principe di Biscari, 1781, *Viaggio per tutte le antichità della Sicilia*, Napoli.

17. Goethe (von) J.W., 2017, *Travel in Italy*, Mondadori, Milan. Johann Wolfgang Goethe, the famous German scholar and traveller, was in Sicily during his Grand Tour in Italy, coming from Naples, from 2 April to 17 May 1787 AD. From 2–17 April he was in Palermo (on 9 April in Bagheria, 10 April in Monreale), 18–19 Aprilin Alcamo, 20 April in Segesta, 21 April in Castelvetrano, 22 April in Sciacca, 23–27 April in Agrigento, 28 April in Caltanissetta, 29 April in Castrogiovanni, 2–3 May in Catania, 4 May in Aci Castello, 5 May on Etna, 7 May in Taormina, 10–13 May in Messina, and between 13 and 17 May returned by ship to Naples.

18. *Idem.*

19. The first name is that of the Phoenician/Punic settlement.

20. Liv. XXI, 49–50.

21. Thucid. VI, 4, 3–4 [3. Gela was built in the forty-fifth year after Syracuse, by Antiphemus, who brought a colony out of Rhodes, and by Entymus, that did the like out of Crete, jointly. This city was named after the river Gela; and the place where now the city standeth, and which at first they walled in, was called Lindii. 4. And the laws which they established were the Doric.]

22. In 131, Eraclea Minoa was refounded as a Roman colony and repopulated by the praetor Publius Rupilius.

23. For the history and archaeology of Gelas: Panvini R., 1996, *Gelas. Storia e archeologia dell'antica Gela*, SEI, Torino.

24. Henna was later conquered by the Mamertines, but thanks to the Corinthian Timoleon, who had killed the tyrant of Syracuse, regained its freedom, which was, however, lost again under Agathocles. While the latter was fighting in Africa against the Carthaginians, the city-state of Akragas began to dominate Sicily. Once Akragas surrendered, Henna regained its freedom. After the murder of Tiberius Sempronius Gracchus in 133, the Senate of Rome sent a delegation of ten members to the Sanctuary of Ceres in Henna.

25. Cic. *Verr.* II, IV, 108, describes the centre of the cult of Ceres in Henna as a '*pulcherrimum et magnificentissimum templum*' (very beautiful and magnificent temple), and adds that '*nec solum Siculi, verum etiam ceterae gentes nationesque Hennensem Cererem maxime colunt*' (it is revered and made a pilgrimage destination not only by the Sicels, but also by all other peoples and nations).

26. Liv. XXIV, 37–39.

27. Procelli E., 1989, *Aspetti e problemi dell'ellenizzazionecalcidese nella Sicilia orientale*, in '*Melanges de l'Ecole française de Rome (Antiquité)*',

pp.679–89. Sjoeqvist E., 1962, *I Greci a Morgantina*, in '*Kokalos*', pp.52–68.

Chapter 6: Grain, Slaves and Banditry

1. D.S. 34–35, 2, 1 [When the affairs of Sicily, after the overthrow of Carthage, had remained successful and prosperous for the space of sixty years, at length war with the slaves broke out for the following reasons. The Sicilians, through the enjoyment of a long peace, grew very rich, and bought up an abundance of slaves; who being driven in droves like so many herds of cattle from the different places where they were bred and brought up, were branded with certain marks burnt on their bodies.] The flourishing urban revival between the reigns of the Syracusan autocrats Timoleon and Hiero, dating around the end of the fourth and the third century, was said to have been followed by a progressive decline under Roman rule. That is not correct. Roman Sicily provides a highly differentiated picture of change as well as shifting traditions, concepts, mentalities and perceptions. This was shown by the monumentalization of many cities, which occurred from the second century onwards and reflected a considerable vitality of civic life.

2. The large estates considered were a very extensive land unit, or a set of properties brought together in the hands of a single tenant, consisting of large farms, having a composite and diversified structure, with a rustic villa, vineyards, gardens, livestock and farms. The Romans called them *latifundia*, in the singular *latifundium*.

3. The land owned by the Roman people. It was economically exploited in various ways, one of which was the establishment of leases.

4. The *confarreatio* was the religious rite with which they celebrated the archaic Roman wedding, a tradition that was traced back to the legendary Romulus, the founder and first king of Rome. It was officiated only on the occasion of the marriage of patricians and was characterized by the spreading of a batter made of spelt flour on the immolated victim and a cake, also made of spelt, among the *nubendi* (those about to marry), in front of the altar.

5. It seems likely that, in the middle of the first century, Rome already had well over 500,000 inhabitants. That would remain the number of inhabitants of the city up to the Principate. Later, the number of inhabitants of Rome would have grown, since the Aurelian Walls – built in the second half of the third century AD – enclosed 1,370 hectares

and left many suburbs unprotected. In the fourth century AD there would have been 1,200,000. Gibbon, E., 1849, *The decline and fall of the Roman Empire*, 1st ed., p.1,126.

6. Between a minimum of 200,000 and a maximum of 400,000 tons in the Imperial period. For the lower limit of this estimate: Garnsey, P., 1983, 'Grain for Rome', in Garnsey, P., Hopkins, K. and Whittaker, R., (eds.), *Trade in Ancient Economy*, London, pp.126–28. For the upper limit: Casson, L., 1980, 'The Role of the State in Rome's Grain Trade', in D'Arms, J.H. and Kopff, E.C. (eds.), *The Seaborne Commerce: Studies in Archaeology and History*, Roma, pp.21–33.

7. Gianfrotta, P.A., 1989, 'Le vie di comunicazione', in AA.VV., *Storia di Roma, 4. Caratteri e morfologie*, Giulio Einaudi Editore, Torino, pp.301–19, v. in part. p.315.

8. Mocchegiani Carpano, C., 1984, 'Il Tevere: archeologia e commercio', in '*BNum*'2.2, pp.21–81. Castagnoli, F., 1980, 'Installazioni portuali a Roma', in '*MAAR*', XXXVI, pp.35–42. Cressedi, G., 1949–51, *I porti fluviali in Roma antica*, in De Dominicis M., 1924, *La 'statio annonae urbis Romae'*, in '*Bullettino della Commissione Archeologica di Roma*' LII, pp.135–49.

9. Pisani Sertorio, G., Colini, A.M., Bozzetti, C., 1986, *Portus Tiberinus*, in *Il Tevere e le altre vie d'acqua del Lazio antico*, in '*Archeologia Laziale*', VII, 2 (QCAEI 12), pp.157–97.

10. Coarelli, F., 1988, *Il Foro Boario dalle origini alla fine della Repubblica*, Roma. Hulsen, C., 1896, *Il foro Boario e le sue adiacenze nell'antichità*, in '*Dissertazioni della Pontificia Accademia romana di archeologia*', 2, II, pp.175–248.

11. Coarelli, F., 1968, *Navalia, Tarentum e la topografia del campo Marzio meridionale*, in '*Quaderni dell' Istituto di topografia antica dell' Università di Roma*' 5, pp.27–37.

12. Gatti, G., 1936, *L'arginatura del Tevere a Marmorata (un manoscritto inedito del P. Luigi M. Bruzza)*, in '*Bullettino della Commissione Archeologica di Roma*' LXIV, pp.55–82. Colini, A.M., 1938, *Deposito di marmi presso il Tevere*, in '*Bullettino della Commissione Archeologica di Roma*', pp.299–300.

13. Colini, A.M., 1980, '*Il porto fluviale del Foro Boario a Roma*', in '*MAAR*' XXXVI, pp.43–53.

14. Gatti, G., 1934, '*Saepta Iulia' e 'Porticus Aemilia' nella 'Forma' Severiana*, in '*BullCom*', pp.123–49.

15. In the beginning the complex was called Horrea Sulpicia, later it was renamed Horrea Galbana. To remember his builder, Servius Sulpicius Galba, consul in 108, placed his grave right in front of the complex.

16. Some scholars have raised the problem of whether the term Syrian, used by Diodorus Siculus in Book XXXIV of his *Library of the Ancient World*, was interchangeable with Assyrian (because 'the same dialect still exists on both sides of the Euphrates' – Str. 2.1. 31) as well as with people from anywhere in the Syrio-Palestine region: Dickie, M.W., 2001, *Magic and Magicians in the Graeco-Roman World*, London, p.101; Millar, F., 1993, *The Roman Near East 31 BC–AD 337*, Cambridge, pp.227, 454–55; Steel, C., 2001, *Cicero, Rhetoric and Empire*, Oxford, p.50

17. Shaw, B.D., 2001, *Spartacus and the Slave Wars: A Brief History with Documents*, Boston, p.9. For those enslaved between 262 and 133: Toynbee, A.I., 1965, *Hannibal's Legacy*, Vol. 2, London, pp.171–73.

18. *Cfr.* Hunt, P., 2018, *Ancient Greek and Roman Slavery*, Wiley Blackwell, pp.169–70.

19. According to Verbrugghe, G.P., 1974, *Slave rebellion or Sicily in revolt?*, in '*Kokalos*' 20, pp.46–60, see in part pp.51–52, not only were there large numbers of Syrian slaves on the market, but the Sicilian land-owners also favoured these slaves over any other.

20. Diodorus of Sicily reports that the maladministration of the province was due to equestrian control of the courts. This is an error, an anachronism based on confusion with the Second Slave War. In the 130s the equites didn't yet have control of the courts. They gained it under the tribunates of Caius Sempronius Gracchus (123–122).

21. The state of insecurity in the countryside and the inertia of the Roman authorities with regard to the crimes accomplished by slaves by instigation or by order of their masters, if the latter were large estate owners, were included in D.S. XXXIV, 28–31.

Chapter 7: The Insurgency of Henna

1. Today Asi Nehri.
2. For this news: Le Bohec, 2018, *Spartaco, signore della guerra*, Carocci Editore, Roma, p.83.
3. Dumont, J.-Ch., 1987, *Servus. Rome et l'esclavage sous la Republique*, Ecole Française de Rome, Rome.

4. The Capitolium was one of the two summits of the Campidoglio hill in Rome. The other summit was called Arx.

5. D. S. XXXIV, 34–38 [34 There was one Damophilus of Enna, who was wealthy, but very proud and arrogant; this man cultivated a large area of land, had a vast stock of cattle, and imitated the luxury and cruelty of the Italians towards their slaves. He traversed the country up and down, travelling in a coach drawn by stately horses, and guarded by a company of armed slaves; he likewise always carried about with him many beautiful boys, flatterers and parasites. 35 In the city and in the villages he had finely engraved silver vessels, and all sorts of purple carpets of very great value; and he held magnificent feasts and entertainments, rivalling the state and grandeur of a king; in pomp and expense he far surpassed the luxury of the Persians, and his pride and arrogance were excessive. He was uncouth, and brought up without learning, or any liberal education; and having heaped up a great deal of wealth, he abandoned himself to self-indulgent licentiousness. At first this fullness and plenty made him insolent; and at length he was a plague to himself, and the occasion of bringing many miseries and calamities upon his country. 36 For having bought many slaves, he abused them in the highest degree; and those that were free born in their own country, and taken captives in war, he branded on their cheeks with the sharp points of iron pins. Some of these he bound in fetters and put in slave pens; and to others that were ordered to look after the cattle in the fields, he allowed neither clothing nor food sufficient to satisfy nature. 37 The barbarity and cruelty of this Damophilus was such, that never a day passed without him scourging his slaves, without the least cause or occasion. And his wife Megallis was as cruel as himself, towards the maid servants, and other slaves that fell into her hands. Therefore his slaves, being provoked by this cruelty of their master and mistress, concluded that nothing could bring them into a worse condition than they already were; [and they suddenly rose up in revolt]. 38 Some naked slaves once went to Damophilus of Enna and complained that they did not have clothes; but he did not listen to their complaints. 'What then,' he said to them, 'do the travellers in the countryside walk naked along the roads, so that you can not take the clothes off them?' He then attached them to pillars, beat them cruelly, and haughtily dismissed them.]

6. *The Bible, Sirach*, 25: '16. The wickedness of a woman will add to its appearance, make it a dark face like that of a bear.'

7. The year of Eunus' uprising is uncertain. Some historians speak of 138, others of 136 or even 135. For the date of 136: Kovaliov, S.I., 2011, *Storia di Roma – I. La Repubblica*, P. Greco Edizioni, Milano (tit. orig.: *Istoria Rima*), p.340.
8. D. S. XXXIV, 11–12.
9. D. S., XXXIV, 41.
10. Vogt, J., 2013, *L'uomo e lo schiavo nel mondo antico*, Res Gestae, Milano (tit. orig.: *Sklavesci und Humanitat*), p.56.
11. D. S., XXXIV, 13–14.
12. D. S., XXXIV, 15.
13. D. S., XXXIV, 39.
14. D. S., XXXIV, 16 [And Eunus himself killed his own master Antigenes and Phyton.]
15. D. S., XXXIV, 15 [When he had therefore been made general, with absolute power to order and dispose of all things as he pleased, an assembly was called, and he put all the prisoners from Enna to death except those that were skilful in making of weapons, whom he fettered and set to work.]

Chapter 8: The Birth of a Kingdom

1. D. S., XXXIV, 14.
2. D. S., XXXIV, 24 [This Eunus king of the robbers called himself Antiochus and all his followers Syrians.]
3. From all this it is possible to deduce that the insurgence of Henna would be considered a nationalistic uprising of Syrian slaves held in Sicily, possibly influenced by the Maccabean war of liberation, in which also the cult of Atargatis would have played a role. Vogt, J., 1965, *Sklaverei und Humanität: Studien zur antiken Sklaverei und ihrer Erforschung*, Wiesbaden, pp.29–30 & pp.40–43.
4. Ando, C., 2011, *Law, Language, and Empire in the Roman Tradition*, University of Pennsylvania Press, p.29.
5. Vogt, J., 2013, *L'uomo e lo schiavo nel mondo antico*, Res Gestae, Milano, p.40, where Atargatis is called Sira (tit. orig.: 1965, *Sklaverei und Humanität: Studien zur antiken Sklaverei und ihrer Erforschung*, Wiesbaden; in English: 1974, *Ancient Slavery and the Ideal of Man*, Oxford). *Contra* Merton, P., p.42, who notes that 'the coinage of King Antiochus does not contain any features that would link him or his kingdom to Seleucid practices apart from his name and the title

basileus, indeed he depicts himself through his coinage as positively Sicilian'.

6. Kunz, H., 2006, *Sicilia: Religionsgeschichte des römischen Sizilien*, Tübingen, pp.329–48, notes that the cult of Atargatis had a fundamental role in uniting the insurgents and building Eunus' kingship.

7. Vogt, J., 2013, *L'uomo e lo schiavo nel mondo antico*, Res Gestae, Milano, p.68, where Atargatis is called Sira (tit. orig.: 1965, *Sklaverei und Humanität: Studien zur antiken Sklaverei und ihrer Erforschung*, Wiesbaden; in English: 1974, *Ancient Slavery and the Ideal of Man*, Oxford).

8. D. S., XXXIV, 22.

9. In Roman Sicily, the circulation of coinage was carried out by five main mints: Syracuse, Messina, Morgantina, Catana and Rome. The minor, local mints did not play any significant part. Nothing is said about the institution of a mint in Enna in book XXXIV of the *Historical Library* of Diodorus Siculus, but this is evident from the discovery in Sicily of many coins attributed to the reign of '*basileus Antiochos*'.

10. A gold coin showing a long-haired god or ruler, of 8.58 grams, allegedly excavated near the town of Morgantina in Sicily. It bears the inscription ΦΙΛΙΠΠΕΙΟΝ, which seems ineffective, but may have been chosen to confer legitimacy on gold. Berk, H.J. & Bendall, S., 1994, *Eunus/Antiochus: Slave Revolt in Sicily*, in '*The Celator*' 8, Number 2, p.6 ss., reported in Gorny & Mosch Auktionskatalog 207, p.28, published at https://issuu.com/gorny_und_mosch/docs/gm_auktion_207_katalog. It has been suggested that it was struck by Eunus and shows him as King Antiochus. Peter Morton and Keith Rutter, however, suggest it is forgery. For an in-depth analysis of the monetary issues of *basileus Antìochos*: Merton, P., *Refiguring the Sicilian Slave Wars: from Servile Unrest to Civic Disquiet and Social Disorder*, Volumes 1 and 2, Phd in Classics, University of Edinburgh, 2012. See in particular Vol. 2, Appendices 1–4, pp.205–11.

Chapter 9: King Antiochus' Army and its Commanders.
Looting and Taking Cities. The Joining of Free Proletarians

1. For these considerations: Le Bohec, Y., 2016, *Spartaco, signore della guerra*, Carocci editore, Roma, p.71.

2. D. S., XXXIV, 17 [In the mean time, a Cilician called Cleon instigated another defection of the slaves, and now all were hoping that this unruly rabble would come to blows one with another, and so Sicily would be rid of them through their mutual slaughters and destruction of each other. But contrary to all men's hopes and expectations, they joined forces together. Cleon followed the commands of Eunus in every respect, and served his prince as general, having five thousand of his own soldiers.] D. S., XXXIV, 43 [About the same time another rebellion of the slaves broke out. Cleon, a Cilician from near Mount Taurus, who was inured to robberies from a boy and had been appointed to look after the horses in their pastures in Sicily, used to attack travellers on the highways and committed various heinous murders. This man, hearing of the good fortune of Eunus and his followers, persuaded some of the neighbouring slaves to join with him in a sudden revolt. They overran the city of Agrigentum and all the neighbouring country round about.]

3. For this identification of the poor in the Roman world: Knapp, R., 2013, *Invisible Romans*, Profile Books, London, p.98.

4. Of these armies, outside Greece, only a fraction were of Greek origin, the rest being allied contingents and conscripts from the local population. The lack of manpower was a serious concern for many Hellenistic rulers, for whom a defeat might cripple their manpower base for a generation. Many states had to rely on mercenaries to bulk up their citizen forces. In order to overcome this, these kingdoms set up military colonies, known as *Klerouchoi*, to settle mercenaries and others from Greece. The system allowed for the colonists to be given a plot of land and in return they would provide military service when needed.

Chapter 10: Like a Fire Driven by an Impetuous Wind, the Rebellion Spreads

1. The *Fasti consulares* was a list of consuls known to have held office, from the beginning of the Roman Republic to the latest, including those magistrates who were appointed in place of consuls who died or resigned, called *consul suffectus*, or who superseded consular authority for a limited period, called *dictator*. It was kept and continuously updated by the college of pontiffs.

2. This date is uncertain. See Brennan, T. C., 1993, *The Commanders in the First Sicilian Slave War*, in '*Rivista di Filologia ed Istruzione*

Classica (RFIC)' 121, p.176, for arguments in favour of 135; and Keaveney, A., 1998, *Three Roman chronological problems (141–132 B.C.)*, in '*Klio*' 80, pp.76–80, for arguments in favour of 134. For the praetorship of Hypsaeus: D. S., XXXIV, 17–18 [Thirty days had now passed since the first beginning of this rebellion: and presently the slaves fought a battle with Lucius Hypsaeus, who had come from Rome and commanded eight thousand Sicilians. In this fight the rebels won the day; they were then twenty thousand in number, and very soon afterwards their army increased to two hundred thousand men. And although they fought against the Romans themselves, yet they often came off as conquerors, and were very seldom defeated.]

3. For this chronological reference: D.S., XXXIV, 17 [... Thirty days had now passed since the first beginning of this rebellion.]

4. Florus II, 7. [... *Quin illud quoque ultimum dedecus belli, capta sunt castra praetorum – nec nominare ipsos pudet – castra Manli, Lentuli, Pisonis, Hypsaei. Itaque qui per fugitivarios abstrahi debuisset, praetorios duces profugos proelio ipsi sequebantur.*] gives a list of defeated Roman commanders, but the sequence of changes is not clear. It is equally possible that Lentulus was governor of Sicily in 136 or 135, as a praetor and (or) propraetor after his praetorship; and that Titus Manlius had been in charge the same year or in the previous ones. A tentative reconstruction of such commands has been made by Brennan, T.C., 1993, *The Commanders in the First Sicilian Slave War*, in '*Rivista di Filologia ed Istruzione Classica (RFIC)*' 121, pp.153–84. See also Keaveney, A., 1998, *Three Roman chronological problems (141–132 B.C.)*, in '*Klio*' 80, pp.66–90. In 137, the governor of Sicily was the praetor Titus Manlius. His first successor, (Lucius?) Cornelius Lentulus, was in office in 136 as a praetor, and in 135 as a propraetor. They tried to fight the insurgents, but faced a series of failures.

5. The Celtiberians were the Lobetani, Lusoni, Pelendoni, Berendones, Arevaci, Belli, and Titthi. These hispanics, as the name says, were born from the physical mixing and cultural osmosis of groups of native Iberians and groups of Celtic invaders/immigrants. They had maintained Celtic writing and religion, and shared with the other Celts a tradition of richly ornamented clothing and weapons. Basically, their settlements were small villages scattered around the countryside, fortified and located on hilltops. Some of their settlements were larger and more developed. One of them was Numantia, a proto-urban centre of 4,000–8,000 people which grew next to a crossing of the River

Douro. The Celtiberians were a warrior people, proudly independent. Their fighters were lightly armoured. Mainly they were equipped with a single-edged and slightly curved sword, and heavy throwing spears. They were redoubtable, courageous, ferocious and irreducible, and developed an aptitude for guerrilla warfare.

6. Before 134/133, the Romans had fought against the Celtiberians twice already: from 181–77 (First Celtiberian War) and 154–52 (Second Celtiberian War). In the latter war at least three tribes of Celtiberians were involved: the Titthi, the Belli (towns of Segeda and Nertobriga) and the Arevaci (towns of Numantia, Axinum and Ocilis). The war was won by the consul Marcus Claudius Marcellus. The next consul, Lucius Licinius Lucullus, successor to Claudius Marcellus as governor of Hispania Citerior, attacked the Vaccaei, a hispanic tribe living in the central Douro valley which had not been at war with Rome, with the excuse that they had mistreated the Carpetani, friends and allies of the Romans. In 143 the Celtiberians formed a federation and resumed hostilities against the Romans. The war had dragged on with alternating events. From all evidence, its outcome was linked to the fate of Numantia. It was for this that this was called the Numantine War.

7. D. S., XXXIV, 18 [and presently the slaves fought a battle with Lucius Hypsaeus, who had come from Rome and commanded eight thousand Sicilians. In this fight the rebels won the day; they were then twenty thousand in number, and very soon afterwards their army increased to two hundred thousand men. And although they fought against the Romans themselves, yet they often came off as conquerors, and were very seldom defeated.]

8. Morton, P., 2014, *The Geography of Rebellion: Strategy and Supply in the Two Sicilian Slave Wars*, in '*Bulletin of The Institute of Classical Studies*', volume 57, Issue 1, pp.20–38. See, in particular: I. iii. 135–132 BC: Strategy and Supply.

9. The Sicilian cities were all accessible from the sea and connected to each other by simple mule tracks, even with paved roads. The network of roads favoured the coast, not inland, and was controlled by Agrigentum in the south, Thermae in the north, Castrum Henna in the centre, and either Messana or Tauromenium in the north-east. Two roads had been built by the Romans before the second century, all the others were Greek or Carthaginian. One of them ran from Agrigentum to Thermae, through Castrum Henna; another from

Messana to Lilybaeum; a third from Agyrium to Halaesa, branching
the route from Catana to Castrum Henna. One further road ran from
Agrigentum to Syracuse, or to Catana. Other roads linked Thermae
to Castrum Henna and on to Catana, and Thermae to Messana, going
down to the east coast through Tauromenium and Catana. In addition
there were long coastal routes, and other roads criss-crossing the area
of Leontinoi.

10. D. S., XXXVI, 6 [At the same time great disorders, and an Iliad of
calamities, spread over the whole of Sicily. Not only slaves, but also
impoverished freemen committed all sorts of robbery and acts of
wickedness; for they shamelessly killed all they met, whether slaves or
free, so that none might be left to inform on them. As a result, the
inhabitants of the cities felt that they scarcely owned what was with them
within the walls; but as for that which was outside, it was all lost, falling
as prey to the lawless rule of violence. Many other outrageous deeds
were impudently committed throughout Sicily, by many different
persons.]

Chapter 11: The Reasons of Rome

1. Tantillio, I., *Gli uomini e le risorse*, in Giardina, A. (ed.), 2014, *Roma
   Antica*, Laterza, Roma-Bari, p.100. On the recurrent famines in the
   Roman world and on the popular movements connected to them:
   Virlouvet, C., 1985, *Famines et émeutes à Rome des origines de la
   Rèpublique à la mor de Neron* (Collection de l'École française de Rome
   87), Rome.
2. Oros., V, 9, 4 [4 *Orta praeterea in Sicilia belli servilis contagio multas
   late infecit provincias. nam et Minturnis CCCCL servi in crucem acti et
   Sinuessae ad quattuor milia servorum a Q. Metello et Cn. Seruilio Caepione
   oppressa sunt.*]
3. Oros., V, 9, 5 [5 *in metallis quoque Atheniensium idem tumultus servilis
   ab Heraclito praetore discussus est; apud Delon etiam servi nouo motu
   intumescentes oppidanis praevenientibus pressi sunt, absque illo primo
   Siciliensis mali fomite, a quo istae velut scintillae emicantes, diversa haec
   incendia seminarunt.*]
4. Bread riots is the name traditionally given to various popular movements
   coinciding with periods of famine.
5. In 137, the Numantians gained a new victory, in which 20,000
   Romans surrendered to them.

6. Sometimes the most perceived consciences questioned themselves on why Rome preferred to resort to violence so often, as if it could not do without it, as if it needed to fight because it was 'drugged' by war. Some Roman intellectuals, in learning the brutal cruelties perpetrated systematically by the Roman conquerors, also questioned the ruthlessness, which sometimes appeared to be an end in itself. But, again, not all evil comes to harm. While Roman conquests often had led to slavery, death and destruction, the supremacy of Rome was not only made up of legions, but also of roads and bridges, and above all, of security. Rome was capable of annexing new peoples so that they felt bound to it. It did so – for example – by respecting and even integrating into its own official religion the gods of others, and by making sure that the elites of the conquered and subjugated societies became part of its ruling class, and even of its governmental machine. Rome did not only create slaves and oppressed, but also dominated those who identified with their rulers.

Chapter 12: A Hole in Water

1. The Flaccus family moved to Rome from Tusculum (Tuscolo), a town located not far away, in the Roman Castles (in the Alban hills). Together with the families Bambalius, Centumalus, Curvus, Gillus, Nacca, Nobilior, Paetinus and Veratius, or Neratius, it composed the *gens Fulvia*.As it was a senatorial and consular family, despite its plebeian extraction, it was an integral part of the noblesse. Since the plebs were permitted to enter the consulate, which happened with the approval of the *lex Genucia de magistratibus* in 342, about sixteen *Flacci*, among the most enterprising and fortunate, crossed the line of the highest magistracy. One – Quintus Fulvius Flaccus – was consul four times (in 237, 224, 212 and 209). There were also other consuls: Quintus Fulvius Flaccus in 180 *(consul suffectus)* and Servius Fulvius Flaccus in 135. Caius Fulvius Flaccus, consul of 134, was the son of the *consul suffectus* of 180.

2. Scipio Aemilianus took the volunteeers to Spain. When he arrived, he added them to the two legions stationed there, that his predecessors used to carry on the war, and to a contingent of Numidian auxiliaries, composed of light cavalry and squadrons of war elephants. He fought in northern–central Spain against some 8,000 Celtiberians, barricaded in the fortress–city of Numantia, and broke their resistance after a siege of fifteen months.

3. Perhaps the praetor of Flaccus was T. Manlius. See for this Brennan T. C., 1993, *The Commanders in the First Sicilian Slave War*, in '*Rivista di Filologia ed Istruzione Classica (RFIC)*' 121, p.177.

4. For Scylla: Hom., *Od.*, XII, 85–100; Ov., *Metamorphoses* XIII, vv. 738–44.

5. Hom., *Od.*, XII, 104–05.

6. Odorizzi, G., 2018, *Ulisse*, Einaudi, Torino, p.78.

7. Galena was the main ore of lead; in some deposits it contains about 1–2 per cent silver.

8. Flaccus led a powerful army to Sicily. However, primary sources speak little of the expedition. Liv., *Per.*, LVI is silent about the possible successes of the consul [*Bellum servile in Sicilia ortum cum opprimi a praetoribus non potuisset, C. Fulvio cos. mandatum est.*].Oros. 5, 9, 6 cites the consul Flaccus in passing when he speaks of the victory achieved by the consul Piso Frugi in the Battle of Curcuraci [*In Sicilia enim post Fulvium consulem Piso consul Mamertium oppidum expugnavit, ubi octo milia fugitivorum interfecit, quos autem capere potuit, patibulo suffixit.*] Obseq. 27 reports to 134 the outbreak of a slave revolt in Sicily and the repression of a similar episode in Italy [*Fugitivorum bellum in Sicilia exortum, coniuratione servorum in Italia oppressa*].

Chapter 13: Chasing the Final Victory

1. Kaufman, D.B., 1932, *Poisons and Poisoning among the Romans*, in '*Classical Philology*' Vol. 27, No. 2, pp.156–67.

2. Quintil., *Inst. or.* 5.11.39 [*Si causam veneficii dicat adultera, non M. Catonis iudicio damnanda videatur, qui nullam adulteram non eandem esse veneficam dixit?*]

3. An indication that Lucius Calpurnius Piso Frugi had been poisoned by his wife is given by the fact that, after his death, his stepson, Quintus Fulvius Flaccus, was appointed as a suffix consul, who had previously attempted, unsuccessfully, to be elected to the consulate. Liv. XL, 37 [*Suspecta consulis erat mors maxime. Necatus a Quarta Hostilia uxore dicebatur. ut quidem filius eius Q. Fuluius Flaccus in locum uitrici consul est declaratus, aliquanto magis infamis mors Pisonis coepit esse*].

4. Liv. XXVII, 6, 1 [*Dictator postquam Romam uenit, C. Sempronium Blaesum legatum quem ad Capuam habuerat in Etruriam provinciam ad exercitum misit in locum C. Calpurni praetoris, quem ut Capuae exercituique suo praeesset litteris excivit. ipse comitia in quem diem primum potuit edixit; quae certamine inter tribunos dictatoremque iniecto perfici non*

potuerunt.] Earl, D.C., 1960, *Calpurnii Pisones in the II century 8.C.,* in *Athenaeum*, pp.283–98, spec. 285 ss., followed by Astin, A.E., 1967, *Scipio Aemilianus*, Oxford, p.317.

5. The support of the Fulvii Flacci to the Calpurnii Pisones may have already failed in 180 when Quintus Fulvius Flaccus, son of the first wife of Caius Calpurnius Piso, was beaten by his stepfather to the elections for the renewal of the consulate. Astin, A.E., 1967, *Scipio Aemilianus*, Oxford, p.317.

6. On the second-century *Annales*: Chassignet, M., 1999, *L'Annalistique romaine. Tome II. L'Annalistique moyenne (fragments)*, Paris. For Lucius Calpurnius Piso Frugi Censorinus, historical annalist: Forsythe, G., 1990, *The Historian, L. Calpurnius Piso Frugi, and the Roman Annalistic Tradition*, Lanham. On his literary production: Cardinali, L., 1988, *Quanti libri scrisse L. Calpurnio Piso Frugi? Congetture sull' estensione dell'opera*, in 'Maia' 40, pp.45–55.

7. Born around 146, L. Cassio Hemina wrote in Latin a history of Rome, from its origins to current affairs, of which there remain about forty fragments, known through the works of Sallust, Pliny the Elder and grammarians. He tended to deal with traditions of the foundations of cities, religions and their rituals, customs and institutions, as well as Greek history.

8. Cnaeus Gellius (second half of the second century) was an accurate chronologer and diligent investigator of ancient usages, and was *triumvir monetalis* in 138. He wrote a history of Rome in at least ninety-seven books, from the earliest epoch, extending at least to 145. He described the Rape of the Sabines, the reign of Titus Tatius and the Second Punic War. He also devoted much space to the legend of the origins of Rome.

9. For the first time in the judicial history of Rome, a major magistrate – in this specific case, the pilgrim magistrate, competent to judge on the quarrels between Roman and foreign citizens – was obliged by law to decide in accordance with the opinion of another organ. Previously, the pilgrim magistrate could ask his *consilium* to express a non-binding opinion.

10. Cf. Arena Primo P., 1841, *Storia Civile di Messina*, Vol. I, Parte I, Lorenzo Dato, Palermo, p.181).

11. Oros. 5.9.6 [*In Sicilia enim post Fulvium consulem Piso consul Mamertium oppidum expugnavit, ubi octo milia fugitivorum interfecit, quos autem capere potuit, patibulo suffixit.*]

12. V. Max. 4.3.10.

13. Or. 5, 9, 6. Morgantiam is preferred to Mamertium, which creates some perplexity since Oros. 5.6.4 excludes Messana from the number of cities involved in the *bellum servile* [*Igitur in Sicilia bellum servile ortum est, quod adeo grave et atrox multitudine servorum, instructu copiarum, magnitudine virium fuit, ut, non dicam praetores Romanos, quos penitus profligavit, sed consules quoque terruerit. Nam LXX milia servorum tunc in arma conspirantium fuisse referuntur, excepta urbe Messana, quae servos liberaliter habitos in pace continuit.*]. See Verbrugghe, G.P., 1974, *Slave rebellion or Sicily in revolt?*, in *Kokalos* 46, 60, spec. 56, n.26.

14. The attack of Piso against Henna is not attested by literary sources, but could be documented by some 'acorn' lead missiles found in the territory of the ancient city, bearing the inscription L. PISO L. F. I COS. (AL p.2.847): see also Manganaro G., 1982, *Inscribed coins and acorns of rebel slaves in Sicily*, in '*Chiron*', pp.237–43, spec. 24.2;/ Val. Max. 2.7.9, 4.3.10 and Frontin. 4.1.26 confirm the presence of slingers in the army of Piso. It is also possible that no attack was brought from Piso to Henna and that the acorns found were instead used by the consul of 132, Rupilius, who, in this case, would have used bullets already available to his predecessor. In fact acorns with the name of Rupilius were not found at Henna. Val. Max. II,7.9, e IV, 3, 10, cit., and Frontin. IV,1,26, cit., mention some anecdotes about the continence of the consul in Sicily and the discipline that he knew how to keep among his troops. Such anecdotes could derive from the *Annals* of Piso. *Cfr.* Cardinali L., 1988, *How many books did L. Calpurnio Piso Frugi write? Conjectures on the extension of the work*, in '*Maia*', pp.45–55. CIL 12.847 (lead glandes from Henna, reading: L. Piso L. f. | cos.), cf. Cic. Ver. 4.108.

15. V. Max. 2.7.9; Front., *Str.* 4.1.26.

16. On Tiberius Gracchus and his brother Caius: Barca, N., 2019, I Gracchi. Quando la politica finisce in tragedia, L'Erma di Bretschneider, Roma; Perelli, L., 1993, *I Gracchi*, Roma; Gabba, E., 1990, *Il tentativo dei Gracchi*, in *Storia di Roma*, 2, Einaudi, Torino, pp.671–89; Schiavone, A., 1987, *Giuristi e nobili nella repubblica romana*, Bari, pp.16–17; Scullard, H.H., 1982, *From the Gracchi to Nero: A History of Rome from 133 B.C. to A.D. 68*, London and New York, pp.1–33; Stockton, D., 1979, *The Gracchi*, Oxford; Stockton, D.L., 1981, *From the Gracchi to Sulla: Sources for Roman History, 133–80 B.C.*, London (2nd ed., London 1991); Rossi, R.F., 1980, *Dai Gracchi a Silla,*

Cappelli, Bologna; Stockton, D.L., 1979, *The Gracchi*, Oxford and New York; Richardson, K., 1976, *Daggers in the Forum*, Littlehampton Book Services Ltd, Faraday Cl., Worthing; Badian, E., 1972, *Tiberius Gracchus and the Beginning of the Roman Revolution*, in *'ANRW'* 1.1, Berlin, pp.668–731; De Sanctis, G., 1921, *Rivoluzione e reazione nell'età dei Gracchi*, ora in *Scritti Minori*, IV, Roma, 1976; Nagle, D.B., 1970, *The Failure of the Roman Political Process*, in *'Athenaeum'*, LVIII; Boren, H.C., 1968, *The Gracchi*, New York; Nicolet, C., 1967, *Les Gracques ou crise agraire et révolution à Rome*, Paris; Carcopino, J., 1967, *Autour des Gracques*, a cura di C. Nicolet, Paris; Gabba, E., 1967, *I Gracchi* (*'I Protagonisti'* 2), Milano; Earl, D.C., 1963, *Tiberius Gracchus: A Study in Politics*, Brussels; Last, H., 1932, *Capp. I e II* in *'CAH'*; Greenidge, A.H.J. & Clay, A.M., 1903, *Sources for Roman History, 133–70 B.C.*, 2nd ed. 1960, rev. E.W. Gray, Oxford, 1–24.

Chapter 14: The Turning Point

1. Flor. II.7.
2. An *ovatio* was a minor form of triumph.
3. D.S., XXXV, 8 [The Syrian slaves cut off the hands of those they took prisoners, not at the wrists, but hands and arms together.]
4. *Lapis Pollae*, ILLRP 454 [*viam fecei ab regio ad capvam et in ea via ponteis omneis miliarios tabelariosqve poseivei hince svnt nouceriam meilia li capuam xxciiii muranum lxxiiii cosentiam cxxiii valentiam clxxx ad fretvm ad statuam ccxxxi regium ccxxxvii suma af capua regium meilia cccxxi et eidem praetor in sicilia fugiteivos italicorvm conquaeisivei redideique homines dccccxvii eidemque primvs fecei vt de agro poplico aratoribvs cederent paastores forum aedisque poplicas heic fecei.*]
5. It is uncertain whether the road was built by Titus Annius Luscus in 153, as suggested by a milestone inscription found in the Vibonese, or started and finished by the consul Popilio Lenate in 133, or begun by the latter and finished by Titus Annius Rufus, praetor in 131, son of Titus Annius Luscus. The main centres touched by the road are indicated in an engraved epigraph in Latin, measuring 70x74cm, found in San Pietro di Polla (Salerno) and known among scholars as the Cippo di Polla.
6. Oros. V, 9, 6 [*in Sicilia enim post Fulvium consulem Piso consul Mamertium oppidum expugnavit, ubi octo milia fugitivorum interfecit, quos autem capere potuit, patibulo suffixit.*]

Chapter 15: A Bloodbath

1. The history of the siege of Tauromenium is narrated in D.S., XXXIV, 20–21 [But in Sicily the disorders increased more and more; for cities were taken, and their inhabitants made slaves, and many armies were routed by the rebels, until such time as Rupilius the Roman general recovered Tauromenium. The besieged had been reduced to such an extremity of famine by a sharp and close siege, that they began to eat their own children, and the men their wives; and at length they butchered one another for food. There Rupilius captured Comanus the brother of Cleon, who was endeavouring to escape out of the city while it was besieged. At last Sarapion, a Syrian, betrayed the citadel, and all the fugitives fell into his hands. Rupilius had them scourged and thrown over a cliff.]

2. Oros. V, 9, 7 [*Cui cum Rutilius consul successisset, idem quoque Tauromenium et Hennam, firmissima fugitiuorum refugia, bello recepit: amplius quam XX milia tunc seruorum trucidata referuntur.*]

3. The Battle of Henna and the subsequent capture and death of King Antiochus are narrated in D.S., XXXIV, 21–23.

4. Plb., 29,17.

5. Posidonius 169 F 1, 19.2. See also Plu., *Aem.*, 19.

6. P. Morton, in *Eunus: the Cowardly King*, writes 'that suggests that the construction of the narrative of Eunus' death was serving a very specific purpose in the overall story of the revolt'.

7. A. Keaveney and J.A. Madden, '*Phthiriasis and its victims*', SO 57 (1982), pp.87–99.

8. We do not know the content of the *lex Rupilia* apart from what can be deduced from Cic., *Verr.* II.2.13.32 [*Verum ut totum genus amplectamini iudiciorum, prius iura Siculorum, deinde istius instituta cognoscite. Siculi hoc iure sunt ut, quod civis cum cive agat, domi certet suis legibus, quod Siculus cum Siculo non eiusdem civitatis, ut de eo practor iudices ex P. Rupili decreto, quod is de decem legatorum sententia statuit, quam illi legem Rupiliam vocant, sortiatur. Quod privatus a populo petit aut populus a privato, senatus ex aliqua civirate qui iudicet datur, cum alternae civitates reiectae sunt; quod civis Romanus a Siculo petit, Siculus iudex, quod Siculus a civi Romano, civis Romanus datur; ceterarum rerum selecti iudices ex conventu civium Romanorum proponi solent. Inter aratores et decumanos lege frumentaria, quam Hieroicam appellant, iudicia fiunt.*]

9. D.S., XXXV, 11.

Chapter 16: Twenty-Eight Years Later

1. Not even at Cannae (216), fighting against the Carthaginians of Hannibal, had the Romans lost so many men. There they had deployed on the battlefield eight legions of Roman citizens and eight auxiliary legions, a total of 86,000 men, under the command of the consuls Lucius Aemilius Paullus and Caius Terentius Varro. They lost the battle because of a brilliant pincer movement by Hannibal, who had held them in a vice. At the end of the fighting the Romans had lost at least 68,000 men, including 48,000 killed. Another estimate speaks of 76,000 deaths and 10,000 prisoners. One of the victims was the consul Aemilius Paullus.

2. Membership in the Senate was not linked to belonging to a particular social class. There were therefore patrician and plebeian senators, and together they – and their families – formed the Roman nobility. In theory, anyone could become a senator. This could happen by succession or following election to the *curulis aedilitas* or to the public office of rank immediately superior to *aedilitas*, the praetorship.

3. Ramsey, J.T., 1999, *Mithridates, the Banner of Ch'ih-Yu, and the Comet Coin*, in '*Harvard Studies in Classical Philology*' *(HSCP)* 99, pp.197–253 – part. pp.237–43 – does not exclude that the *lex Sempronia provinciae Asiae* may also have established the annexation of Little Phrygia, disputed between Pontus and Bithynia.

4. Merola, G.D., 2001, *Autonomia locale governo imperiale. Fiscalità e amministrazione nelle province asiane* (Pragmateiai 5), Bari, p.38. Ramsey, J.T., 1999, *Mithridates, the Banner of Ch'ih-Yu, and the Comet Coin*, in '*Harvard Studies in Classical Philology*' *(HSCP)* 99, pp.197–253, part. pp.237–43. Perelli, L., 1990, *Questioni graccane*, in '*Rivista di filologia e di istruzione classica*' *(RFIC)* 118, pp.237–52.

5. On the companies of publicans in Sicily: Scaramuzza, V., 1937, *Publican Societies in Sicily in 73–71 B.C.*, in '*Classical Philology*' *(CPh)* 32, pp.152–55.

6. D.S., XXXVI, 3, 1–3 [As part of the command of Marius against the Cimbrians, the senate had given him a commission to raise men from the countries beyond the seas; to which end, Marius sent envoys to Nicomedes king of Bithynia, requesting him to send some men as auxiliaries; but Nicomedes replied that most of the Bithynians had been taken away as slaves by the tax-collectors, and were dispersed throughout the provinces. Upon hearing this, the senate decreed that no freeman

belonging to any of the Roman allies should in any province be forced to be a slave, and that the praetors should take care to see that they were all set free. In pursuance of this order Licinius Nerva, then praetor in Sicily, appointed hearings and set free so many slaves that in a few days above eight hundred gained their liberty; so that all the slaves in Sicily were hereby encouraged and grew confident in their hope of liberty. The most eminent Sicilians therefore approached the the praetor, and asked him to desist from making any more free. Whereupon he (whether bribed, or to gain favour) withdrew his support for the hearings, and if any others came to him in the hope of being made free, he dismissed them with harsh words and sent them back to their masters. Upon this the slaves entered into a conspiracy; they left Syracuse, and gathered together at the grove of the Palici, where they discussed their intended rebellion.]

Chapter 17: The Rebirth of the Phoenix Arab

1. D.S., XXXVI, 4, 1–3.
2. D.S., XXXVI, 4, 4.
3. Finley, M.I., 1968, *Ancient Sicily to the Arab Conquest*, London, p.144.
4. *Ibidem.*
5. D.S., XXXVI, 5–6.
6. Morton, P.C.F., 2012, *Refiguring the Sicilian Slave Wars: from servile unrest to civic disquiet and social disorder*, Thesis, PhD in Classics, University of Edinburgh, pp.154–55.
7. D.S., XXXVI, 7, 1 [Salvius likewise, who had besieged Morgantina, after harassing all the country, as far as the territories of Leontini, mustered his army there, consisting of above thirty thousand fighting men.]
8. D.S., XXXVI, 8.
9. D.S., XXXVI, 5, 1 [After this, all the slaves in the territories of Segesta and Lilybaeum were likewise infected with this desire of rebellion. Their leader was one Athenion, a valiant man, and a Cilician. This man, who was the steward of two rich brothers, and an excellent astrologer, first persuaded the slaves, over whom he had some sort of command, to join with him, to the number of two hundred; and afterwards he added those who lived in the neighbouring districts, so that in five days' time there were gathered above one thousand.]
10. D.S., XXXVI, 5, 3–4.
11. Plu., *Cato.* 21, 1.

12. This reconstruction was developed under the direction of the buildings' principal investigator, Dr Brian McConnell, and is based on a detailed analysis of the remains discovered in the excavations undertaken by the Superintendency for Cultural and Environmental Resources of Catania, Sicily. See http://www.learningsites.com/Palike/hestiaterion_home.php.

13. D.S., I, 11, 89 gives us a precise testimony of the sanctuary of the chthonic deities of the Palici (Mineo, near Catania), one of the most important places of worship of the indigenous populations of Sicilian origin. [The myths tell that this sacred enclosure surpassed the others for antiquities ... First there are craters that, from the point of view of greatness are not at all big, but emit impetuous sources from one unspeakable depth. The emission of water is so amazing that it seems that the event is due to a divine force. In fact, the water has the annoying smell of sulphur, and the chasm causes a great rumble to come out, it is frightening ... Because in the sanctuary there is such a divine majesty, here the most important oaths are performed ... The sacred enclosure is located in a plain worthy of a deity, it is also adorned adequately with porticoes and other rooms.]

14. D.S., XXXVI, 5, 2 [They made him king, and placed a diadem upon his head.]

15. D.S., XXXVI, 7, 1 [Then he made a sacrifice to the Palici, the local heroes, and dedicated one of his royal robes, in gratitude for his victories. He caused himself to he proclaimed king, and was given the name Tryphon by the rebels.]

16. D.S., XXXVI, 7, 4.

17. The primary sources on Diodotus Tryphon are the following: 1 Maccabees, 11–15; Diodorus of Sicily, *Library of World History*, 32.9c, 33.4a, 33.28–28a; Flavius Josephus, *Jewish Antiquities*, 13.131–34; Livy, *Periochae*, 52, 55; Strabo, *Geography*, 16.2.10.

18. An advocate or partisan of the monarchical regime in a country where a royal dynasty has been displaced by a coup.

19. D.S., XXXVI, 7, 2 [Since he wished to take possession of Triocala, and there to build a palace, he sent to Athenion, summoning him as a king would summon a general. Every man then thought that Athenion would endeavour to gain the sovereignty for himself, and by that means the rebels would be divided, and so a speedy end would be put to the war. But fortune so ordered the matter, as if to strengthen the armies of the runaway slaves, that the two leaders

fully co-operated with each other. For Tryphon marched speedily with his army to Triocala, and Athenion met him there with three thousand men, in everything observing the commands of Tryphon as king. Athenion had sent the rest of his army away to devastate the countryside, and to bring over as many slaves as they could to join in the revolt. But not long afterwards, Tryphon suspected that Athenion was planning to supplant him in time, and therefore he caused him to be put in custody. The fortress, which was in itself very secure, he made still more strong, and adorned it likewise with many stately buildings.]

20. For this location: Bejor, G., 1975, *Ricerche di topografia e di archeologia nella Sicilia sud-occidentale*, in '*Annali della Scuole Superiore Normale di Pisa, Cl. di Lettere e Filosofia*' *(ASNP)* 5, pp.1275–1303 (esp. 1283–89). See also Manni, E., 1981, *Geografia fisica e politica della Sicilia antica*, Roma, pp.238–39.

21. D.S., XXXVI, 7, 3 [They say that it was called Triocala, because it was remarkable for three fine things (tria kala). First, for springs of excellent sweet water; secondly, for vineyards, and olive plantations, and rich lands for tillage; and thirdly, that it was an impregnable position, built upon a high and inaccessible rock. After he had built a city wall of eight stades round about it, and had surrounded it with a deep trench, he made it his royal capital, filled with an abundance of all things necessary for the life of man. He likewise built there a stately palace and an agora, capable of receiving a vast number of men.]

22. D.S., XXXVI, 7, 2–3 [The fortress, which was in itself very secure, he made still more strong, and adorned it likewise with many stately buildings. ... After he had built a city wall of eight stades round about it, and had surrounded it with a deep trench, he made it the his royal capital, filled with an abundance of all things necessary for the life of man. He likewise built there a stately palace and an agora, capable of receiving a vast number of men.]

23. Bradley, K.R., 1989, *Slavery and Rebellion in the Roman World*, 140 *BC*–70 *BC*, Batsford (reprint 1998), p.80.

24. Morton, P., *The geography of rebellion: strategy and supply in the two 'Sicilian Slave Wars'*, pp.10, 19.

25. D.S., XXXVI, 7, 2 [Athenion had sent the rest of his army away to devastate the countryside, and to bring over as many slaves as they could to join in the revolt. But not long afterwards, Tryphon suspected

that Athenion was planning to supplant him in time, and therefore he caused him to be put in custody.]

Chapter 18: Disorder, Famine, Death

1. This happened in the Republican era, when there was not yet a proper grain supply management system. In the Imperial age, in order for the food supply of the city to be constant and proportionate to its needs, a special public service was instituted, the *Curia Annonae*.
2. This would in the long run have a counterproductive effect, putting the loyalty of the soldiers in the hands of their general rather than the Roman *res publica*.

Chapter 19: Lucullus' Reverse

1. The location of this site is uncertain. Manni, E., 1981, *Geografia fisica e politica della Sicilia antica*, Roma, pp.238–39, and in part, p.222, identifies it as San Carlo, north of Caltabellotta, on the modern SS386 road. For other possible locations: Bejor, G., 1975, *Ricerche di topografia e di archeologia nella Sicilia sud-occidentale*, in '*Annali della Scuole Superiore Normale di Pisa, Cl. di Lettere e Filosofia*' (*ASNP*) 5, pp.1282–83.
2. D.S., XXXVI, 8, 1–5 [At length, Lucius Licinius Lucullus was chosen general by the senate of Rome, to go against the rebels. He took with him fourteen thousand Romans and Italians; eight hundred Bithynians, Thessalians and Acarnanians; six hundred Lucanians, under the command of Cleptius, an expert general, renowned for his valour; and also six hundred from other places; in the whole amounting to (?) seventeen thousand. When he entered Sicily with this army, Tryphon released Athenion, and consulted with him how to manage the war against the Romans. Tryphon was of the opinion that the safest way was to continue at Triocala, and there await the enemy: but Athenion advised that they should fight in the open countryside, rather than allow themselves to be trapped in a siege. As this opinion prevailed, they marched out and encamped near Scirthaea, with no fewer than forty thousand men, twelve stades distant from the Roman camp. At first the armies employed themselves every day in light skirmishes; but at length they engaged in battle. While victory was still undecided, and many were slain on both sides, Athenion fought alongside two hundred of his cavalry, and covered the ground round about him with the bodies of his enemies. But being wounded in both knees, and then receiving a third wound, he was totally unable to continue fighting.

This so discouraged the rebels, that they turned to flight. Athenion lay concealed, as if he were dead, and so feigned himself till night came on, and then stole away. But the Romans, having now gained a glorious victory, forced Tryphon himself to take to his heels, and in the pursuit slew at least twenty thousand men. The rest, taking advantage of the night, got away to Triocala, although the general might easily have killed them too, if he had pressed the pursuit. Upon this rout the slaves were so much discouraged, that it was proposed amongst them that they should return to their masters, and submit themselves wholly into their power. But those who advised to stand it out to the last, and not to surrender themselves to the vengeance of their enemies, prevailed over the other. Nine days later, the Roman praetor began to besiege Triocala; but after much slaughter on both sides, he was obliged to withdraw and leave the place. Upon this the rebels recovered their spirits; the praetor on the other hand, either through sloth and negligence, or corrupted by bribes, neglected entirely the proper conduct of his duty, for which he was afterwards brought to trial by the Romans.]

3. Marcus Terentius Varro Lucullus was consul in 73, then governor of Macedonia, and celebrated a triumph for his victories over a Thracian tribe, that of the Bessi.

Chapter 21: The End of the Story

1. A number of slinghots have been found bearing Athenion's name in several places across Sicily, as well as other slinghots which seem to be related to Salvius/Tryphon. Two of the finds inscribed with Athenion's name have been found near Lentini and in the area of Palermo; the other two come from an unknown site. Thus it would appear that Athenion also commanded operations in the plains of Lentini, between Syracuse and Catania, and around Palermo. See: Manganaro, 1982, *Monete e ghiande inscritte degli schiavi ribelli in Sicilia*, in 'Chiron' 12, pp.237–44; ID., 2000, *Onomastica greca su anelli, pesi da telaio e glandes in Sicilia*, in 'Zeitschrift für Papyrologie und Epigraphik' (ZPE) 133, pp.123–34 (esp. 131–32).

2. Cic. *Verr.* II, 54 [*Athenion qui nullum oppidum coepit*].

3. D.S., XXXVI, 5, 3. [He pretended that by the stars the gods foretold that he should become the king of the whole of Sicily, and therefore he was to refrain from spoiling the country, or destroying the cattle and crops, as they all belonged to him. At length, having now got together above ten thousand men, he was so daring as to besiege Lilybaeum, a city

considered to be impregnable. But since he failed to make any headway, he abandoned the enterprise, pretending he was commanded to do so by the gods, who warned him that, if they continued the siege, they would certainly fall into some sudden misfortune.] From a fragment of Dio, we learn that Athenion had fortified the site of Makella with a wall (27.93.4). The ancient city of Makella is mentioned in the fifth decree of Entella (Entella AI) and is also known from classical historical sources. Recently it was identified with the modern site of Montagnola di Marineo, near Palermo, as attested by three roof tiles inscribed in Greek characters. For such an identification: Spatafora, F., 2011, *Un contributo per l'identificazione di una delle 'città di Sicilia' dei decreti di Entella*, in Ampolo, C. (ed.), *Da un'antica città di Sicilia. I decreti di Entella e Nakone*, pp.111–14; Spatafora, F. and Vassallo, S. (eds), *Das Eigene und das Andere. Griechen, Sikaner und Elymer. Neue archailogische Forschungen im antiken Sizilien*, Palermo, p.108 nos 208/209.

4. D.S., XXIII, 4, 2. [Though the Romans kept Makella and the village of Hadranon under siege for many days, they went away without having accomplished their purpose.]

5. Plb. I, 24, 2 [Thus, having disembarked in Sicilia, they freed the inhabitants of Segesta from their siege; then, retiring from Segesta, they took the city of Makella by force.]

6. Liv. 26, 21, 14. The Roman capture of the city is also remembered in an inscription engraved on a rostral column (OL I, 2,1) discovered in Rome in 1565 at the Arch of Septimius Severus. In that epigraph it is read, in the list of the accomplished enterprises in Sicily from Caio Duilio, '*Macellamque oppidum pugnando cepet*'.

7. The trial brought by the sons of Lucullus against Servilius the Augur took place in 91 and ended with the acquittal of the accused in a climate of violence, which caused many deaths and injuries: Cic. *Prov.* 22; Cic. *Off.* 2.50; Cic. *Arch.* 6.

8. Silius Italicus, XIV, 270 [And then Triokala was destroyed during the Servile War].

9. D.S., XXXVI, 10, 1 [In the following year, Caius Marius was elected as consul at Rome for the fifth time, and with him Manius Aquillius. Aquilius was sent as general against the rebels; and through his personal valour he defeated them in a great battle; like a hero, he fought hand to hand with Athenion the king of the rebels, and killed him, but himself suffered a wound on the head, from which he recovered. Then he marched against the remainder of them, who were about ten thousand;

and though they did not wait for his attack, but fled to their defences, yet Aquilius did not slacken his resolution in the least, until he had overcome them by siege.]

10. Oakley, S.P., 1985, *Single combat in the Roman Republic*, in '*Classical Quarterly*' (CQ) 35.2, pp.392–410.

11. Str. VI, 2, 6, tells that, in his time, a certain Sélourós, called 'son of Etna', was conducted to Rome, because he had headed an armed band and for a long time had made raids for the purpose of robbery in the regions around Etna. He himself saw him torn by wild beasts during a fight of gladiators in the Forum. They had placed him on a stage, which was to represent Etna, with the excuse of having him watch the fight. The stage was collapsed and Sélourós fell into the cages that had been placed under it, where there were wild beasts. The episode took place in 35.

Conclusions

1. Bejor, G. (ed.), 1988, *Diodoro Siculo, II, XXI-XL*, Rusconi, Milano.

2. Flor. 2, 8, 1–2. The translation shown in the text is the one found in Brizzi, G., *Ribelli contro Roma, Gli schiavi, Spartaco, l'altra Italia*, Il Mulino, Bologna, p.7.

3. Morton, P.C.F., 2012, *Refiguring the Sicilian Slave Wars: from servile unrest to civic disquiet and social disorder*, Thesis, PhD in Classics, University of Edimburgh, p.iv.

4. In the beginning, the Seleucid Empire embraced Anatolia, Syria, Mesopotamia, Persia and other Asiatic territories. It had to renounce Anatolia west of the Taurus mountains after having lost a war against Rome, Pergamon and Rhodes (Syrian War, 192–188). Later it also lost further territories, torn from it by the Parthians.

5. We refer to three Celtic tribes, originally from the Danube valley, which, in about the middle of the third century, the King of Pontus agreed to settle in Western Phrygia (central Anatolia) and to rule over the local populations, to reward them for having fought for him as mercenaries. The Greeks called these Celtics Galatians; consequently the land of the Galatians was called Galatia. The Galatians constituted a confederation of three states, on the model of the similar formations of Greece, usually improperly referred to as the league (Peloponnesian League, L. corinthia, L. beotica, L. panhellenica, L. achaeian, L. aetolica, etc.). In the beginning each state was organized into four cantons and governed by a tetrarch, which was endowed with

absolute powers and, for the exercise of its functions, could use a judge, a military commander and two deputy commanders. A political institution of the confederation was a council of 300 members in charge of the administration of justice. For about a century Galatia constituted an anti-war protective wall both for the Kingdom of Pontus and the Kingdom of Bithynia against the attempts of territorial expansion of the Seleucids. In the meantime the cantonal organization failed and was replaced by a unitary state. At first the three tetrarchs were reduced to two and finally to one, who became king.

Appendix

1. Plutarch speaks in these terms of Spartacus, the protagonist of the revolt (Third Slave War, 73–71), saying he was originally from the Maidi tribe.
2. *Cfr.* Le Bohec, Y., 2018, *Spartaco, signore della Guerra*, Carocci, Roma (original title: *Spartacus, chef de guerre,* Editions Tallandier 2016).

List of the Primary Sources Cited

Aug. *Civ.* 6.9

Cic. *Arch.* 6
Cic. *Leg.*, 2.37
Cic. *Nat. D.*, II, 62
Cic. *Off.* 2.50
Cic. *Prov.* 22
Cic. *Verr.* II, 2, 13, 32
Cic. *Verr.* II,4, 108
Cic. *Verr.* 54

D.S., I, 11, 89
D.S., XXIII, 4, 2
D.S., XXXIV, 11–12
D.S., XXXIV, 14
D.S., XXXIV, 15
D.S., XXXIV, 16
D.S., XXXIV, 17
D.S., XXXIV, 18
D.S., XXXIV, 20–21
D.S., XXXIV, 21
D.S., XXXIV, 21–23
D.S., XXXIV, 22
D.S., XXXIV, 24
D.S., XXXIV, 34–38
D.S., XXXIV, 39
D.S., XXXIV, 41
D.S., XXXIV, 43
D.S., XXXV, 8
D.S., XXXV, 11
D.S., XXXVI, 3, 1–3

D.S., XXXVI, 4, 1–2
D.S., XXXVI, 4, 1–2, 3
D.S., XXXVI, 4, 2–3
D.S., XXXVI, 4, 4–6
D.S., XXXVI, 4, 6
D.S., XXXVI, 4, 5
D.S., XXXVI, 5, 1
D.S., XXXVI, 5, 2
D.S., XXXVI, 4, 7–8
D.S., XXXVI, 4, 8
D.S., XXXVI, 5, 3
D.S., XXXVI, 5, 3–4
D.S., XXXVI, 6
D.S., XXXVI, 7, 1
D.S., XXXVI, 7, 4
D.S., XXXVI, 7, 2
D.S., XXXVI, 7, 1–2
D.S., XXXVI, 8, 1–5
D.S., XXXVI, 10, 1
Ephorus of Cyme in Fr. 135 Kakoby

Flor. II, 7
Flor. II, 8, 1–2

Frontin. IV, 1, 2–6

Hdt. VI, 138

Hom. *Od.*, XII, 85–100
Hom. *Od.*, XII, 104–105
Hom. *Od.*, XIV, vv. 15–30

IG X 2.1.141

ILLPP 454

Liv. XXI, 49–50
Liv. XXII, 33
Liv. XXIV, 37–39

Liv. XXVII, 6.1
Liv. XXXII, 26
Liv. XXXIX, 8–19
Liv. XXXIX, 14–18
Liv. XXXIX, 29, 8–10
Liv. XL, 37
Liv. XLI, 6–7
Liv. XLV, 34

Oros. V, 9, 4
Oros. V, 9, 6

Ov. *Metamorphoses* XIII–XIV, vv. 738–744
Pindar, *Pythian Ode* 1, 19–25

Plb. I, 15, 1–9
Plb. I, 15, 10
Plb. I, 24, 2
Plb. II, 3, 8
Plb. IV, 38
Plb. VII, 6
Plb. IX, 27, 11
Plb. XXIX, 18
Plb. XXX, 15, 1

Plu. *Aem.*, 19
Plu. *Cato*, 21, 1
Plu. *Cimon*, 8, 3

Posidonius 169 F 1, 19, 2

Quint. *Inst. or.* V, 11, 39

Silius Italicus XIX, 270

Str. V, 1, 8, 3–4
Str. V, 3, 11
Str. VI, 2, 1
Str. VI, 2, 3

Str. VI, 2, 6
Str. VI, 2, 97–99
Str. VI, 3
Str. VI, 7, 3
Str. X, 2, 2
Str. XIV, 5, 2

Thu. I, 55

V. Max. II, 7
V. Max. IV, 3, 10

Zon. VIII, 11, 6–7
Zon. VIII, 11, 7–12
Zon. VIII, 11, 8–9

References

Andreau, J. and Descat, R., 2009, *Gli schiavi nel mondo greco e romano*, Il Mulino, Bologna, p.84 (originally published in France as *Esclave en Grèce et à Rome*, Paris, Hachette Littératures, 2006).

Andreau, J. and Descat, R., 2011, *The Slave in Greece and Rome*, University of Wisconsin Press, Madison (originally published in France as *Esclave en Grèce et à Rome*, Hachette Littératures, 2006), p.145.

Arena-Primo, P., 1841, *Storia civile di Messina*, Vol. 1, Part 1, Lorenzo Dato, Palermo, p.181.

Astin, A.E., 1967, *Scipio Aemilianus*, Oxford, p.317.

Bejor, G., 1975, *Ricerche di topografia e di archeologia nella Sicilia sud-occidentale*, in '*Annali della Scuole Superiore Normale di Pisa, Cl. di Lettere e Filosofia*' (*ASNP*) 5, pp.1275–1303, in part. pp.1282–83, e pp.1283–89.

Berrendonner, C., 2007, *Mercenarius dans le sources litteraires*, in Andreau, J. & Chankowki, V., *Vocabulaire et expressions de l'economie dan le monde romain*, Ellipse Editions, Paris, pp.215–21.

Bradley, K.R., 1989, *Slavery and Rebellion in the Roman World, 140 BC –70 BC*, Batsford (reprint 1998), p.80.

Brennan, T.C., 1993, *The Commanders in the First Sicilian Slave War*, in '*Rivista di Filologia ed Istruzione Classica (RFIC)*' 121, pp.153–84.

Capozza, M., 1967, *Movimenti servili nel mondo romano in età repubblicana, I. Dal 501 al 184 a. Cr.*, L'Erma di Bretschneider, Roma, pp.95–100.

Cardinali, L., 1988, *Quanti libri scrisse L. Calpurnio Piso Frugi? Congetture sull'estensione dell'opera*, in '*Maia*' 40, pp.45–55.

Casson, L., 1980, *The Role of the State in Rome's Grain Trade*, in D'Arms, J.H. and Kopff, E.C.(eds), *The Seaborne Commerce: Studies in Archaeology and History*, Roma, pp.21–33.

Castagnoli, F., 1980, *Installazioni portuali a Roma*, in '*Memoirs of the American Academy in Rome*' (*MAAR*) XXXVI, pp.35–42.

Chassignet, M., 1999, *L'Annalistique romaine. Tome II. L'Annalistique moyenne (fragments)*, Paris.

Coarelli, F., 1988, *Il Foro Boario dalle origini alla fine della Repubblica*, Roma.

Coarelli, F., 1968, *Navalia, Tarentum e la topografia del campo Marzio meridionale*, in 'Quaderni dell' Istituto di topografia antica dell' Università di Roma' 5, pp.27–37.

Colini, A.M., 1980, *Il porto fluviale del Foro Boario a Roma*, in 'Memoirs of the American Academy in Rome' (*MAAR*) XXXVI, pp.43–53.

Colini, A.M., 1938, *Deposito di marmi presso il Tevere*, in 'Bullettino della Commissione Archeologica comunale di Roma' (*Bull Comm*), pp.299–300.

Cressedi, G., 1949–51, *I porti fluviali in Roma antica*, in De Dominicis, M., 1924, *La 'statio annonae urbis Romae'*, in 'Bullettino della Commissione Archeologica comunale di Roma' (*Bull Comm*) LII, pp.135–49.

Cristofori, A., 2016, *Lavoro e identità sociale*, in Marcone, C. (ed.), 2016, *Storia del lavoro in Italia. L'Età Romana. Liberi, Semiliberi e schiavi in una società premoderna*, Castelvecchi, Roma, pp.150, 151, 153.

Earl, D.C., 1960, *'Calpurnii Pisones' in the second century B.C.*, in 'Athenaeum' 48 (= N.S. 38), pp.283–98, esp. 285 ss.

Finley, M.I., 1981, *Economy and Society in Ancient Greece*, Chatto and Windus, London, ch. 5.

Forsythe, G., 1990, *The Historian, L. Calpurnius Piso Frugi, and the Roman Annalistic Tradition*, Lanham.

Garnsey, P., 1983, *Grain for Rome*, in Garnsey, P., Hopkins, K. and Whittaker, R., (eds), *Trade in Ancient Economy*, London, pp.126–28.

Gatti, G., 1936, *L'arginatura del Tevere a Marmorata (un manoscritto inedito del P. Luigi M. Bruzza)*, in 'Bullettino della Commissione Archeologica comunale di Roma' (*Bull Comm*) LXIV, pp.55–82.

Gatti, G., 1934, *'Saepta Iulia' e 'Porticus Aemilia' nella 'Forma' Severiana*, in 'Bull Comm', pp.123–49.

Gianfrotta, P.A., 1989, *Le vie di comunicazione*, in AA.VV., *Storia di Roma, 4. Caratteri e morfologie*, Giulio Einaudi Editore, Torino, pp.301–19, v. in part. p.315.

Gibbon, E., 1849, *The decline and fall of the Roman Empire*, 1st ed., p.1126.

Goethe (von), J.W., 2017, *Viaggio in Italia*, Mondadori, Milano.

Hulsen, C., 1896, *Il foro Boario e le sue adiacenze nell'antichità*, in 'Dissertazioni della Pontificia Accademia romana di archeologia' 2, II, pp.175–248.

Keaveney, A., 1998, *Three Roman chronological problems (141–132 B.C.)*, in 'Klio' 80, pp.66–90.

Kovaliov, S.I., 2011, *Storia di Roma – I. La Repubblica*, PGreco Edizioni, Milano (tit. orig. *Istoria Rima*), p.340.

Manganaro, G., 1982, *Monete e ghiande inscritte degli schiavi ribelli in Sicilia*, in '*Chiron*' 12, pp.237–44.

Manganaro, G., 2000, *Onomastica greca su anelli, pesi da telaio e glandes in Sicilia*, in '*Zeitschrift für Papyrologie und Epigraphik*' (*ZPE*) 133, pp.123–34 (esp. 131–32).

Manni, E., 1981, *Geografia fisica e politica della Sicilia antica*, Roma, pp.222, 238–39.

Merola, G.D., 2001, *Autonomia locale governo imperiale. Fiscalità e amministrazione nelle province asiane* (Pragmateiai 5), Bari, p.38.

Mocchegiani Carpano, C., 1984, *Il Tevere: archeologia e commercio*, in '*BNum*' 2.2, pp.21–81.

Oakley, S.P., 1985, *Single combat in the Roman Republic*, in '*Classical Quarterly*' (*CQ*) 35.2., pp.392–410.

Paternò, I., Principe di Biscari, 1781, *Viaggio per tutte le antichità della Sicilia*, Napoli.

Perelli, L., 1990, *Questioni graccane*, in '*Rivista di filologia e di istruzione classica*' (*RFIC*) 118, pp.237–52.

Pisani Sertorio, G., Colini, A.M. and Bozzetti, C., 1986, *Portus Tiberinus*, in *Il Tevere e le altre vie d'acqua del Lazio antico*, in '*Archeologia Laziale*' VII, 2 (QCAEI 12), pp.157–97.

Ramsey, J.T., 1999, *Mithridates, the Banner of Ch'ih-Yu, and the Comet Coin*, in '*Harvard Studies in Classical Philology*' (*HSCP*) 99, pp.197–253, in part. pp.237–43.

Rickman, G., 1971, *Roman Granaries and Store Buildings*, Cambridge.

Scaramuzza, V., 1937, *Publican Societies in Sicily in 73–71 B.C.*, in '*Classical Philology*' (*CPh*) 32, pp.152–55.

Spatafora, F., 2011, *Un contributo per l'identificazione di una delle 'città di Sicilia' dei decreti di Entella*, in Ampolo, C. (ed.), *Da un'antica città di Sicilia. I decreti di Entella e Nakone*, pp.111–14.

Spatafora, F. and Vassallo, S. (eds), *Das Eigene und das Andere. Griechen, Sikaner und Elymer. Neue archailogische Forschungen im antiken Sizilien*, Palermo, p.108 nos 208/209.

Tantillio, I., *Gli uomini e le risorse*, in Giardina, A. (ed.), 2014, *Roma Antica*, Laterza, Roma-Bari, p.100.

Virlouvet, C., 1985, *Famines et émeutes à Rome des origines de la Rèpublique à la mort de Neron* (Collection de l'École française de Rome 87), Rome.

Vogt J., 2013, *L'uomo e lo schiavo nel mondo antico*, Res Gestae, Milano (tit. orig. *Sklavesci und Humanitat*), pp.56, 68.

Further Literature

Piracy

On the piracy in antiquity: ORMEROD, H.A., 1924 (reprint: 1969), *Piracy in the Ancient World. An Essay in Mediterranean History*, Liverpool-London. SESTIER, J., 1880, *La Piraterie dans l'Antiquité*, Paris. **On the piracy in the Graeco-Roman world:** DE SOUZA, P., 1999, *Piracy in the Graeco-Roman World*, Cambridge University Press, Cambridge. PERINET, C.H., 1968, *La Piraterie dans la latinité*, in *Caesaroudunum* 2, pp.75–80. **On merchants, sailors and pirates:** RAUH, N.K., 2003, *Merchants, Sailors & Pirates in the Roman World*, Tempus. GIANFROTTA, P.A., 1981, *Commerci e pirateria*, in *Mèlanges d'archéologie et d'histoire de l'Ecole française Rome* (*MEFRA*) 93, pp.227–42. **On the pirates:** BUTI, G. and HRODEJ, P.H., 2013, *Dictionnaire des corsaires et pirates*, Parigi, CNRES éditions. REDIKER M., 2011, *Pirates de tous le pays*, Paris. **On the pirate as everyone's enemy:** HELLER-ROAZEN, D., 2010, *L'Ennemi de tous, le pirate contre les nations*, Le Seuils, Paris. FRAMONTI, S., 1994, *Hostis commmunes omnium. La pirateria e la fine della Repubblica Romana, 145–33 a.C.*, Ferrara. MacMULLEN, R., 1967, *Enemies of the Roman Order*, Cambridge. **On the pirates of north-western Europe:** DETALLE, M-P., 2002, *La Piraterie en Europe du Nord Ouest à l'epoque romaine*, British Archaeological Reports, IS 1806. **On the Greek pirates:** GARLAN, Y., 1978, *Signification historique de la piraterie grecque*, in 'Dialogues d'histoire ancienne' 4, pp.1–16. **On the Cretan pirates:** BRULE, P., 1978, *La piraterie crétoise hellénistique*, Paris. **On the Cilician pirates:** ARRAYÁS MORALES, I., 2010, *Bandidaje y piratería en la Anatolia meridional: definición y circunstancias en el marco de las guerras mitridáticas*, in *Studia historica. Historia antigua. Salamanca*, XXVIII, pp.31–55. AVIDOV, A., 1997, *Were the Cilicians a Nation of Pirates?*, in 'Mediterranean Historical Review' 2, pp.5–55 POHL, H., 1993, *Die römische Politik und die Piraterie im östlichen Mittelmeer vom 3. bis zum 1. Jh. v.Chr.*, Berlin-New York, pp.216–56. LEWIN, A., 1991, *Banditismo e civilitas nella Cilicia Tracheia antica e tardoantica*, in 'Quaderni di storia' LXXVI, pp.167–84. MARASCO, G.,

1987, *Roma e la pirateria cilicia*, in '*Rivista Storica Italiana*' XCIX, pp.122–46. MITFORD, T.B., 1980, *Roman Rough Cilicia*, in *Aufstieg und Niedergang der romischer Welt* II.7.2., pp.1230–61. **More generally on the Cilicia:** cfr. DESIDERI, P., 1991, *Cilicia ellenistica. Scambi e identità Culturale*, in '*Quaderni di Storia*' LXXVI, pp.141–65. **On the brigandage and piracy in the Roman world (Republican Period):** CLAVEL-LÉVEQUE, M., 1978, *Brigandage et piraterie: représentations idèologiques et pratiques impérialistes au dernier siècle de la République*, in '*Dialogues d'histoire ancienne*' 4, pp.17–31. **On the naval policies of Rome:** POHL, H., 1993, *Die romische Politik und die Piraterie im ostlichen Mittelmer vom 3. Bis zum 1.Jr v. Chr.*, Berlin-New York. COURTOIS, C.H., 1939, *Les Politiques navales de l'Empire romain*, in '*Revue historique*' 186, pp.17–47, 225–59.

Slavery

On the slavery in antiquity: McKEOWN, N., 2007, *The Invention of Ancient Slavery*, 'Duckworth Classical Essays', Duckworth, London. FINLEY, M., 1981, *Ancient Slavery and Modern Ideology* (*Schiavitù antica e ideologie moderne*), Laterza, Roma-Bari. VOGT, J., 1972, *Sklaverei und Humanitat: Studien zur antiken Sklaverei und ihrer Erforschung*, in 'Historia Einzelschriften' 8, Steiner, Wiesbaden, 2nd ed. VOGT, J., 1965, *Sklaverei und Humanität: Studien zur antiken Sklaverei und ihrer Erforschung*, Wiesbaden. Published in English (1974) as *Ancient Slavery and the Ideal of Man*, Wiedemann, T. (trans.), Oxford. SECHI, M., 1969, *L'uomo e lo schiavo nel mondo antico*, Silva, Roma.

On the slavery in archaeology: WEBSTER, J., 2005, *Archeologies of Slavery and Servitude: Bringing 'New World' Perspectives to Roman Britain*, in '*Journal of Roman Archaeology*' (*JRS*) 18, 1, pp.161–79. THOMPSON, F.H., 2003, *The Archaeology of Greek and Roman Slavery*, Duckworth, London.

On the slavery in the Greek and Roman worlds: JONGMAN, W., 2003, *Slavery and the Growth of Rome. Transformation of Italy in the Second and First Centuries BCE*, in EDWARDS, C. and WOOLF, G. (eds), *Rome the Cosmopolis*, Cambridge University Press, Cambridge, pp.100–221. MASSEY, M. and MORELAND, P., 2001, *Slavery in Ancient Rome*, Bristol Classical Press, London. DUMONT, Ch., 1987, *Servus. Rome et l'esclavage sous la république*, Ecole Française de Rome, Rome. WIEDMANN, T., 1981, *Greek and Roman Slavery*, Routledge, London. HOPKINS, K., 1978, *Conquerors and Slaves. Sociological Studies in Roman History* (trad. it.

Conquistatori e schiavi. Sociologia dell'impero romano), Boringhieri, Torino, 1984. **On the origin and provenance of the Roman slaves:** HARRIS, W.V., 1999, *Demography, Geography and the Sources of Roman Slaves*, in '*Journal of Roman Studies*' (*JRS*) 89. **On the Roman slave trade:** BODEL, J., 2005, *Caveat emptor: towards a Study of Roman Slave-Traders*, in '*Journal of Roman Archaeology*' (*JRA*) 18, pp.181–95. HARRIS W.R., 1999, *Demography, Geography and the Sources of Roman Slaves*, in '*Journal of Roman Studies*' (*JRS*) 89, pp.62–75. SCHEIDEL, W., 1997, *Quantifying the Souces of Slaves in the Early Roman Empire*, in '*Journal of Roman Studies*' (*JRS*) 87, pp.156–69. MUSTI, D., 1980, *Il commercio degli schiavi e del grano: il caso di Puteoli*, in *The Seaborne Commerce of Ancient Rome. Studies in Archaeology and History* (eds J. D'Arms and E. Kopff), in '*Memoirs of the American Academy in Rome*' (*MAAR*) XXXVI, Rome, pp.197–215. **On the slave labour in Rome:** AUGENTI, E.D., 2008, *Il lavoro schiavile a Roma (=Arti e mestieri nel mondo romano, 3)*, Roma. **On the employment of Roman slaves in the sectors of economic and productive activity:** ROSAFIO, P., 2016, *Lavoro e status giuridico: lavoro libero e lavoro servile nelle campagne dell' Italia romana in età repubblicana*, in Marcone, A., *Storia del lavoro in Italia, 'Età Romana. Liberi, semiliberi e schiavi in una società premoderna*, Castelvecchi, Roma, pp.91–112. BODEL, J., 2008, *Slave Labour and Roman Society*, in Bradley, K. and Cartledge, P. (eds), *The Cambridge World History of Slavery*, Volume 1, Cambridge University Press, Cambridge. GIARDINA, A. & SCHIAVONE, A. (eds), 1981, *Società romana e produzione schiavistica*, Laterza, Roma-Bari.

Hellenistic Sicily

On the Roman *provincia* **of Sicily:** SALMERI, G., 2015, *Sicilia, Sardegna e Corsica*, in Letta, C. and Segenni, S. (eds), *Roma e le sue province. Dalla prima guerra punica a Diocleziano*, Carocci, Roma, pp.87–100. MANGANARO, G., 2012, *Pace e guerra nella Sicilia tardo-ellenistica e romana (215 a.C. – 14 d.C.)*, Bonn. PRAG, J.R.W., 2009, *Identità siciliana in età romano repubblicana*, in C. Michelini (ed.), *Immagine e immagini della Sicilia e di altre isole del Mediterraneo antico. Atti delle Seste Giornate Internazionale di studi sull'area elima e la Sicilia occidentale (Erice, 12–16 ottobre 2006)*, Vol. 1, Pisa, pp.87–100. PERKINS, P., 2007, '*Aliud in Sicilia? Cultural development in Rome's first province*', in P. Van Dommelen and N. Terrenato (eds), *Articulating Local Cultures. Power and Identity under the Expanding Roman Republic*, in '*JRA*' suppl. 63, Portsmouth, pp.33–53.

PRAG, J.R.W., 2007, *Auxilia and gymnasia: a Sicilian model of Roman imperialism*, in '*JRS*' 97, pp.68–100. PRAG, J.R.W., 2007, *Ciceronian Sicily: the epigraphic dimension*, in J. Dubouloz and S. Pittia (eds), *La Sicile de Cicéron, lectures des Verrines*, Besançon, pp.245–72. PÉRÉ-NOGUÈS, S., 2006, '*Les "identités" siciliennes durant les guerres puniques: entre culture et politique*', in P. Francois, P. Moret and S. Péré-Noguès (eds), *L'hellénisation en Méditerranée occidentale au temps des guerres puniques (260–180 av. J.C.). Actes du colloque international (Toulouse, 31 mars–2 avril 2005)*, Toulouse, pp.57–70. PRAG, J.R.W., 2006, 'Poenus plane est – but who were the "Punickes"?', in '*Papers of the British School at Rome*' (PBSR) 74, pp.1–37. CAMPAGNA, L., 2006, *L'architettura di età ellenistica in Sicilia: per una rilettura del quadro generale*, in M. Osanna & M. Torelli (eds), *Sicilia ellenistica, consuetudo Italica. Alle origini dell'architettura ellenistica d'occidente*, Rome, pp.15–34. FREY-KUPPER, S., 2006, *Aspects de la production et de la circulation monétaires en Sicile (300–180 av. J.-C.): continuités et ruptures*, Pallas 70, pp.27–56. KUNZ, H., 2006, *Sicilia: Religionsgeschichte des römischen Sizilien*, Tübingen. LA TORRE, G.F., 2004, *Il processo di 'romanizzazione' della Sicilia: il caso di Tindari*, in '*Sicilia Antiqua*' 1, pp.111–46. ANTONACCIO, C.M., 2001, *Ethnicity and colonization*, in I. Malkin (ed.), *Ancient Perceptions of Greek Ethnicity*, Cambridge, pp.113–57. LOMAS, K., 2000, *Between Greece and Italy: an external perspective on culture in Roman Sicily*, in C. Smith and J. Serrati (eds), *Sicily from Aeneas to Augustus*, Edinburgh, pp.161–73. PINZONE, A., 2000, *La 'romanizzazione' della Sicilia occidentale in età repubblicana*, in *Terze giornate internazionali di studi sull'area elima (Gibellina-Erice-Contessa Entellina, 23–26 ottobre 1997). Atti*, Pisa, 2, pp.849–78. RUTTER, N.K., 2000, *Coin types and identity: Greek cities in Sicily*, in C. Smith & J. Serrati (eds), *Sicily from Aeneas to Augustus*, Edinburgh, pp.73–83. WILSON, R.J.A., 2000, *Ciceronian Sicily: an archaeological perspective*, in C. Smith and J. Serrati (eds), *Sicily from Aeneas to Augustus*, Edinburgh, pp.134–60. PINZONE A., 1999, '*Provincia Sicilia*'. *Ricerche di storia della Sicilia romana da Gaio Flaminio a Gregorio Magno*, Edizioni del Prisma, Catania. SARTORI, F., 1981, *Storia costituzionale della Sicilia antica*, in '*Kokalos*' 26–27, pp.263–84. MANGANARO, G., 1980, *La provincia romana*, in E. Gabba & G.Vallet (eds), *La Sicilia antica*, Naples, II.ii, pp.411–61. CALDERONE, S., 1976–77, *Storia della Sicilia romana*, in '*Kokalos*' 22–23, pp.363–84. VERBRUGGHE, G.P., 1972, *Sicily 210–70 BC: Livy, Cicero and Diodorus*, in '*Transactions of the American Philological Association*' 103, pp.535–59. FINLEY, M.I., 1968, *Ancient Sicily to the Arab Conquest*,

London. CALDERONE, S., 1964–65, *Problemi dell' organizzazione della 'provincia' di Sicilia*, in '*Kokalos*' 10–11, pp.63–98. CALDERONE, S., 1960, *Il problema delle città censorie e la storia agraria della Sicilia romana*, in '*Kokalos*' 6, pp.3–25.

On Dionysus: KERENY, K., *Dionysos. Urbild des unzerstorbaren Lebens*, (rist. 1976), Trad. it. *Dioniso*, rist. Milano 2010. Vd. anche: FRONTISI-DUCROIX, F., 1997, *Dioniso e il suo culto*, in S. Settis (ed.), 1997, *I greci*, vol. II, 2, Einaudi, Torino. On the repression of the *Bacchanalia*:BAUMAN, R.A., 1990, *The Suppression of the Bacchanals: Five Questions*, in '*Historia*' 39, pp.334–48. GRUEN, E.S., 1990, '*The Bacchanalian Affair*', in *Studies in Greek Culture and Roman Policy*, Berkeley and Los Angeles, pp.34–78. PAILLER, J-M., 1988, *Bacchanalia: la répression de 186 av. J.-C. à Rome et en Italie. Vestiges, images, tradition*, École française de Rome, Roma. COVA, P.V., 1974, *Livio e la repressione dei Baccanali*, in '*Athenaeum*' n.s., LII, pp.82–109. DUMEZIL, G., 1970, *Archaic Roman Religion*, Chicago, II, pp.407–31, 512–25. TOYNBEE, A.J., 1965, *Hannibal's Legacy*, London, New York and Toronto, II, pp.387–402. GELZER, M., 1964, *Die Unterdruckung der Bacchanalien bei Livius*, ora in ID., *Kleine Schriften*, III, Wiesbaden, pp.256–69. BRUHL, A., 1953, *Liber Pater*, Paris, pp.82–116 (in French). McDONALD, A.H., 1944, *Rome and the Italian Confederation*, in '*Journal of Roman Studies*' (*JRS*) 34, pp.11– 34. FRAENKEL, E., 1932, 33. ACCAME, S., 1938, *Il senatusconsultum de Bacchanalibus*, in '*Rivista di Filologia e di Istruzione Classica*' (*RFIC*), n. s., XVI, pp.225–34. FRAENKEL, E., 1932, *Senatus Consultum de Bacchanalibus*, in '*Hermes*' 67, pp.369–96 (in German). FRANK, T., 1927, *The Bacchanalian Cult of 186 B.C.*, in '*Classical Quarterly*' (*CQ*) 21, pp.128–32. FOWLER, W.W., 1911, *The Religious Experience of the Roman People*, London, pp.335–56. On the repression of servile movements in Puglia of 185/184 BC: CAPOZZA, M., 1966, *Movimenti servili nel mondo romano in età repubblicana, I. Dal 509 al 184 av. C.*, Roma, pp.143–59.

On the cult of Demeter in Sicily: HINZ, V., 1998, *Der Kult von Demeter und Kore auf Sizilien und in der Magna Graecia*, Wiesbaden. WHITE, D., 1964, *Demeter's Sicilian cult as a political instrument*, in '*Greek, Roman and Byzantine Studies*' 5, pp.261–79.

On Morgantina: PIRAINO, M.T., 1959, *Morgantine e Murgentia*, in '*Kokalos*' 5, pp.174 ss.

On Leontinoi (Leontini, Lentini): FRASCA, M., 2004, '*La porta verso i campi detti leontini*', in M. Frasca (ed.), *Leontini. Il mare, il fiume, la città, Atti della giornata di studio, Lentini, 4 maggio 2002*, Siracusa, pp.87–98. FRASCA, M., 2009, *Leontinoi. Archeologia di una colonia greca*, '*Archeologica*' 152, Roma. KARLSSON, L., 1992, *Fortification Towers and Masonry Techniques in the Hegemony of Syracuse, 405–211 BC*, Stockholm. MUSUMECI, M., 2011, '*Leontinoi tra IV e III secolo a.C.*', in '*Archivio Storico Siracusano*' 46, pp.389–423. ORSI, P., 1930, '*Scavi di Leontini-Lentini*', in '*Atti Memorie Società Magna Grecia*' 3, pp.3–39. RIZZA, G., 1955, '*Leontini. Campagne di scavi 1950–51 e 1951–52. La necropoli della Valle San Mauro; le fortificazioni meridionali della città e la porta di Siracusa*', in *Notizie degli Scavi*, pp.281–376. RIZZA, G., 1990, '*Lentini. Storia della ricerca archeologica*', in G. Vallet and G. Nenci (eds), *Bibliografia Topografica della Colonizzazione Greca in Italia e nelle Isole tirreniche* 8, Pisa, pp.533–38. RIZZA, S., 2000, *Studi sulle fortificazioni greche di Leontini*, in *Studi e Materiali di Archeologia Greca* 7, Catania.

On Montagnola di Marineo (Palikè): SPATAFORA, F., 1993–94, *La Montagnola di Marineo. Campagna di scavi 1991*, in '*Kokalos*' XXXIX–XL, pp.1187–98. SPATAFORA, F. *et alii*, 1997, *La Montagnola di Marineo. Nuovi scavi nell'abitato (1991–1993)*, in *Archeologia e Territorio (Beni Culturali – Palermo)*, Palermo, pp.111–235. SPATAFORA, F., 2000, *Indigeni, Punici e Greci in età arcaica e tardo-arcaica sulla Montagnola di Marineo e nella valle dell'Eleuterio*, in *Terze Giornate Internazionali di Studi sull'Area Elima. Atti II (ottobre 1997)*, Pisa-Gibellina, pp.895–918. SPATAFORA, F., 2002, *La Montagnola – Makella*, in *Sicani, Elimi e Greci. Storie di contatti e terre di frontiera*, Palermo, pp.86–90. SPATAFORA, F., 1997–98, *La Montagnola di Marineo. Campagna di scavi 1996*, in '*Kokalos*' XLIII–XLIV, II, 2, pp.703–19. TAMBURELLO, I., 1991, s.v. *Marineo*, in '*Bibliografia Topografica della Colonizzazione Greca in Italia e nelle Isole Tirreniche (Pisa, 1977)*' (*BTCGI*), IX, pp.365–75.

Slave Revolts

On the slave revolts in antiquity: URBAINCZYK, T.H., 2014, *Slave Revolts in Antiquity*, Routledge, Oxford, 2014; see also: URBAINCZYK, T., 2008, *Slave Revolts in Antiquity*, Stocksfield). STRAUSS, B., 2010, *Slaves Wars in Greece and Rome*, in *Makers of ancient strategy*, in Hanson, V.D. (ed.), Oxford, pp.185–205. BUSSI, S., 1998, *Rivolte servili e bagliori di 'lealismo' ellenistico*, in '*Rivista italiana di numismatica e scienze affini*' (*RIN*), pp.15–27.

On Rome's slave revolts: DONALDSON, A., 2012, *Peasant and Slave Rebellion in the Roman Republic*, Unpublished PhD dissertation,

University of Arizona. BRADLEY, K.R., 2011, *Resisting slavery at Rome*, in K.R. Bradley and P. Cartledge (eds), *The Cambridge World History of Slavery. Volume 1: The Ancient Mediterranean World*, New York, pp.362–84. BRADLEY, K.R., 1989 (1990), *Slavery and Rebellion in the Roman World, 140 B.C.– 27. BRADLEY, K. 70 B.C.*, University of Indiana Press, Bloomington (Ind.). BRADLEY, K.R., 1984, *Slaves and Masters in the Roman Empire: A Study in Social Control*, Latomus, Brussels. MAHAFFY, J.P., 1890, *The slave wars against Rome*, in '*Hermathena*' 7.

On the revolts of the Ancient and Middle Republic: DONALDSON, A., 2012, *Peasant and Slave Rebellion in the Roman Republic*, Unpublished PhD dissertation, University of Arizona. SHAW, B., 2001, *Spartacus and the Slave Wars: A Brief History With Documents*, Palgrave Macmillan, London. BUSSI, S., 1998, *Rivolte servili e bagliori di 'lealismo' ellenistico*, in '*Rivista italiana di numismatica e scienze affini*', pp.15–27. BRADLEY, K.R.,1990, *Slavery and Rebellion in the Roman World, 140 B.C – 70 B.C.*, Bloomington, Indiana University Press. CROOK, J.A. *et alii* (eds), 1985, *The Cambridge Ancient History IX: The Last Age of the Roman Republic, 146–43 B.C.*, Cambridge University Press, Cambridge. BALDWIN, B., 1967, '*Two aspects of the Spartacus slave revolt*', in '*The Classical Journal*' (*CJ*) 62. CAPOZZA, M., 1966, *Movimenti servili nel mondo romano in età repubblicana*, vol. I: dal 501 AL 184 A.CR. (Università degli Studi di Padova, Pubblicazioni dell'Istituto di Storia Antica, 5), L'Erma di Bretschneider, Roma.

Rome's Sicilian Slave Wars

On Rome's Sicilian Slave Wars: MORTON, P., 2018, *Filling in the Gaps: Studying Anachronism in Diodorus Siculus' narrative of the First Sicilian 'Slave War'*, in '*Histos*' Supplement 8, pp.115–43. MORTON, P., 2012, *Refiguring the Sicilian Slave Wars: From Servile Unrest to Civic Disquiet and Social Disorder*, Unpublished University of Edinburgh PhD thesis. WIRTH, G., 2004, *Sklaven und Helden: zur Darstellung der sizilischen Aufstände bei Diodor*, in H. Heftner and K. Tomaschitz (eds), *Ad Fontes!*, Wien, pp.81–85. MANGANARO, G., 2012, *Pace e guerra nella Sicilia tardo-ellenistica e romana (215 a.C. – 14 d.C.)*, Bonn. MANGANARO, G., 1990, *Due studi di numismatica greca*, in '*Annali della Scuole Superiore di Pisa*' (*ASNSP*) 20, pp.409–27. BEJOR, G. (ed.), 1988, *Diodoro Siculo, II, XXI–XL*, Rusconi, Milano. BRADLEY, K.R., 1984, '*Slave kingdoms and slave rebellions in ancient Sicily*', in '*Historical Reflections*' 10. MANGANARO,

G., 1983, *Ancora sulle rivolte 'servili' in Sicilia*, in '*Chiron*' 13, pp.405–09. MANGANARO, G., 1967, *Über die zwei Sklavenaufstände in Sizilien*, in '*Helikon*' 7, pp.205–22. WALTON, F.R. (ed. and trans.), 1967, *Diodorus of Sicily*,12 vols, Cambridge, 1963–67, XII.

On the First Slave War (Revolt of Eunus): MORTON, P., 2013, *Eunus: the cowardly king*, in '*The Classical Quarterly*' 63. MORTON, P., 2012, *Refiguring the Sicilian Slave Wars: From Servile Unrest to Civic Disquiet and Social Disorder*, Unpublished University of Edinburgh PhD thesis. ENGELS, D., 2011, *Ein syrisches Sizilien? Seleukidische Aspekte des ersten sizilischen Sklavenkriegs und der Herrschaft des Eunus-Antiochus*, in '*Polifemo*' 11, pp.233–51. MORTON, P., 2008, *Rebels and Slaves: Reinterpreting the First Sicilian Slave War*, Unpublished University of Edinburgh MSc thesis. LA ROCCA, A., 2004, *Liberi e schiavi nella prima guerra servile di Sicilia*, in '*Studi Storici*', Anno 45, No. 1, Gli 'Spazi' del tardoantico (Jan. – Mar.), pp.149–67 SÁNCHEZ LEÓN, M.L., 2004, *La amonedación del Basileus Antíoco en Sicilia (siglo II a.C.)*, in F. Chaves Tristán and F.J. García Fernández (eds), *Moneta qua scripta. La moneda como soporte de escritura*, Sevilla, pp.223–28. BERK, H.J. and BENDALL, S., 1994, *Eunus/Antiochus: slave revolt in Sicily*, in '*The Celator Feb.*', pp.6–8. COREY BRENNAN, T., 1993, *The commanders in the First Sicilian Slave War*, in '*Rivista di Filologia e di Istruzione Classica*' 121, pp.153–84. CANFORA, L. (ed.), 1990, *Diodoro Siculo: la rivolta degli schiavi in Sicilia*, Palermo. MANGANARO, G., 1990, *Due studi di numismatica greca*, in '*Annali della Scuola Superiore Normale di Pisa*' (*ASNSP*) 20, pp.409–27. SACKS, K.S., 1990, *Diodorus Siculus and the First Century*, Princeton (New Jersey), v. in part. CAP. V., *Diodorus on Rome: The First Sicilian Slave War*, pp.142–54. GARNSEY, P. & RATHBONE, D., 1985, *The background to the grain law of Caius Gracchus*, in '*The Journal of Roman Studies*' (*JRS*) 75. BRADLEY, K.R., 1984, '*Slave kingdoms and slave rebellions in ancient Sicily*', in '*Historical Reflections*' 10. CANFORA, L., 1983, *La rivolta dei dannati della terra*, in L. Canfora (ed.), Diodoro, *La rivolta degli schiavi in Sicilia*, Sellerio, Palermo. MANGANARO, G., 1983, *Ancora sulle rivolte 'servili' in Sicilia*, in '*Chiron*' 13, pp.405–09. MANGANARO, G., (1982), *Monete e ghiande inscritte degli schiavi ribelli Sicilia*, in '*Chiron*' 12, pp.237–44. VERBRUGGHE, G.P., 1974, *Slave Rebellion or Sicily in Revolt?*, in '*Kokalos*' 20, p.46 ss. VERBRUGGHE, G.P., 1973, *The elogium from Polla and the First Slave War*, in '*Classical Philology*' 68. MANGANARO, G., 1967, *Über die zwei Sklavenaufstände in Sizilien*, in '*Helikon*' 7, pp.205–22. STINTON, T.C.W., 1962, *The First Sicilian Slave War*, in '*Past and*

Present' 22, pp.87–93. GREEN, P., 1961, *The First Sicilian Slave War*, in *'Past and Present'* (*P&P*) 20, p.10 ss. DONALDSON, A., 1920, 'E.S.G.R.', *Antiochus, king of slaves*, in *'The Numismatic Chronicle and Journal of the Royal Numismatic Society'* 4S.20.

Rebellion of Spartacus

On the Rebellion of Spartacus: SHAW, B.D., 2001, *Spartacus and the Slave Wars. A brief History with Documents*, Bedford/St Martins, Boston and New York (see also: Palgrave Macmillan, London). BALDWIN, B., 1967, *Two aspects of the Spartacus slave revolt*, in *'The Classical Journal'* (*CJ*) 62.

Republican Rome

On the demographic aspects of the impetuous development of late-Republican Rome: TANTILLO, I., *Gli uomini e le risorse*, in A. Giardina (ed.), 2014, *Roma Antica*, Laterza, Roma-Bari, pp.85–111. There is a bibliography on the subject. PURCELL, N., 1994, *The City of Rome and the Plebs Urbana in the Late Republica*, in J. Crook, A. Lintott and E. Rawson (eds), *The Cambridge Ancient History*, vol. IX, *The Last Age of the Roman Republic 146–43 BC*, pp.644–88, in part. 648–55. HOPKINS, K., 1978, *Conquerors and Slaves*, pp.96–98.

For the ranking of the most important cities: AA.VV., 1989, *Storia di Roma*, Vol. IV, Cap. I - *I Caratteri e le Morfologie* (A. Schiavone), Einaudi, Torino, p.26.

On the markets of Rome: COARELLI, F., 1988, *Il Foro Boario dalle origini alla fine della repubblica*, Quasar, Roma.

On the river ports of the urban area of Rome: MOCCHEGIANI CARPANO, C., 1984, *Il Tevere: archeologia e commercio*, in *'Bollettino di Numismatica'* (*BNum*) 2.2, pp.21–81. CASTAGNOLI, F., 1980, *Installazioni portuali a Roma*, in *'Memoirs of the American Academy in Rome'* (*MAAR*) XXXVI, pp.35–42. CRESSEDI, G., 1949–51, *I porti fluviali in Roma antica*, in M. De Dominicis, 1924, *La 'statio annonae urbis Romae'*, in *'Bullettino della Commissione Archeologica di Roma'* (*BullComm*) LII, pp.135–49. PISANI SERTORIO, G., COLINI, A.M. and BOZZETTI, C., 1986, *Portus Tiberinus*, in *Il Tevere e le altre vie d'acqua del Lazio antico*, in *'Archeologia Laziale'* VII, 2 (QCAEI 12), pp.157–97. COARELLI, F., 1988, *Il Foro Boario dalle origini alla fine della Repubblica*, Roma. HULSEN, C., 1896, *Il foro Boario e le sue adiacenze nell'antichità*, in *'Dissertazioni della*

Pontificia Accademia romana di archeologia' (*DissPontAcc*) 2, II, pp.175–248. COARELLI, F., 1968, *Navalia, Tarentum e la topografia del campo Marzio meridionale*, in '*Quaderni dell' Istituto di topografia antica della Università di Roma*' (*Quaderni Ist. Topogr.)* 5, pp.27–37. GATTI, G., 1936, *L'arginatura del Tevere a Marmorata (un manoscritto inedito del P. Luigi M. Bruzza)*, in '*Bullettino della Commissione Archeologica di Roma*' (*BullComm*) LXIV, pp.55–82. COLINI, A.M., 1938, *Deposito di marmi presso il Tevere*, in '*Bullettino della Commissione Archeologica di Roma*' (*BullComm*), pp.299–300. COLINI, A.M., 1980, '*Il porto fluviale del Foro Boario a Roma*', in '*Memoirs of the American Academy in Rome*' (*MAAR*) XXXVI, pp.43–53.

On the *Porticus Aemilia*: GATTI, G., 1934, '*Saepta Iulia' e 'Porticus Aemilia' nella 'Forma' Severiana*, in '*BullCom*', pp.123–49. RICKMAN, G., 1971, *Roman Granaries and Store Buildings*, Cambridge.

On the Roman food supply system: TCHERNIA, A., 2003, *Le ravitaillement de Rome: les reponses aux contraintes de le géographie*, in B. Marin and C. Virlouvet (eds), *Nourrir les cités de la Méditérranée-Temps mondermes*, Maison-neuve & Larose, Paris, pp.45–60. VIRLOUVET, C., 2003, *L'approvvisionnemnet de Rome en denrées alimentaires de a République au Haut-Empire*, in B. Marin and C. Virlouvet (eds), *Nourrir les cités de la Méditérranée-Temps modernes*, Maison-neuve & Larose, Paris, pp.61–82. GARNESY, P., 1999, *Food and Society*, in *Classical Antiquity*, Cambridge University Press, Cambridge. GARNESEY, P. and RATHBONE, D., 1985, *The background to the grain law of Caius Gracchus*, in '*Journal of Roman Studies*' (*JRS*) 75.

On the *quaestor ostiensis*: CHANDLER, D.C., 1978, *Questor Ostiensis*, in '*Historia: Zeitschrift fur Alte Geschichte*', Bd. 27, H. 2 (2nd Qtr), pp.328–35.

On the tonnage of ancient ships: TCHERNIA, A. and POMEY, P., 1980–81, *Il tonnellaggio massimo delle navi mercantili romane*, in '*Puteoli*' IVV (Atti del convegno 'Studi e ricerche su Puteoli romana', Napoli, 1979), pp.29–57. CASSON, L., 1971, *Ships and seamanship in the ancient world*, Princeton. CASSON, L., 1956, *The size of ancient merchant ships*, in *Studi in onore di A. Calderini e R. Paribeni*, I., Milano, pp.231–38.

On the port of Pozzuoli: FREDERIKSEN, M., 1980–81, *Puteoli e il commercio del grano in età romana*, Puteoli, IV–V, 1 (Atti del convegno 'Studi e ricerche su Puteoli romana', Napoli, 1979), pp.5–27. SOMMELLA, P., 1980, *Forma eurbanistica di Pozzuoli romana*, Napoli.

On the grain warehouses at Emporium (main river port of Rome): CASTAGNOLI, F., 1980, *Installazioni portuali a Roma*, in D'ARMS, J. and KOPFF, E. (eds), *The Seaborne Commerce of Ancient Rome. Studies in*

Archaeology and History, Rome (MAAR, XXXVI), pp.35–42. RICKMAN, G., 1971, *Roman granaries and store buildings,* Cambridge.

On wheat imports in Rome: SALTINI, A., 1996, *I semi della civiltà. Frumento, riso e mais nella storia delle società umane,* Bologna (Nuova edizione 2010). GARNSEY, P., 1988, *Famine and Food Supply in the Greco-Roman World: Responses to Risk and Crisis,* Cambridge University Press, Cambridge. GARNSEY, P., GALLANT, T. and RATHBONE, D., 1984, *Thessaly and the Grain Supply of Rome during the II Cent. B.C.,* in '*JRS*' 74, 1984, pp.30–44. GARNSEY, P., 1983, *Grain for Rome,* in P. Garnsey, K. Hopkins and C.R. Whittaker (eds), *Trade in the Ancient Economy,* Chatto & Windus, London. RICKMAN, G., 1980, *The corn supply of ancient Rome,* Cambridge. SCULLARD, H.H., 1973, *Roman Politics 220–150 B.C.,* Oxford. OLIVA, A., 1930, *La politica granaria di Roma antica dal 265 a. C. al 410 d. C.,* Federazione Italiana dei Consorzi Agrari, Piacenza. DE ROMANIS, F., *L'approvvigionamento annonario nella Roma imperiale.*

On the famines in Rome in the Republican Period: VIRLOUVET, C., 1985, *Famines et émeutes à Rome des origines de la république à la mort de Néron,* Collection de l'Ecole Française de Rome LXXXVII, Ecole Française, Rome.

On the protection of public order in Rome: NIPPEL, W., 1995, *Public Order in Ancient Rome,* Cambridge University Press, Cambridge.

On the equipment of the Roman army: GOLDSWORTHY, A.K., 1996, *The Roman Army at War 100 BC – AD 200,* pp.83–84, 209–19. BISHOP, M.C. and COULSTON, J.C.N., 1993, *Roman Military Equipment from the Punic Wars to the Fall of Rome,* Oxbow Books, Oxford. CONNOLY, P., 1981, *Greece and Rome at War,* Macdonald, London. FEUGERE, M. (ed.), 1997, *L'Equipment Militaire et l'Armement de la Republique,* in '*Journal of Roman Military Equipment Studies*' (*JRMS*) 8.

Index

All dates are BC, unless otherwise stated.

1. INDIVIDUAL

2. COLLECTIVE

3 . GEOGRAPHICAL

4. GREEK AND LATIN WORDS

aediles (Roman magistrates), 64, 102

ager publicus populi romanorum (the Roman state property), 39, 48, 169, 183

agora (Greek name for the main square of a city), 48, 55, 59–60, 144, 184, 206

ala (auxiliary troops), 105

amnis Petronia, 21

Annales (historical work), 114, 199

archegetes (Greek word that meant leader or founder), 50

asylum (the protection granted by a State to the refugees), 7, 73

auxilia (auxiliary troops), 105, 131, 148, 152, 224

bacchanalia (rites in honor of Bacchus), 22, 138, 179–80, 225

ballista (missile weapon), 41, 93, 152

basileus Antìochos, , 80, 192, 228
    see also, King Antiochus (former Eunus)

bouleterion (assembly house), 60

caligae (type of military shoes), 106

centuriae (Roman troop formations), 93, 105

chiliarchos (Macedonian commander), 79

chlamys (cloak), 78

civitates censoriae (the legal position of some cities with respect to their relations with Rome), 42

civitates decumanae (see above), 40, 42

civitates liberae et foederatae (see above), 40, 96

civitates liberae et immunae (see above), 40

cognomen (family name), 91

confarreatio (the way to celebrate the patricians' wedding in Rome), 62, 187

consilium (advisory body), 83, 199

dediticius/dediticii (the condition of a conquered people who did not individually lose their freedom, but as a community lost all political existence as the result of a deditio, an unconditional surrender), 16

diadochi (Alexander's successors), 78, 88
    see also, epigonoi

duumviri (the board of two notables who served as mayor), 81

eisangeleus (Greek term for chamberlain), 78

epigonoi (Greek term for successors, synonim of Diadochi), 88

ergastula (accommodation for slaves), 65–6

eunous (Greek term), 76

ex officio (by virtue of one's position or status), 132

fasces lictorii (symbols of the power of life or death), 91

Fasti consulares (list of consuls), 91, 193

foedus, pl. foedera (contracts of association), 37, 40